Jerusalem
a walk through time

Yad Izhak Ben-Zvi is grateful to the following experts in the various periods of the history of Jerusalem for their insights and instructive comments: Dr. Dan Bahat, Dr. Mordechai Bar-On, Dr. Gabriel Barkay, Prof. Yossi Ben-Artzi, Prof. Haggai Ben-Shammai, Yitzhak Bezalel, Prof. Gideon Biger, Yaakov Billig, Prof. Amnon Cohen, Prof. Israel Eph'al, Dr. Ronnie Ellenblum, Prof. Ora Limor, Dr. Roni Reich, Dr. Shaul Sapir, Avraham Zvi Schwartz, Prof. Daniel Schwartz, Prof. Ephraim Stern and Dr. Hana Taragan.

Jerusalem
a walk through time

Yad Ben-Zvi's Walking-Tour Guide

Editor: Eyal Meiron

VOLUME ONE

From Ancient Times to the End of the Middle Ages

Yad Ben-Zvi Press ▪ Jerusalem

Published with the generous support of the Beracha Foundation

Translation: Edward Levin

Text editing: Robert Amoils, Heather Rockman

Drawings: David Harel

Tour maps: Tamar Sofer, Ronald Basford

Graphics and Design: Studio David Harel, Jerusalem

Cover photos: Albatross Aerial Photography

Editorial Coordination: Yohai Goell

Printed in Israel

ISBN 965-217-165-4

Who has ever seen Jerusalem naked?
Not even the archaeological.
Jerusalem never gets completely undressed
but always puts on new houses
over the shabby and broken ones.

YEHUDA AMICHAI

Preface

There are many ways to lead the visitor through the streets and byways of Jerusalem. In this guide we have chosen to present the sites of Jerusalem in their historical sequence. This enables the reader to place in time the sites and events that he encounters as he walks through the city. Jerusalem, however, does not submit easily to precise definitions. Both within the Old City and without its walls, you will encounter a unique mixture of periods, styles, memories and expectations that lie behind the seemingly silent stones that impart their interesting tales. An episode from the period of Ottoman rule is likely to crop up in proximity to the tomb of a Second Temple period mariner, and it is not inconceivable that both of them "reside" in the heart of a British Mandate period garden neighborhood. And if that does not pose enough of a difficulty, we must also take into account another limitation: each tour should progress along a continuous geographical course that is not too long or tiring, and which does not force the stroller to make unreasonably lengthy jumps from site to site. This guidebook takes all of these limitations into account, offering you a wide spectrum of routes that are organized in the very best and most convenient manner.

The thirty-six tour routes included in the two volumes of *Jerusalem – A Walk through Time* are organized under nine headings, each dealing with a period in the history of Jerusalem from its beginnings as the capital of King David to that of the modern-day State of Israel. Each period is preceded by a concise historical overview that will put its tours in context. The introduction to each tour focuses on the special topic within the wider period on which we will concentrate while following this specific route, and on the major sites we will visit. Here, too, the reader will find a colored map of the route marking the exact location of all the sites. Pertinent details, such as public transportation to the beginning of the route, parking facilities, and visiting hours at some of the sites are also provided on the introductory pages of each tour.

Yad Izhak Ben-Zvi's guides, who prepared these routes, have lent the volume their expertise and experience gained in years of guiding groups to Jerusalem's sites, those that are on the beaten path and are a must for every visitor and those that form part of this old-new city's hidden treasures. The many maps, floor plans, drawings and photos, most of which were prepared especially for this guide, complement the text and impart to the reader the unique atmosphere of Jerusalem.

We hope that first-time visitors to Jerusalem as well as those who frequently tour its diverse sites will find the guide a welcome companion on their walks through the city. May the pleasure sensed by all those involved in its preparation be also the lot of the user.

***

It gives me great pleasure to express my gratitude to all who have made the English edition possible. The specific contributions of many of them have been acknowledged on the verso of the title page, and I take this opportunity to thank them. Many thanks to the staff of Studio David Harel, especially to Ronald Basford who spent many long hours on typesetting and the graphic layout. I am greatly obligated to our colleagues at Yad Izhak Ben-Zvi: Gadi Wexler, tour coordinator at Yad Izhak Ben- Zvi, whose incomparable knowledge of Jerusalem's history and its streets and alleys helped us clarify many points of fact and technical issues, and Ruthy Goldstein who extended a helping hand with transliterations from the Arabic.

The English version is for the most part a translation of its Hebrew counterpart. In the Preface to the Hebrew edition I expressed our gratitude to the many persons and institutions who were so cooperative when we prepared that volume. I wish to take this opportunity to thank them once again.

Eyal Meiron

Contents

VOLUME ONE

From Ancient Times to the End of the Middle Ages

VOLUME TWO

From the Ottoman Conquest to the Present

Tour

VOLUME ONE

*From Ancient Times
to the End of the Middle Ages*

The first known mention of Jerusalem is to be found in Egyptian texts. The name of the city appears in a group of inscriptions on pottery bowls and figurines from the nineteenth century BCE, known as the "Execration Texts" that placed a curse upon potential rebellious city states. Five centuries later, the name Jerusalem was found in archives in el-Amarna, in Middle Egypt, which for a short time was the capital of all Egypt. Among the documents were letters by Abdi Hepa, king of Jerusalem, who sought the aid of the Egyptian monarch in his struggles against his neighbors.

The source of the name Jerusalem is not clear. The city is not mentioned specifically in the Pentateuch. Melchizedek, the king of Salem, who was "priest of God Most High" (Genesis 14:18), may very well have been the monarch of Jerusalem. The name Jerusalem first appears in the Book of Joshua, in a passage about the king of Jerusalem who allied himself with four other kings from the south against the Israelites, who had recently conquered part of the hill country. Joshua also refers to the city as Jebus, inhabited by the Jebusites. The Book of Judges (1:21) relates that "The Benjaminites did not dispossess the Jebusite inhabitants of Jerusalem; so the Jebusites dwelt with the Benjaminites." At that time Jerusalem, like other cities in the land, was a royal city ruled by the Jebusite king. At the beginning of Saul's reign it was a non-Israelite enclave in the hill country. It was included in the territory of the tribe of Benjamin (Joshua 18:21-28).

After David's conquest of the city round about 1004 BCE, Jerusalem became the official royal residence and the capital of the new monarchy. David brought the Ark of the Covenant to the city with the intention of building a Temple to the Lord and making Jerusalem the religious and political capital of the people of Israel. The Bible relates that David was prevented from building the Temple because his hands were stained with blood. It was his son Solomon who erected the Temple, north of the royal quarter, on the site of the threshing floor purchased by David from Ornan the Jebusite, which is identified as Mount Moriah (II Chronicles 3:1). Once the Temple was dedicated, the city became the spiritual center that united the entire nation and to which the masses came on pilgrimages. This was "the place that He would choose," where people came to pay homage to the Lord of Hosts. After the monarchy was divided following Solomon's death (ca. 930 BCE), Jerusalem remained the capital of the kingdom of Judah, whereas the capital of the kingdom of Israel changed a number of times, as one dynasty supplanted another. The kings of Israel sought a surrogate Temple for their subjects. At times peace reigned between the kingdoms of Judah and Israel, while during other periods they were hostile to each other.

The two kingdoms mutually influenced each other in several spheres, from language, architecture, and commercial ties, to intermarriage between the ruling dynasties, which both strengthened the relationship between them and introduced foreign cults into Jerusalem. These cults exerted great influence upon the inhabitants of the city, leading the prophets to decry the idolatry that had spread throughout the capital. The archaeological evidence in Jerusalem together with historical documents from Mesopotamia and Egypt, provide us with information about this period in the city's history. It was in Jerusalem that some of the prophets, in addition to advising kings, warned of the dangers awaiting the Temple and the city. Portions of the Bible were probably written in Jerusalem in this period. In 720 BCE, when the kingdom of Israel fell to the Assyrian army, some refugees apparently arrived in Jerusalem as well. Nineteen years later, under the leadership of King Hezekiah, Jerusalem successfully withstood the siege by the Assyrian monarch Sennacherib. The story of the city's miraculous deliverance contributed to the concept of Jerusalem's sanctity and immunity

The Assyrian Empire was conquered by the Babylonians in the late seventh century. The king of Jerusalem, Jehoiakim, seized the opportunity to rebel against Babylonian rule, but the Babylonians advanced on the city and conquered it in 589 BCE. They took its king captive and installed Zedekiah in his stead. The new king, however, made an alliance with Egypt against his Babylonian patrons. This political misreckoning once again brought the Babylonian army, commanded by Nebuzaradan, to the Land of Israel, and the Babylonians conquered Jerusalem after a protracted siege. The city was looted and destroyed, and its Temple put to the torch. This took place in the fifth month (Av) of the year 586 BCE. Many of the city's inhabitants were exiled to Babylonia. Thus ended the First Temple period.

For a map of Jerusalem in this period, see p. 207.

Aerial view of the City of David excavations ➤

FIRST TEMPLE PERIOD

The City of David

THE TERM "CITY OF DAVID" is somewhat misleading, since the ancient city extended over a very small area, in comparison with modern cities. Ranging between several dozen and a few hundred dunams (one dunam = 1,000 sq. meters), this area was inhabited by a few thousand people, who earned their livelihood from commerce and agriculture. It is estimated that in David's time some 1,500 people lived on the narrow ridge south of Mount Moriah, an area of about 60 dunams which is about the size of a single small quarter in modern Jerusalem.

What led these people to establish their city precisely on this site? There were two prerequisites for the founding of a city in antiquity: the presence of a nearby source of water, and natural topographical defenses. Both conditions were filled by the hill of the City of David: the Gihon Spring issued forth on the lower part of its eastern slope, and the site was well protected by the Kidron Valley to the east, the Central Valley to the west, and the juncture of these valleys to the south. The north, which lacked any natural barriers, was the weak point in the city's defenses. The valleys around the city trapped the fertile soil carried down by rainwater, enabling its inhabitants to develop agriculture and ensuring Jerusalem's food supply.

Jerusalem was also located within a reasonable distance from the trade route that passed through the nearby hill country to the area of the present-day railroad station. This was one of the important routes which traversed the length of the Land of Israel.

According to some authorities, the Temple Mount had already been a sacred site in the Canaanite period, about a thousand years before the time of David. If this is correct, it may have increased the attractiveness of the area adjoining the Mount.

The most intensively excavated site in Israel is the limited area of the City of David, whose secrets have not yet been fully disclosed. From the little that has been revealed, however, we can envisage life in the city during the First Temple period, and even prior to that, in the time of the Jebusites and Canaanites who preceded the Israelites. Thus we will see the remains of a large Canaanite fortress, whose foundations attest to its might; we will hear the story of seal impressions from the municipal archives of the time of the prophet Jeremiah; we will gaze into the depths of the ancient "Warren's Shaft" and finally, we will refresh ourselves in the cool waters of the Siloam Channel, which empty into the "King's Garden" to the south of the City of David.

The Old City

Ophel Road

Dung Gate

1

2

3

4

5

6

7

8

9

City of David Wall

City of David Ascent

City of David

Hezekiah's Tunnel

Siloam Channel

Village of Silwan

Hinnom Valley

10

11

12

13

14

0   100m

N

The route: the tour begins at the Dung Gate. From there we shall descend to the City of David and its sites, then pass through the Siloam Pool before returning to the Dung Gate.

Duration of the tour: about an hour and a half. For those opting to walk along Hezekiah's Tunnel – more than two hours.

Public transportation: bus no. 1 to the Western Wall plaza, or bus no. 38 to the Jewish Quarter. Walk down from there to the Dung Gate.

By private car: the parking lot outside the Dung Gate, to the south of the road.

Visiting hours: Area G and Warren's Shaft:
Sun–Thur: 9:00 a.m–5:00 p.m.
Friday: 9:00 a.m.–1:00 p.m.
Entrance fee for the Shaft and the Tunnel.

Note: for a walk through the tunnel, bring a flashlight and dress suitably for wading in water.

Southern Wall, Temple Mount

Southern wall of the Old City

Russian Church of the Ascension

Jewish cemetery on the Mount of Olives

Seven Arches Hotel (formerly: Intercontinental)

Central Valley

Southern Wall excavations

View to the east from the Dung Gate

1   OUTSIDE THE DUNG GATE

THE PANORAMA above will help orient us as we look to the east: The Central Valley, which is the western boundary of the City of David (also called "Zion" in the Bible), fairly closely follows the road leading south to the Siloam Pool. The valley then heads northward, toward the Western Wall plaza,

The Dung Gate

continuing to Damascus Gate. It is hardly visible today, since the alluvium and refuse deposited in it over the centuries have raised the ground level. Beyond the parking lot is the ridge on which stood Jebus – the City of David. The road next to us turns to the left. The end of this bend marks the northeastern limit of the City of David. This gives us an idea of its width: only about 150 meters at its widest point. On the other side of the ridge is the dry bed of the Kidron, with the Mount of Olives beyond it. The gravestones of the Jewish cemetery cover the slope, above which is the Seven Arches Hotel (formerly the Intercontinental), built during the period of Jordanian rule, that can be identified by its arches.

We'll follow the road down to the east, as we traverse the City of David breadthwise, until we come to its end above the Kidron Valley. To our left is the

The **Ophel** is the name of the area between the City of David and the Temple Mount. The Ophel is first mentioned by name in the time of King Jotham (II Chronicles 27:3).

fenced-off area of the Southern Wall excavations. Impressive finds from the First Temple, Second Temple, Byzantine, and Muslim periods were revealed here (see Tour 4).

Jerusalem expanded into this area, known as the **Ophel**, in the time of King Solomon, when the Temple was built atop the Temple Mount to the north. The excavations near the road uncovered a large house ❷ which, according to one view, was used after Solomon's time as a gatehouse, providing access from the City of David to the Ophel.

THE VIEW TO THE KIDRON VALLEY   **3**

T**HE STEEP CHANNEL** of the Kidron, which continues to the south before turning east toward the Dead Sea, is revealed to us in all its splendor. Here the riverbed begins to cut through the limestone to form cliffs. In the First Temple period it was about 20 meters lower in some sections, but its level has risen over the years. Before us are the dwellings of the Arab village of Silwan, jutting out from the steep rock. Note especially the step-like construction of the houses. We may assume that the City of David had a similar appearance 3,000 years ago, and the village is a sort of latter-day mirror image of the ancient city. Many square apertures were hewn in the cliff beneath the village, and many

City of David – proposed reconstruction

more are scattered among the houses of Silwan. These were the entrances to the burial caves carved out of the rock for Jerusalem's notables of the First Temple period, and part of the "belt of tombs" that encompassed the city. Some of these tombs would later be incorporated in the houses of the village, while others were turned into cesspits.

Some tombs were dug out of and separated from the surrounding bedrock. On the facade of one of them is an engraved inscription which puts a curse on anyone daring to break into the tomb: "This is [the tomb of ...] **yahu,** caretaker of the house. There is no silver or gold here, [but] only [his bones] and the bones of his maidservant with him. Cursed be the man who will open this!" The name of the tomb's

Looting of tombs is a very old phenomenon, and is known to us also from ancient Egypt. The very existence of the "**...yahu,** caretaker of the house" inscription teaches us an interesting detail about the educational level of thieves in ancient Jerusalem: we can safely assume that they knew how to read and write, otherwise there would have been no purpose in affixing such an inscription to the facade of the tomb.

occupant is damaged and only the last letters remain: "...yahu." Who was "...yahu, caretaker of the house"? Some believe him to have been "Shebna, who is over the house," the royal steward mentioned in the prophecy of Isaiah (22:15).

At the end of a row of houses on the left we can see a cube-like structure cut into the bedrock, with an entrance facing in our direction ◄4. This, too, is a tomb from the First Temple period, which is popularly known as the Tomb of Pharaoh's Daughter (who was Solomon's wife). It apparently had been topped by a stone pyramid, which was later destroyed. Remnants of an inscription in ancient Hebrew script were also discovered here. The pyramid was probably the source of the tomb's popular name. In the upper valley to the north (to the left) are a number of funerary monuments cut in the bedrock, dating from the Second Temple period, such as Zechariah's Tomb, the Tomb of the Sons of Hezir, and Absalom's Tomb (see Tour 5). Before leaving, let's take a look at the village's southernmost houses. Some of them were built in the 1880s, when Yemenite Jews who had immigrated to Eretz Israel (the Land of Israel) settled in the village of Silwan. Jews continued to live here until August 1938, when the last of them were forced to leave due to attacks by their neighbors and the deteriorating security situation.

We will walk down the path to the right, enter the excavations area, and go down to Area G.

---

5   AREA "G"

N OW WE ARE INSIDE the City of David, in the area which the archaeologists denoted with the letter "G." The city wall to the east is at the foot of the slope behind us. The area where we are standing was probably the nerve center of the ancient city for many years: the administrative, municipal, and governmental center, with the royal residence possibly nearby. This lasted until the time of King Solomon, who moved the seat of government northward, to the Ophel. The stepped stone wall facing us was probably the massive retaining wall of a large structure (the royal palace? the citadel?) which had been built atop the steep slope during the Canaanite period (possibly in the thirteenth century BCE). This structure may very well have been the "stronghold of Zion" taken by David when he conquered the Jebusite city (II Samuel 5:7). It was later destroyed but we do not know how or why: did an earthquake cause its collapse, or was this the deed of some enemy? The southern side of the retaining wall also began to disintegrate. Under it we can see the crosswise walls that served as its foundation. During the First

Proposed reconstruction of the House of Ahiel

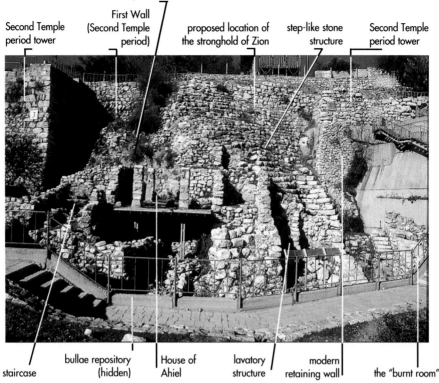

foundation of the step-like stone structure

Second Temple period tower | First Wall (Second Temple period) | proposed location of the stronghold of Zion | step-like stone structure | Second Temple period tower

staircase | bullae repository (hidden) | House of Ahiel | lavatory structure | modern retaining wall | the "burnt room"

Temple period the city's houses began to "climb" upon the structure, and were built over it. Since the slope is especially steep here, the engineers of the time had to level the area by building large stone terraces, which are visible under the ruins of the colonnaded house opposite us. This building is known as "the House of Ahiel," since it contained sherds (possibly from a cooking vessel) bearing the name Ahiel, but we cannot be certain that this was the name of its owner. The house, which was built in the seventh century BCE and continued to exist until the destruction of the city in 586 BCE, is fashioned in the style of the **four-room house**, which was common in Eretz Israel during the First Temple period. The illustration on the opposite page contains a proposed reconstruction of this house.

◆ The **four-room house** is so
◆ named because the
◆ arrangement of the columns
◆ in the courtyard forms three
◆ longitudinal spaces (in the
◆ House of Ahiel with a
◆ north-south orientation) to
◆ which a fourth chamber,
◆ perpendicular to the first
◆ three, is attached.

In one of the pits to the right of the House of Ahiel we can see a square stone with a hole in its center. It is a stone toilet seat which had once been affixed to the top of the cesspit and is now at its bottom. This is the earliest toilet ever discovered in Eretz Israel.

In the house on the right, the excavations revealed signs of a conflagration, which attest to the destruction that was the fate of Jerusalem in 586 BCE. The ruins of the house contained remnants of a burnt piece of wooden furniture which botanists identified as wood from the boxwood tree that grows in Syria. This attests to the commercial ties between Eretz Israel and Syria in that period.

Another building, of which only a narrow strip of the floor at the bottom of the excavations is visible, contained a treasure trove of about fifty clay seal impressions (*bullae* in Latin) that had been affixed to parchment or papyrus documents which were consumed in the conflagration. The flames fired the pieces of clay and preserved them. One of them was found to bear the seal impression of Gemariah son of Shaphan, possibly the scribe of King Zedekiah, who is mentioned in the Bible (Jeremiah 36:10). This might have been the royal

archives, in which documents, writs, and contracts were kept.

Document with *bullae* affixed (reconstruction)

When the Jews exiled to Babylonia returned to Jerusalem and began to rebuild its walls, Nehemiah the governor conducted a nocturnal

inspection tour of the ruined city walls. He writes: "I went out by the Valley Gate, at night, toward the Jackals' Spring and the Dung Gate; and I surveyed the walls of Jerusalem that were breached, and its gates, consumed by fire. I proceeded to the Fountain Gate and to the King's Pool, where there was no room for the beast under me to continue" (Nehemiah 2:13-14). The difficulties encountered by Nehemiah and his beast in traversing the area were caused by the heaps of debris from the destruction that

Bulla **bearing the name Benaiah son of Hoshaiahu** had accumulated along the eastern slope. These piles of rubble forced him to abandon the original line of the wall at the foot of the slope, and to build the new wall higher up. Consequently, the area where we are standing remained outside the new wall. This was to be of great consequence, since new construction did not take place here during the Second Temple and later periods, and the ancient ruins were thus preserved for thousands of years.

Now we will leave through the gate in the southern part of Area G, and continue along the stepped path (about two-thirds of the way down the stairs is a turn to the right, toward a single-story building that contains the entrance to Warren's Shaft, which we will shortly enter). As we continue to descend the stairs, we see on the left a pit with vegetation, above which are stone terraces.

6   THE CANAANITE WALL

FACING US, on the bedrock, we can see the large unhewn stones of the Canaanite city wall from the eighteenth century BCE, about 800 years before the time of David. This wall apparently was

Proposed reconstruction of the gate tower

still in use in the time of the Jebusites, from whom David **wrested control of the city,** and which he and his men saw as they stood at the foot of the city. Above

it is an additional wall, also built of unhewn, but smaller, stones. This is the Israelite wall of the First Temple period, probably from the days of King Uzziah, who is said to have built and fortified towers in Jerusalem. Above the wall we see stone terraces, which bear no relation to the city walls. They were erected by the excavators to prevent a cave-in during the unearthing of the Canaanite wall.

We shall now retrace our steps, climb the stairs, and reenter the city. According to one opinion, the modern staircase is built over a gate that had existed in the wall. This may have been the site of the "Water Gate" through which, in times of peace, the maidens of Jerusalem went down to the Gihon Spring to bring water. But what did they do when Jerusalem was besieged, since the source of its water supply, the Gihon, was located outside the city walls? To answer this question, we must turn left, toward the building to which we are directed by the sign "Warren's Shaft."

The Canaanite wall, with the Israelite wall

WARREN'S SHAFT 7

WHAT WAS THE appearance of Jerusalem in the First Temple period, and what impression did it make on those who saw it? The illustration hanging in the entrance room to Warren's Shaft attempts to answer this question on the basis of the archaeological evidence. In it we can see the step-like stone structure (Area G), the graduated houses of the city, the wall, the

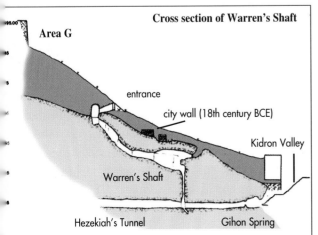

Cross section of Warren's Shaft

Area G

entrance

city wall (18th century BCE)

Kidron Valley

Warren's Shaft

Hezekiah's Tunnel

Gihon Spring

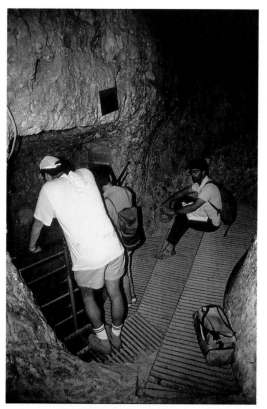
Warren's Shaft

"Water Gate," and the deep Kidron Valley with its vegetable gardens and orchards. Note the apertures along the cliff underneath the wall, through which water apparently flowed to irrigate the gardens. These outlets are located along the length of a water channel from the First Temple period known as the Siloam Channel (not to be confused with the later Hezekiah's Tunnel). We will see one of the outlets from this channel later on, in the Kidron Valley.

In the other part of the room is a model of the ancient waterworks known as "Warren's Shaft," named after its discoverer, Captain Charles Warren, who conducted excavations in Jerusalem in 1867.

The fact that the Gihon Spring is located outside the city walls endangered the city's inhabitants in time of siege, since the enemy controlled the water source and prevented access to it. Many cities faced the same problem in antiquity. In order to forestall such crises in the future, it was common practice to dig an underground tunnel linking the city to its water source. Projects of this sort were found in Gibeon, Gezer, Hazor, and other cities. In some cases they led to a spring, and in others to the groundwater level in the vicinity of the city.

A similar solution was adopted here in Jerusalem. We can see from this plastic model before us how the tunnel passes under the city wall before ending in a vertical shaft, through which a bucket on a rope could be lowered.

We will go down to the bottom floor, where there is a selection of photographs taken during the last major excavation conducted in the City of David, headed by Yigal Shiloh (1978-85), including finds from the area. We will continue along the modern concrete tunnel until we reach a room with a vaulted ceiling. This chamber was apparently built during the Second Temple period. A narrow passage, with a gabled ceiling of stone slabs, also dating from the same period, leads to it on the right. Now we will descend the modern iron stairs within the original waterworks tunnel. The original entrance has not been preserved. At the bottom of the staircase we see the remains of stairs cut in the bedrock, and behind them a short modern staircase which was built to enable one to reach the top of a cliff more than 2.5 meters high. In the past, a wooden ladder had probably been placed here, which could have been removed if an enemy sought to gain entrance to the city through the waterworks. We continue along a horizontal section in which signs of stonecutting are visible. The tunnel is much higher than is necessary for people to pass through, and is quite tortuous. This leads us to conjecture that it is actually made up of a series of natural chambers that were connected and widened by man. The tunnel turns, and next to the railing we walk on several rock-cut steps. The tunnel ends in a vertical shaft 15.6 meters deep. Spring water flowed to the bottom of this shaft through a rock-cut channel. The maidens who drew water would descend all the way with empty water jugs on their heads. They stood here, drew the water from the bottom of the shaft, and began the trip back with lighting far inferior to what we have today, the only light coming from candles placed in niches in the rock.

Soon after the discovery of Warren's Shaft in the nineteenth century, the conjecture was raised that this was the mysterious "water channel" that appears in the narrative of the capture of Jerusalem by David: The king and his men set out for Jerusalem against the Jebusites who inhabited the region. David was told, "You will never get in here! Even the blind and the lame will turn you back." (They meant: David will never enter here.) But David captured the stronghold of Zion; it is now the City of David. On that occasion David said, "Those who attack the Jebusites shall reach the water channel ..." (II Samuel 5:68).

According to this hypothesis, David's warriors successfully scaled Warren's Shaft and thus entered the city. If this theory is correct, then Warren's Shaft must have already been in existence before the time of David, and such a possibility cannot be rejected on archaeological or geological grounds. Nonetheless, some scholars give a later date for the digging of the waterworks, the ninth century BCE (that is, after the time of David), on the basis of comparison with the other waterworks in Israel known to us from this period.

We will leave the waterworks and descend the stairs to the Kidron Valley, toward the Gihon Spring.

THE GIHON SPRING   8

THE STEEP STAIRCASE leads to a plaza, to the left of which is a Muslim prayer niche *(mihrab)* facing Mecca. According to a Muslim legend, the waters of the Gihon Spring that gush forth here flow underground all the way to Mecca. Christian tradition identifies this as the place where Mary, the mother of Jesus, was baptized. The spring issues forth in a cavity under the stairs, several meters below us. At present, the spring is lower than the level of the Kidron Valley streambed. In the distant past, however, when the level of the Kidron was much lower, the spring flowed above it. The Gihon Spring apparently is a **karst spring,** whose waters in the past gushed irregularly. The name of the spring may derive from the "bursting forth" [*gihah* in Hebrew] of its water. A recent study has shown that the activity of the spring is no longer spasmodic, but produces a regular flow of water, about 2,000 cubic meters per day.

A **karst spring** receives its water from large underground cavities. When these cavities are filled with water, it gushes forth, after which the flow ceases or lessens until the cavities fill up again.

The Gihon Spring supplied three water systems that were in operation during the First Temple period: Warren's Shaft, the

Hezekiah's Tunnel

Siloam Channel (the entrance of which is located to the left of the sixth step above the spring), and Hezekiah's Tunnel (the latest of the three). The first twenty meters of the tunnel that begins at the spring channeled its water to the bottom of Warren's Shaft; this section of the tunnel must therefore have been hewn at the same time as the shaft. As we advance a bit further into the tunnel, we see that the water is currently blocked from entering the bottom of Warren's Shaft by a small stone wall. As the continuation of this first tunnel section, a 513-meter-long tunnel was dug, apparently in the time of King Hezekiah. This enabled the water to flow underground, safe from any enemy, to the Central Valley just west of the City of David where a special reservoir, the Siloam Pool, had been prepared. The digging of this tunnel was one of the steps taken by Hezekiah to prepare his city for war after he rebelled against King Sennacherib of Assyria (see Tour 2). At that time he also encompassed the Western Hill of the city with a broad wall that joined the City of David wall, so that by diverting the spring water to the other side of the City of David he ensured a supply of water within the city walls. When this operation was completed, the eastern entrance to the Gihon Spring was sealed, to conceal it from the view of the enemy. Hezekiah's water diversion project is described in the Bible, and a reading of this passage illustrates the anxiety of the city's inhabitants in the face of a possible Assyrian siege:

When Hezekiah saw that Sennacherib had come, intent on making war against Jerusalem, he consulted with his officers and warriors about stopping the flow of the springs outside the city and they supported him... for otherwise, they thought, the king of Assyria would come and find water in abundance... It was Hezekiah who stopped up the spring of water of Upper Gihon, leading it downward west of the City of David (II Chronicles 32:230).

The height differential between the spring and the aperture of the long winding tunnel was only 33 centimeters, an incline of only about six-tenths of one percent – a remarkable achievement even using modern technology. How was the tunnel dug? How did the tunnelers succeed in maintaining such a moderate incline? How were they supplied with air to breathe? And why does the tunnel follow such a meandering course? An inscription

Apertures in the Siloam Channel

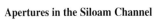

found in 1880 close to the opening of the tunnel describes the digging operation in these words:

[... when] (the tunnel) was driven through. And this was the way in which it was cut through: While [...] (were) still [...] axe(s), each man toward his fellow, and while there were still three cubits to be cut through, [there was heard] the voice of a man calling to his fellow, for there was an overlap [zada] in the rock from the right [and from the left]. And when the tunnel was driven through, the

Copy of the Siloam inscription

quarrymen hewed [the rock], each man toward his fellow, axe against axe; and the water flowed from the spring toward the reservoir for 1,200 cubits, and the height of the rock above the head(s) of the quarrymen was 100 cubits.

It is clear from the wording of the inscription that two teams of workers were engaged in the tunneling operation, digging simultaneously from either end ("from the right and from the left"). This testimony raises yet another question: how did the two teams manage to meet deep within the rock without the use of a compass? Many solutions have been suggested for these questions. The most likely is that Hezekiah's Tunnel is only an extension of a system of natural chambers in the rock. This would have enabled the two teams enlarging the natural chambers to meet with such precision, while adhering to the original course of the chambers and receiving a supply of fresh air from each end. According to some researchers, the unknown term *zada* that appears in the inscription refers to these natural chambers.

Enter the tunnel and follow in the footsteps of Hezekiah's quarriers. Those who prefer to stay dry will climb back up to the Kidron Valley and continue south, along the foot of the eastern slope.

The walk along the road in the Kidron Valley channel passes through one of the most fascinating areas in all Jerusalem. To our left are the houses of Silwan with the entrances to the burial caves visible beneath them. To our right, as we look eastward, the City of David, built on the steep slope, is revealed in all its splendor. We are passing by a number of sections ◀9▶ in which the excavations uncovered the Canaanite wall, with the Israelite wall above it. They continue the line of the wall that we saw at stop no. 6 on this tour. Both behind and in front of the wall we can see houses from the late First Temple period. Further on, to our left, is an orchard with fig trees and field crops. To our right, we can see one of the irrigation outlets of the Siloam Channel ◀10▶. The "King's Garden," which drew its water from the Siloam Channel, apparently extended to the left of the road. It should be mentioned that the Siloam Channel fell into disuse when Hezekiah's Tunnel was dug. At the bend in the road we will turn to the right where, beyond the iron railing, we can see a rock-cut water channel ⓫ which led overflow water from the Siloam Pool to gardens outside the City of David.

The large orchard ⓬ to the west is known as Birkat al-Hamra. It is located on the site of a large reservoir, to which the water of the Gihon flowed via the Siloam Channel prior to the hewing of Hezekiah's Tunnel. A look at the map of the city (see p. 207) shows that the Siloam Pool is located between the City of David wall and the Western Hill wall, which led some authorities to identify it with the "basin between the two walls" mentioned in the Bible (Isaiah 22:11).

Let us go down the steps to the Siloam Pool.

13 ◆ THE SILOAM POOL

THE SILOAM POOL is carved out of the rock at the end of the tunnel. The fragments of columns scattered in the pool are remnants from the Byzantine period, when the site was occupied by the Siloam Church which had been erected by Empress Eudocia in the fifth century CE. This church, built on the site of one of Jesus' miracles (John 9), also appears in the Madaba Map (see Tour 9). Interestingly enough, in the Second Temple period the location of the Gihon Spring apparently had been forgotten, and the mouth of Hezekiah's Tunnel was erroneously identified as the Siloam Spring.

We will leave the pool and return to the path from which we came, turning left to the houses of the quarter built over the City of David. To the east is a quarry from the Second Temple period ⓮. Two rock-cut chambers were discovered here at the beginning of the century, and they are still visible. The archaeologist

The rock-cut chambers

R. Weill proposed identifying them with the **tombs of the House of David** that, as the Bible relates, were within the city. Weill claimed that the Siloam Channel took a wide turn to avoid passing under the tombs located here. Scholarly research does not support this assumption, and it has recently been suggested that these chambers are Second Temple period storerooms.

◆ An early tradition places **David's tomb** on Mount Zion (which, during David's time, was outside the City of David). Some scholars are of the opinion that even if David himself is not buried on Mount Zion, other kings of the Davidic line may have been interred there.

Weill also found here a stone tablet bearing a Greek inscription that mentions a man named Theodotos son of Vetanos who was an *arche-synagogos,* that is, the head of a synagogue. This is archaeological proof of the existence of synagogues in Jerusalem in the Second Temple period.

From here we will proceed directly to Area G, and return to the Dung Gate the same way we came.

Conduit for overflow water at the Siloam Channel

From Kettef Hinnom to the Jewish Quarter

O N OUR VISIT to the City of David in the preceding tour we took a quick look at Jerusalem in its first days as a capital, focusing on everyday life in the city, the problems of water supply and the solutions adopted by its rulers, as well as public buildings and fortifications. In this tour we will come to know some of the "darker" sides of the city in the late First Temple period, and will learn about the necropolis, the cult of Molech, the miraculous lifting of a terrifying siege, and finally, a revolt and destruction.

The remains of the late First Temple period necropolis include about 140 rock-cut burial caves which encompass the biblical city. We will visit an interesting concentration of tombs overlooking the Hinnom Valley (although not the most magnificent one that has survived).

It is generally assumed that with the exception of the kings of the Davidic dyasty who, according to the Bible, were buried within the city, the dead were interred outside the city for fear of corpse impurity and for health reasons. Accordingly, the location of the tombs that have been uncovered helps us to determine the boundaries of the city and to trace the limits of its expansion.

The style of the tombs and the finds discovered in them shed fascinating light on the period and on the beliefs and customs of the city's inhabitants.

The fact that the tombs tell the story of the living no less, and at times even more, than that of the dead should come as no surprise to us: this is true for every period and time, as we shall learn in the tours that dwell upon burial practices in the Second Temple period (Tour 6) and modern burials on Mount Herzl (Tour 36).

At the Broad Wall site we will learn the story of the international rebellion against the Assyrian superpower, under whose yoke all the nations of the region suffered in the eighth century BCE. Immediately afterwards, we will leap about 120 years forward in our time machine, as we descend to the depths to see the remains of a a fortified tower whose stones are silent testimony to the city's last battle and its destruction by the Babylonians.

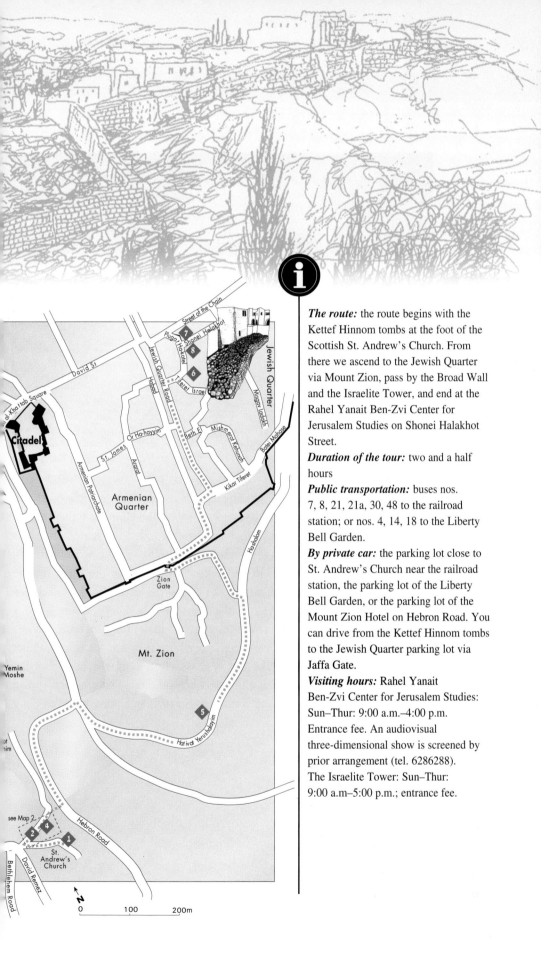

The route: the route begins with the Kettef Hinnom tombs at the foot of the Scottish St. Andrew's Church. From there we ascend to the Jewish Quarter via Mount Zion, pass by the Broad Wall and the Israelite Tower, and end at the Rahel Yanait Ben-Zvi Center for Jerusalem Studies on Shonei Halakhot Street.

Duration of the tour: two and a half hours

Public transportation: buses nos. 7, 8, 21, 21a, 30, 48 to the railroad station; or nos. 4, 14, 18 to the Liberty Bell Garden.

By private car: the parking lot close to St. Andrew's Church near the railroad station, the parking lot of the Liberty Bell Garden, or the parking lot of the Mount Zion Hotel on Hebron Road. You can drive from the Kettef Hinnom tombs to the Jewish Quarter parking lot via Jaffa Gate.

Visiting hours: Rahel Yanait Ben-Zvi Center for Jerusalem Studies: Sun–Thur: 9:00 a.m.–4:00 p.m. Entrance fee. An audiovisual three-dimensional show is screened by prior arrangement (tel. 6286288). The Israelite Tower: Sun–Thur: 9:00 a.m–5:00 p.m.; entrance fee.

The Path at the Foot of St Andrew's Church

Hinnom Valley cliffs

THE HIGH SPOT where we are standing affords us an excellent view of Mount Zion and the wall of the Old City. At their foot is the Hinnom Valley, which is already mentioned in the Book of Joshua, in the period of the settlement of the Israelite tribes in Eretz Israel, as the boundary between the tribe of Benjamin in the north and the tribe of Judah in the south (Joshua 15:8). In the First Temple period, the valley was infamous as the site of the rite of the idol Molech (an Ammonite god), which, according to the testimony of the Bible, included a ceremony in which boys and girls were "consigned" to the fire. According to one opinion, this meant that children were actually burnt alive as sacrifices. Other authorities, however, maintain that this was merely a symbolic act or, at the most, the burning of the bodies of children who had died. This practice spread among the inhabitants of Judah and Jerusalem (to such an extent that even King

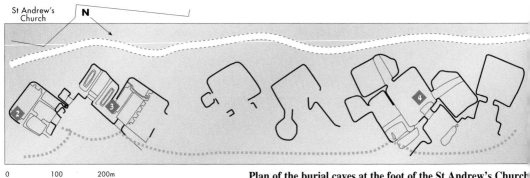

Plan of the burial caves at the foot of the St Andrew's Church

Ahaz consigned his son to the fire during his war with Aram) and aroused the ire of the prophets, who attacked it. King Josiah eliminated this practice at the end of the seventh century BCE, when he instituted religious reforms: "He also defiled Topheth, which is in the Valley of Hinnom, so that no one might consign his son or daughter to the fire of Molech" (II Kings 23:10). The origin of the name "Valley of Hinnom" is not known, and may have been derived from the name of an early owner of the land. In later traditions it was transformed from a geographical term to an abstract religious concept: "Gehenna," as a synonym for Hell. Thus, for example, the Hebrew sages state that "there are two palm trees in the Valley of Hinnom, between which smoke ascends... and this is the entrance to Gehenna" (*Babylonian Talmud,* Sukkah 32b). Knowledge of the practise of the ancient fire rite, together with the proximity of the tombs of Jerusalemites, may very well have contributed to the creation and establishment of the tradition that this was the location of Hell, where the wicked are punished after their death.

We proceed southward, along the tombs to our right, until the last burial cave.

THE KETTEF HINNOM TOMBS   2

HOW MANY PEOPLE LIVED and died in Jerusalem during the 400 years (about sixteen generations) of the First Temple period? Some archaeologists estimate their number at about 200,000. We know of some 140 tombs from this period cut in the bedrock. These served as family tombs over the course of many generations, and we may assume that, at most, a few thousand individuals were buried in them. If so, where are the tombs of the tens of thousands of others? The main explanation seems to be that the commoners were buried in simple graves dug in the earth, of which there are no remains. Some of the tombs of kings and the upper classes, which were hewn in the bedrock, were destroyed by later rulers, and many others simply await discovery. The tombs before us did not escape the destruction that was the fate of many others: their upper part was quarried and is missing, leaving their interiors exposed to the elements.

A typical burial chamber would generally contain three rock-cut shelves adjoining

Partial reconstruction of a burial cave

three of its four walls. The bodies of the deceased were laid supine on these shelves. At times we find that a sort of raised stone pillow was cut in the rock, featuring a carved headrest with an opening for the neck. The fashioning of the

Jerusalem City hall

David's Village neighborhood (formerly Mamilla)

San Salvador Church

the Citadel (David's Tower)

Greek Orthodox mon

Yemin Moshe neighborhood

Sultan's Pool

Hinnom Valley

burial shelf in the tomb before us teaches that four corpses were placed here head-to-toe. The burial shelf was a sort of bed, and the headrests probably simulated a portable wooden piece of furniture which was placed on the beds of people in this period, as is known from Egypt. The picture that emerges is that death may have been perceived at the time as a period of extended slumber in a dwelling fashioned like a house from the world of the living. Better preserved burial caves to the north of Damascus Gate indicate that the interior of the "eternal abode" was fashioned as a copy of sumptuous palaces: with engraved cornices, niches for door pivots, and even engravings on the stone walls imitating the wood overlays covering palace walls. Oil lamps, utensils for food and drink, and personal belongings such as jewelry, seals, etc. were placed alongside the corpse.

Row of headrests in a burial cave

In the next tomb 3, we see an especially wide shelf, with a row of six headrests. The sunken passage between the shelves enabled the burial attendants to stand comfortably within the cave while dealing with the corpse.

A considerable number of tombs from the First Temple period served as family burial sites over the course of several generations. This made economic sense, since the hewing and fashioning of a burial cave must have been quite expensive. Thus we find in the same tomb the grandfather, grandson, and great-grandson. The young people, who were familiar with

Dormition Abbey   American Institute for Holyland Research   Protestant graveyard

"Pope's Rd"   **Panoramic view from the Scottish church area**

the family tomb, knew that when their time came they would join the long line of their ancestors. We may assume that the knowledge that the unity of the protective family would continue beyond life in this world imparted a sense of security and consolation.

When all the burial shelves were filled with the dead, leaving no room for the burial of an additional family member, the accumulated bones would be cleared from the shelves and transferred for secondary burial in a large chamber dug under one of the shelves, along with the personal belongings of the dead.

The expression commonly used by the Bible in reference to death is "gathered" (as in "I will gather you to your fathers" – II Samuel 22:20; or "And all that generation were likewise gathered to their fathers" – Judges 2:10). This wording apparently refers to the first phase, when the body was brought to the tomb, while the second phase, when the bones were collected from the shelf and placed in the underground chamber, is termed "burial."

The remains of at least ninety-five corpses were found in the subterranean chamber before us, along with a treasure trove of glass jars, small pottery bottles, arrowheads, needles, makeup pencils, pot handles, earrings, silver rings, and gold jewelry in diverse patterns. The large quantity of jewelry attests to the wealth of those interred in this tomb and teaches us about their artistic tastes.

The most fascinating finds to have been uncovered here are two thin silver tablets, rolled up like scrolls. When they were opened, the researchers discovered engraved on them the Priestly Blessing known to us from the Bible (Numbers 6:24-26), with a few changes. This is the earliest biblical text to have been found in archaeological excavations, and it is dated to the seventh century BCE (according to another opinion, the sixth century BCE). The excavators are of the opinion that the scrolls were worn around the neck as an amulet. If this is correct, we are tempted to think that the wearing of an object containing verses from the

Torah was the beginning of the practice of wearing phylacteries. We will see a copy of one of these small tablets later on, in the Rahel Yanait Ben-Zvi Center for Jerusalem Studies.

We will continue along the path to another **cave** ◀4▶. One of its burial chambers was

In this **cave** the excavators discovered the remains of dozens of rifles, military uniform buttons, rank insignia, fragments of pipes, dice, horseshoes, and other items. It was learned from these finds that the cave was used as a weapons and ammunition store during the Ottoman period, and an army unit was probably stationed in the cave.

hewn at a lower level than the others, and its entrance is under a wide burial shelf. Such a "split-level" burial is rare. If you want to know how high the ceiling of the cave was, nothing could be simpler: the remains of an angular cornice cut at the junction of the walls and the ceiling are still visible at a height of two meters. Similar cornices are familiar to us from other tombs in Jerusalem, and also from the magnificent tombs of the kings of ancient Ararat in eastern Turkey.

We will leave the excavation site, go down Hebron Road, and then up Hativat Yerushalayim Street. On the way, to the left of the road, we see archaeological remains ◀5▶. These are the ruins of a tower which most likely formed part of the city wall during the First Temple period. The location of the tower teaches that the slopes of Mount Zion, which presently are to the south of and outside the Ottoman city wall, were encompassed by the city wall in the First Temple period. We will now enter the Jewish Quarter through Zion Gate. In the Quarter, we will walk along the main street (Rehov Ha-yehudim – Jewish Quarter Road) until the intersection with Plugat Ha-kotel Street, where we turn right for our next stop.

6 ◆ THE BROAD WALL

Plugat Ha-kotel Street

WHEN THE RUINS of the Broad Wall in the Jewish Quarter are viewed from above, a number of questions come to mind which undoubtedly troubled the excavators who uncovered it in the early 1970s, during the reconstruction of the Quarter. What was the purpose of such a massive wall in the heart of the city? Who built it? Why is it so broad? What was its original height? Why is its line so contorted? Do we know where it continued from here? Is there any hint of this wall in the Bible?

If we look at the map of the First Temple period city hanging at the site, we see that this wall is merely a portion of a long wall that extends from the Temple Mount area, encompasses the Western Hill of the city, and touches the City of David wall, in the process surrounding and protecting the Siloam Pool to the southwest of the City of David. The reconstruction of the course of the wall was based mainly on topographical considerations, while making use of the sparse remains of additional fortifications discovered alongside the Western Hill. The wall was probably built by King Hezekiah of Judah in the late eighth century BCE. Hezekiah was a leader of the international coalition of kings who rebelled against the rule of Assyria, a major power. As part of his preparations for the impending military confrontation, he took steps to fortify the cities and fortresses of the kingdom. He dug the Siloam Tunnel in Jerusalem (see Tour 1), and surrounded the outlying neighborhoods on the Western Hill with a defensive wall. The base of the wall at our feet exceeds seven meters in width. These exceptional dimensions led the researchers to identify it with the "broad wall" mentioned in the Book of Nehemiah (3:8). The gigantic yardstick on the wall of the facing building reconstructs its estimated original height (about eight meters). This may not seem so high from where we are, but we should remember that we are standing on the piles of refuse and debris that were heaped up here over thousands of years. The occupational level in the time of Hezekiah was much lower (look at the mark on the concrete wall opposite us), and from down there the wall must have seemed much more impressive. Was the wall so broad along its entire length? Not necessarily. Its builder may have been forced to widen the wall only on the northern side of the city, where we are, because it lacked natural topographical defenses, while a narrower wall would have sufficed for the other parts of the city, which were encompassed by deep valleys. The bend in the wall

The Broad Wall

before us was necessary in order to prevent the descent into the small riverbed that passes along here.

Look at the western end of the wall, that cuts through and destroys the remains of a house that stood there. The house evidently belonged to the unwalled neighborhood that had existed here before the wall was built. It seems that Hezekiah's engineers, who discovered that the house stood in the way of the planned wall, evicted its occupants by means of a royal edict, and possibly also dismantled some of its stones, which were then used in the fortification of the new wall. The prophet Isaiah, who was active in the city at the time, may have been referring to this phenomenon when he reproached the inhabitants of Jerusalem: "and you counted the houses of Jerusalem and pulled houses down to fortify the wall" (Isaiah 22:10) – an early instance of eviction for urban renewal.

In 701 BCE the wall was put to the test, when the troops of Sennacherib king of

Assyria, who had taken Judah by storm and left devastation and ruin in their wake, stood at the gates of Jerusalem. The Bible relates that Rabshakeh, the Assyrian commander, sought to avoid a battle and attempted to persuade the beleaguered Jerusalemites to surrender. His speech in front of the walls is a masterpiece of psychological warfare, incorporating both threats and enticements, as he sought to undermine the fighting spirit of the defenders and their faith in Hezekiah and his politics:

Then Rabshakeh said to them, "You tell Hezekiah... on whom are you relying, that you have rebelled against me? You rely, of all things, on Egypt, that splintered reed of a staff, which enters and punctures the palm of anyone who leans on it! That's what Pharaoh king of Egypt is like to all who rely on him.... The Lord Himself told me: Go up against that land and destroy it.... Don't listen to Hezekiah... come out to me... until I come and take you away to a land like your own, a land of grain [fields] and vineyards, of bread and wine, of olive oil and honey, so that you may live and not die. Don't listen to Hezekiah, who misleads you by saying, 'The Lord will save us'" (II Kings 18:19-32).

The Bible further notes that he delivered the entire speech in Hebrew, and not in Aramaic, which was the international diplomatic language (as is English today), in order to influence the masses who heard him.

Then there is a dramatic turn of events: "That night an angel of the Lord went out and struck down one hundred and eighty-five thousand in the Assyrian camp, and the following morning they were all dead corpses. So King Sennacherib of Assyria broke camp and retreated, and stayed in Nineveh" (II Kings 19:35-36). Jerusalem was left in peace, and the Assyrian soldiers did not set foot on its soil. The Assyrian sources describing these events also relate that Sennacherib did not conquer the city, which submitted and paid a heavy tribute. What really happened in this strange episode? Did a plague break out in the Assyrian camp? Did Hezekiah yield to their monetary demands and thereby save the city? Perhaps Sennacherib left the city untouched, because he had to contend with another military threat somewhere else within his empire, as the Bible hints in another passage (II Kings 19:7-9)? In any event, the story of the deliverance of Jerusalem became an important factor in the sanctification of the city in the consciousness of the people of Israel, in that and the following generations.

7   THE ISRAELITE TOWER

Shonei Halakhot Street

MANY OF US HAVE OFTEN seen glass bottles with a model of a large sailing ship inside, and have probably wondered how the craftsman managed to insert into the bottle an object larger than the width of its neck. You may also wonder about the presence of this massive tower under a modern building. In this case, however, the explanation is much simpler: after the Six-Day War, when archaeological excavations began at this site, which was strewn with ruins and debris, and remains of early fortifications were found, it was decided to cover them temporarily. A modern house was built over them, and only then were the fortifications uncovered for a second time and prepared for display.

When we stand with our backs to the wall, we can discern – even if we aren't expert archaeologists – that these are fortifications from two different periods: the tower on the right, which is built of **unhewn stones**, similar to those used in the Broad Wall, was most likely a gate tower from the late First Temple period (also known as the Israelite period, from which it derives its name: the "Israelite Tower"). Adjoining this tower, on the left, is one from the Second Temple period, belonging to the "First Wall" of the three walls described by Josephus in this period (see Tour 3). The masonry of this tower consists of ashlars characteristic of Hasmonean structures. The black mark on the floor denotes its continuation beneath our feet.

◆ **Unhewn stones** are
◆ unworked fieldstones,
◆ while ashlars are
◆ dressed stones.

The maps and drawings on the wall teach us that the Israelite Tower and the

Israelite Tower

section of the Broad Wall are two different fortifications, and probably were not in use at the same time. The tower, the later of the two, is built within the streambed which was skirted by the Broad Wall.

Advance to the end of the hall, and look beyond the railing. On the dirt floor at the foot of the tower we can see remains of ashes and soot, attesting to the conflagration that raged here when the Babylonian army broke into the city in 586 BCE, at the conclusion of a siege that lasted a year and a half. Did a torch thrown from one of the positions on the tower set fire to a Babylonian siege engine when it approached too close to the wall? A group of arrow-heads, which were found in the layer of soot, has been reconstructed and is on display. Three of them are made of iron and have flat heads, of the type used by the army of Judah. The fourth arrowhead, polygonal in shape, is made of bronze and was used by the foreign armies that fought in the Land of Israel. A photograph of the original arrowheads can be seen in the lighted display cases on the wall.

The conquest of Jerusalem by Nebuchadnezzar king of Babylon was accompanied by great destruction: "He burned the House of the Lord, the king's palace, and all the houses of Jerusalem; he burned down the house of every notable person.... [They] tore down the walls of Jerusalem on every side" (II Kings 25:9-10).

Zedekiah, the rebel king of the city, who attempted to escape, was seized by the Babylonians and suffered an especially bitter fate: "They captured the king and brought him before the king of Babylon... and they put him on trial. They slaughtered Zedekiah's sons before his eyes; then Zedekiah's eyes were put out. He was chained in bronze fetters and he was brought to Babylon" (II Kings 25:6-7).

The destruction of the city and the deportation of its inhabitants brought to a conclusion the four hundred years of the First Temple period, which had begun when David conquered the city and made it his capital.

8 — THE ARIEL CENTER

Plugat Ha-kotel Street, corner of Shonei Halakhot Street

ARIEL – THE CENTER FOR JERUSALEM in the First Temple Period was opened in 1987 by Yad Izhak Ben-Zvi, under the academic aegis of outstanding scholars, headed by Dr. Rivka Gonen. In the center of the exhibit is a large model, covering an area of 35 square meters, which presents a bird's-eye view of most of the current archaeological information regarding the topography, fortifications, residential structures and waterworks of the First Temple period city. The model was built by Yehudah and Shirley Levi-Aldema. The Center provides us with a good opportunity to sum up what we have learned about Jerusalem in the first two tours. An audio-visual three-dimensional show which surveys the development of the city in the First Temple period is screened here. In the hall with the model there is a second model depicting the Assyrian army breaching the wall of a city in Judah in the eighth century BCE. It is based on Assyrian reliefs and written historical sources. Alongside this model is an exact copy of the Siloam inscription (see Tour 1).

Model of besieged city in the Center for Jerusalem in the First Temple Period

In the adjoining hall are copies of important finds, such as the tablet with the Priestly Blessing found in the Kettef Hinnom tombs, a collection of seal impressions from the City of David, an ivory pomegranate which researchers attribute to the Temple of Solomon, and a model of a burial cave. The exhibits cast light on various aspects of daily life in the city, such as the script in use at the time, the form of burial, and manifestations of paganism. The Center conducts educational activities on these topics for schoolchildren of different ages and for families. Our tour ends here.

Copy of the Priestly Blessing

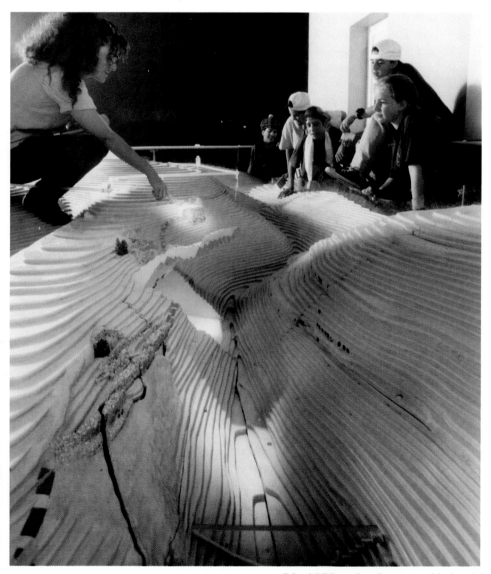

Schoolchildren view the topographical model

The Second Temple period begins with the dedication of the Second Temple (516 BCE) by the returnees from Babylon and ends with its destruction on the Ninth of Av, 70 CE. During this span of more than five hundred years, the city came under the rule of different conquerors: Persians, Greeks, and Romans. This period was also marked by eighty years of Jewish independence, under the reign of the Hasmoneans.

The declaration by Cyrus king of Persia in 539 BCE brought the first returnees from Babylon to Jerusalem, about half a century after they had been exiled from the city. Those returning to Zion erected the Second Temple while contending with attacks by the Cutheans (Samaritans) who had been settled by the Assyrians in the region of Samaria. "Many of the priests and Levites and the chiefs of the clans, the old men who had seen the first house, wept loudly at the sight of the founding of this house. Many others shouted joyously at the top of their voices" (Ezra 3:12).

Nehemiah, the Jewish governor of Judah who had been appointed by Artaxerxes I, came to the Land of Israel in 445 BCE and restored the city walls, despite the incessant disturbances by the peoples dwelling in the land. Some of Nehemiah's activity was revealed in the excavations on the slopes of the City of David.

Jerusalem, the capital of the province of Yehud, was smaller than the city of the late First Temple period, both in area and in population. There are few physical remains from this time.

Palestine underwent an upheaval in 332 BCE, and the conquests of Alexander the Great ushered in a new era – the Hellenistic period. Alexander's sudden death led to the division of his empire between the Ptolemies in Egypt and the Seleucids in Syria. Palestine was ruled initially by the Ptolemies and later by the Seleucids. The country, especially the coastal plain, became a battlefield and the arena for military campaigns.

The idolatrous decrees of Antiochus IV Epiphanes led to the outbreak of the Hasmonean revolt against Seleucid rule. The Books of Maccabees are one of the main sources for our knowledge of this uprising. The successful revolt culminated in the establishment of the Hasmonean state (140 BCE).

Jerusalem, which was now the capital of the independent Hasmonean monarchy, slowly grew and returned to its dimensions of the late First Temple period. The Hasmoneans made use of the remains of the city wall that had survived from the First Temple period. Hellenistic culture exerted ever-growing influence, and was felt in all aspects of daily life. This influence upon Jerusalem and Eretz Israel would extend far beyond this period. After the death of the Hasmonean queen Salome in 67 BCE, the kingdom suffered from internal struggles and civil war between her sons Hyrcanus and Aristobulus, which brought in their wake intervention by the Roman superpower upon the invitation of the warring parties. The Roman army, commanded by Pompey, conquered Jerusalem (63 BCE) and brought an end to the independent Hasmonean kingdom. This was the beginning of Roman rule, in the latter days of the Second Temple period.

The central figure in Jerusalem and the Land of Israel in the late Second Temple period was without question King Herod (37–4 BCE), who assumed power under the aegis of the Romans. His building projects completely changed the face of the city, and its population grew. A considerable portion of the city's inhabitants were priests and those close to the royal house, who lived in the Upper City. Along with the Pharisees and Sadducees, other sects also inhabited the city, such as the Essenes, who probably lived in its southwestern section. The life of Second Temple period Jerusalem centered around the Temple service. The Temple was not only the spiritual and religious focus of the Jewish people, it also constituted the economic basis of the city.

After Herod's death his kingdom was split between his heirs (4 BCE). Some time afterwards, Judea and Jerusalem came under the control of Roman procurators. The city endured years of instability, antigovernment agitation, and internal struggles between the different political factions. Jesus and his disciples were active in Jerusalem at the end of this period.

The great revolt against the Romans began in 66 CE. Four years later Jerusalem fell after a difficult and bloody war. The Temple was burned on the ninth day of the Hebrew month of Av, and a month later, after fierce house-to-house fighting – as attested by the many archaeological finds and the descriptions of Josephus, the historian of the period – the entire city surrendered to the Roman legions commanded by Titus and its remaining inhabitants were sent into exile.

For a map of Jerusalem in this period see p. 208.

Entrance to the Second Temple (model) ⟶

SECOND TEMPLE PERIOD

From the Model of Second Temple Jerusalem to En-Ya'el

ONE OF THE BEST-KNOWN tourist sites in Jerusalem is the model of Jerusalem in the late Second Temple period on the grounds of the Holyland Hotel. As we walk around the model, we feel like Gulliver in the land of the Lilliputians. It gives us a rare opportunity for a birds-eye view of the city, and even more exciting, a glimpse of what it might have looked like in the distant past.

There are several models in Jerusalem that provide a good picture of the city in different periods: the model of the city in the First Temple period located in the Jewish Quarter (see Tour 2); the Temple Mount model in the Western Wall Tunnel (see Tour 4); the model of the modern city used by the city planners, in the new Jerusalem Municipality building; and the various models of the city in the Tower of David Museum (see Tour 30). The model in the Holyland Hotel is undoubtedly the most impressive of them all, due both to its size, artistic level, and scientific accuracy, as well as to the fact that late Second Temple period Jerusalem was a large and very magnificent city. The model was planned by the late Prof. Michael Avi-Yonah of the Hebrew University, designed by Havah Avi-Yonah, and built in 1964–68 by A. Shefler and R. Brozen.The original idea for the model came from the hotel's owner, in memory of his son Zvi who fell in the War of Independence.

The model shows Jerusalem on the eve of the great revolt, after which the city was destroyed by the Roman legions in 70 CE. It is built to a scale of 1:50, that is, every centimeter represents fifty centimeters in reality (by this scale, the height of a person in the model would be less than that of a match). The sources for the reconstruction were the finds from the archaeological excavations conducted in the city, which provided less information when the model was being prepared than is available today. Avi-Yonah also used historical sources, primarily the writings of Josephus and the Mishnaic tractate of *Middot*,

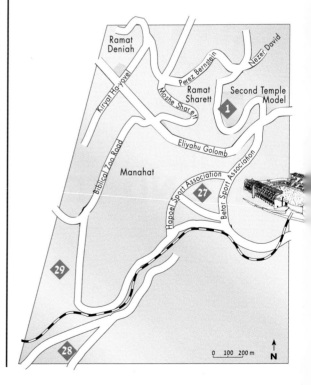

which describes the Temple Mount in detail. He also drew upon considerable available knowledge on construction and urbanization in the classical world, of which, to a great extent, Jerusalem was a part.

It should be borne in mind that Avi-Yonah did not attempt to reconstruct each and every house. The model is more of an effort to present the general character of the city. Where possible, the sites are reconstructed precisely, while in other areas Avi-Yonah used his imagination. The model contains a great deal of information about sites, some of which we will see on the tours dealing with the Second Temple and Roman periods.

The route: the tour begins with the model of Jerusalem in the Holyland Hotel, proceeding from there to En Ya'el by way of the Jerusalem Shopping Mall.

Duration of the tour: about three hours.

Public transportation: buses nos. 21, 21a to the Holyland Hotel. From there, we take a short walk following the signs to the model south of the hotel.

By private car: the parking lot near the model. After the tour of the model, drive to the Jerusalem Shopping Mall via Bernstein St., Moshe Sharett Blvd., and Golomb St.

Visiting hours: model of the city: entire week: 8:00 a.m.–10:00 p.m. Entrance fee.

En-Ya'el: entire week: 9:30 a.m.–4 p.m. Entrance fee. For the guided tour and participation in the activities, call 6413257.

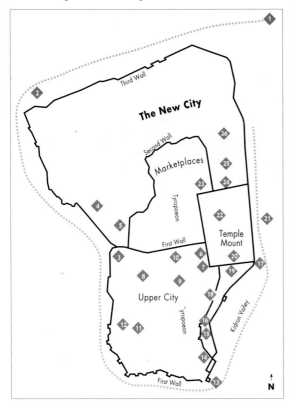

Observation porch north of the model

W HEN ROAMING AROUND A STRANGE CITY, one should be accompanied by one of the locals. We will follow this procedure and let the descriptions of Josephus guide us from our observation point of the model, while referring to the map of the route through the model:

The city was built on two hills which are opposite to one another, and have a valley to divide them asunder... Of these hills, that which contains the upper city is much higher, and in length more direct. Accordingly, it was called the "Citadel" by King David... but it is by us called the "Upper Marketplace." But the other hill, which was called "Acra," and sustains the lower city... over against this was a third hill, but naturally lower than Acra and parted formerly from the other by a broad valley. However, in those times... they filled up that valley with earth, and had a mind to join the city to the Temple. They then took off part of the height of Acra, and reduced it to be of less elevation than it was before, that the Temple might be superior to it (Josephus, *War of the Jews,* 5:4:1).

Josephus describes three hills, which are actually two: to the west (our right), the

Western Hill, on which the Upper City was built; to the east of it we see the hill on which the Temple stood (the third hill); and to its south, the second hill, also known as the "Acra," where the Lower City was located. The Upper City is separated from the Acra hill by a valley which significantly affects the topography of the city. Josephus refers to this valley as the Tyropoeon, which is Greek for "Cheesemaker's Valley." The source of the name is unknown, and it may be a corruption. This valley is no longer a prominent feature, because, like many other places in Jerusalem, the topography of the area changed due to the large quantities of alluvium that accumulated over the course of time and filled in some of its valleys.

From this observation point we can readily discern the differences between the two parts of the city. Visible on the upper part of the Western Hill are the houses of the rich with tile roofs, arranged in a grid pattern while the slope of the Western Hill is covered with dense construction – more humble houses packed close together. The Temple Mount is the most prominent and highest feature of the city. To its north, in the area closer to us, is the new quarter of the city, the "**Bezetha,**" as Josephus calls it. In the model this quarter is built as a neighborhood of villas, with much open space, since it was not fully populated before the destruction of the city. From this point we clearly see the three walls that encircle the city. Once again we refer to the description of Josephus: "The city of Jerusalem was fortified with three walls... Now, of these three walls, the old one... because David and Solomon, and the following kings, were very zealous about this work" (*War of the Jews* 5:4:1-2). Josephus continues with a description of the line of the Second Wall, the most distant from us, which encompasses more than half of the

The term **"Bezetha"** (also rendered Bethesda) is unclear. Some claim that it is a corruption of the Aramaic *beizeita* (the "house of the olive," because of the olive trees that grew there). Others suggest that this is a corruption of the Aramaic term *betza'ta,* which is possibly connected with the term *bitzah,* "pool," because of the pools in the area; or with the Aramaic word *bitzu'a,* meaning smooth, sliced, alluding to Bezetha being a new section of the city.

city. He attributes it to the time of David and Solomon. Today, after the excavations in the Jewish Quarter of the Old City (see the Israelite Tower in Tour 2), it has now become evident that to a certain extent Josephus was right: the wall was not built by David or Solomon, nor by the following kings of Judah, but this essentially is the wall that, from the time of the Bible, surrounded Jerusalem's western quarter.

Herod's palace with a section of the Third Wall

Its builders saw before them the ruins of the city wall from the First Temple period, and they incorporated these remains in their wall.

The Second Wall, which is situated between the other two, started, according to Josephus, "from that gate which they called 'Gennath' [close to the group of towers to the right] which belonged to the first wall; it only encompassed the northern quarter of the city, and reached as far as the tower Antonia [the fortress adjoining the Temple Mount on the north]" (*War of the Jews 5:4:2*).

The Third Wall is the outermost wall, the one closest to us. It too began close to the Gennath Gate and ended at the northern wall of the Temple Mount. The question that naturally arises is, why were three different walls built for the city, when a single long one would have sufficed? The explanation is quite simple: these walls were built over the course of two centuries. Whenever the city expanded and a new neighborhood was built outside the wall, this quarter would eventually be surrounded by a new wall, and so the First Wall was joined by the Second and Third Walls. The First and Second Walls were probably built in the Hasmonean period, while the Third Wall was erected shortly before the destruction of the city, and its construction was hastily completed just before the outbreak of the great revolt against the Romans.

In the last phases the city's expansion was to the north, because its growth to the east and the west was blocked, respectively, by the Kidron and Hinnom Valleys.

Let's descend from the observation point and begin to circle the model of the city from the northwest, moving in a counterclockwise direction.

2 ▸ THE TOWER OF PSEPHINUS

ONE OF THE HIGHEST TOWERS IN JERUSALEM at the time was the Tower of Psephinus, which stood in the northwestern corner of the city wall. We may assume that not everyone was permitted to climb to the top of the tower, which was part of the city's fortifications and undoubtedly housed a garrison. The few who were allowed to ascend, however, must have seen a breathtaking panorama, as Josephus relates: "for being seventy cubits high [35 meters], it both afforded a prospect of Arabia at sun-rising, as well as it did of the Hebrew possessions at the sea westward. Moreover, it was an octagon..." (*War of the Jews 5:4:3*).

From this tower, which apparently stood in the area of the present-day Russian Compound and soared to a height of 35 meters, the region of Moab and the Dead Sea was visible to the east, and the Mediterranean Sea to the west. From where we are standing we have a good view of the new Bezetha quarter. Luxurious houses have been reconstructed here, and the area most likely also contained inns for the many pilgrims who visited the city.

You will note that there are very few **green areas** in the model. This is connected with a "municipal bylaw" prohibiting the establishment of gardens and orchards

It was technically extremely difficult to create **green areas** in the model that would survive heat, rain, and wind. The attempts to include vegetation or areas resembling vegetation were not successful, and the plastic vegetation we see in the model had to be imported from Japan.

within the city limits, as is mentioned in the Babylonian Talmud: "No dunghills should be made there; no kilns should be kept there; neither gardens nor orchards should be cultivated there... no fowls should be raised there" (*Bava Kamma 82b*). This prohibition was probably instituted to prevent the unpleasant odor coming from the manure used to fertilize gardens. Excluded from this prohibition were the rose gardens in the city. This law apparently was not strictly observed in the new, richer neighborhoods, and the reconstructors have added green areas here and there.

HEROD'S PALACE AND THE TOWERS 3

A BOUT WHERE WE ARE STANDING, the Hinnom Valley begins to cut its course southward and forms the western boundary of Jerusalem. Here is where Herod built his palace, which was defended on the north by three towers named after "those three persons who had been the dearest to him. They were his brother [Phasaelus], his friend [Hippicus], and his wife [Mariamne]" (*War of the Jews 5:4:3*).

The three towers of Herod

Today, in the courtyard of the Tower of David Museum, adjacent to Jaffa Gate, you can see the base of a massive tower attributed to the time of Herod, but it is unclear whether this was the Phasael Tower or the Hippicus Tower. Michael Avi-Yonah placed the three towers in a triangular formation, to form a sort of fortified precinct, while other scholars maintain that they stood in a straight line along the wall.

Slightly to the left of the towers we see the funerary monument of the Hasmonean John Hyrcanus 4, who ruled during the years 135–104 BCE. Next to this monument (which, incidentally, has not been revealed in the excavations) is the Pool of the **Towers** 5, which is identified with the still-existing pool close to Jaffa Gate (see Tour 7).

Also visible from here is the Second Wall and the marketplace area that it

> Josephus calls this pool by the Greek name Amygdalon (almonds). This seems to be a corruption of its conjectured Hebrew name, **Ha-Migdalim (towers)** so called because of its proximity to the towers of Herod's Palace.

Herod's Palace and the Upper City

The Hasmonean palace

bounds. Look in the direction of the Temple Mount and its walls. A section of the Western Wall, which is currently used for prayers, is marked by a red line. North of it is an arched bridge (Wilson's Arch) **6** that connects the Temple Mount with the Upper City, and to its south a huge overpass (Robinson's Arch) **7** extends over a paved street running alongside the Western Wall. We will now look at Herod's palace, which is surrounded by round towers. The palace stood on the site of the present-day Tower of David Museum and the Old City police station (the Kishle). The excavations in this area uncovered the foundations of a structure identified with the palace (for the Herodian towers and the palace, see Tour 30).

The Upper City extends behind the palace. Here lived the nobility, the priests, the members of the royal family and those close to them. The large domiciles (we can gain an idea of the splendor and size of these houses during a visit to the Herodian Quarter – see Tour 5), the straight streets arranged in a grid pattern, the stone paving, and the tile roofs all imparted to the city the appearance of an affluent Roman city. Adjoining the palace on the east is a rectangular plaza bounded by a colonnade structure **8**. This is the Agora – the Upper Market – which is reconstructed in the model as a copy of the Agora in Athens. Several structures stand out within the area of the Upper City: we see the semicircular **theater** **9** that is described by Josephus, the exact location of which is unknown. Two towers resembling pagodas mark the Hasmonean palace **10**, which has not been revealed in the excavations and whose exact location has not been determined.

A **theater** was a semicircular structure in which performances were presented, in contrast to the amphitheater, which (as is alluded by the prefix amphi-, which means bi- in Greek) was fully circular in shape – like two theaters joined together. The amphitheaters were generally used for gladiatoral and animal-baiting contests, while the theaters were generally the venue for plays.

The shape of the towers in the model was inspired by structures in Petra. Josephus relates (*Antiquities* 20:8:11) that King Agrippa would recline at his leisure on the roof of this palace and watch the priests as they offered the sacrifices at the altar on the Temple Mount. The priests complained about this practice and raised the western wall of the Temple Courtyard, thereby blocking the king's line of sight. Since the close location of the altar was known to the researchers, they could conclude from this where the palace must have stood, to enable the king to observe the offering of the sacrifices, and accordingly determined its place in the model.

DAVID'S TOMB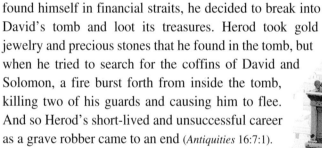

11

T O THE SOUTH OF HEROD'S PALACE is a stone monument topped by a pyramid. We are standing next to the present-day Mount Zion (that is, the part of the Western Hill outside the Ottoman wall that encompasses the Old City). The tradition that places David's Tomb at this site is a relatively late one. The tomb had to have been within the bounds of the City of David, on the Acra hill, but the reconstruction nevertheless relies upon the commonly accepted tradition, until the real site is discovered. Scholars have proposed that, even if David himself is not buried on Mount Zion, other kings of the Davidic dynasty may have been interred here.

David's burial place was known in Herod's time. It is related that when Herod found himself in financial straits, he decided to break into David's tomb and loot its treasures. Herod took gold jewelry and precious stones that he found in the tomb, but when he tried to search for the coffins of David and Solomon, a fire burst forth from inside the tomb, killing two of his guards and causing him to flee. And so Herod's short-lived and unsuccessful career as a grave robber came to an end (*Antiquities* 16:7:1).

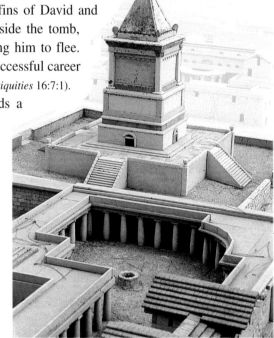

Close to the tomb structure stands a large house **12** whose remains were uncovered in the vicinity of the Dormition Abbey on Mount Zion, outside Zion Gate. Some traditions identify this as the home of the High Priest Caiaphas, in whose time Jesus was active in Jerusalem.

David's Tomb

THE FORK OF stream-beds where we are standing marks the southern end of the city. To the right is the Kidron Valley; in the center, between the Western and Eastern Hills, passes the valley which Josephus termed the Tyropoeon; and to the left, the Hinnom Valley. The Tyropoeon

The Lower City

contains a pool , the Siloam Pool, which received the water of the Gihon Spring that had been diverted by King Hezekiah from the east to the west and into the city (see Tour 1). In the Second Temple period, the fact that the water originated in the spring apparently was forgotten. Since the water continued to flow through the tunnel and emerged in the place known as "Siloam," the location where it emerged was erroneously regarded as the spring itself and was called the "Siloam Spring." Such confusion regarding names is very common in our time as well. The water was brought up from the Siloam Pool to the Temple,

The **Simhat Bet Ha-sho'evah** ceremony was held in the Temple on each of the evenings of the intermediate days during the Festival of Sukkot. It was connected with the libation on the Altar of water which was drawn from the Gihon Spring. The rejoicing was character-ized by much light: "And there was not a courtyard in Jerusalem that was not illumi-nated by the light of the place of the water-drawing" (Mishnah, *Sukkah* 5:3).

for the **Simhat Bet Ha-sho'evah** ceremony ("the rejoicing of the place of water-drawing"). "How was the water libation [performed]? A golden saucer holding three *log*s [a liquid measure] was filled from the Siloam. When they arrived at the Water Gate, they sounded a long blast..." (Mishnah, *Sukkah* 4:9). In winter, much runoff flowed from the valley into the Siloam area. On the eastern slope of

the Western Hill is a graphic reconstruction of a residential quarter of the common people. Some of the houses are built of clay, and the contrast with the sumptuous domiciles on the summit of this hill is striking. This reconstruction apparently was inspired by the village of Silwan, which is situated on the Mount of Olives, to the east of the present-day Old City.

Facing us is the ancient City of David. The line of the eastern wall before us dates from the time of the Return to Zion. In the First Temple period, the wall was located lower down, on the slope of the hill, as we learn from the archaeological excavations. The southernmost of the reconstructed buildings in the City of David is a synagogue . A few Second Temple period sources mention the existence of synagogues in Jerusalem. Thus, for example, we read in the Jerusalem Talmud: "There were four hundred and eighty synagogues in Jerusalem, and each had a school and study hall" (*Megillah* 1c). Synagogues are also mentioned in the New Testament: "Then some of those who belonged to the synagogue of the Freedmen (as it was called), and of the Cyrenians, and of the Alexandrians, and of those from Cilicia and Asia, arose..." (Acts of the Apostles 6:9). But why did the reconstructor decide to place a synagogue here? In 1913 the excavations at the south of the City of David revealed a stone tablet bearing an inscription that mentions an individual named Theodotos son of Vetanos who was an *arche-synagogos* ("the head of a synagogue" in Greek). The tablet was found cast aside in a quarry, and we cannot be sure that a synagogue stood on this spot. Since, however, the tablet was found here, it was decided to locate a synagogue structure at this point.

To the north of the synagogue are two large structures conspicuous for their architectural peculiarity 16. They do not have a stone overlay, and are painted purple and pink. Built in the style of palaces from Mesopotamia, they are the palaces of the royal family of Adiabene (a kingdom in what is now northern Iraq)

who converted to Judaism, and some of whom came to live in Jerusalem (see Tour 6). The palaces were placed here in the model because of an incidental remark by Josephus that when the buildings on the Temple Mount went up in flames in 70 CE, the conflagration also spread to the palaces of the royal family of Adiabene (*War of the Jews* 6:6:3).

The palaces of the royal family of Adiabene

THE CORNER OF THE TEMPLE MOUNT 17

THE HOLYLAND MODEL IS DYNAMIC, and is constantly changing in accordance with new archaeological discoveries in the city. The area to the south and southwest of the Temple Mount in the model has undergone many changes since it was first designed by Prof. Avi-Yonah. In the area of the Western Wall, close to the southwest corner, is the staircase of Robinson's Arch, which is reconstructed in the model as an overpass that extends above a paved street running alongside the Western Wall. Formerly, this arch had been reconstructed as the beginning of an arched bridge leading to the Upper City, but was amended as a result of the finds from the excavations next to the Western Wall. To the south of the Temple Mount stands a large elliptic structure 18. This is the hippodrome (hippo = horse in

Robinson's Arch

The hippodrome

Greek), where horse and chariot races were held. Jerusalem had a hippodrome, but its location has not been determined. It is now clear that it did not stand in this area, but as long as its exact position is not known, it will not be moved in the model. A staircase leads up from the plaza to the south of the Temple Mount to the two Huldah Gates in the southern wall. In the plaza we see a monument topped by a pyramid **19**. This is the funerary monument of Huldah the prophetess which, according to the sources, was within the city (*Tosefta, Bava Batra* 1:11). Its placement here is based on the assumption that the gates were named after the prophetess, whose tomb was located in the vicinity. The excavations conducted at the site, however, have not revealed any traces of a funerary monument. Incidentally, a medieval tradition places Huldah's tomb on the Mount of Olives.

The Huldah Gates led to tunnels through which anyone entering the Mount reached its plaza, and the tunnel exits are visible in the plaza. Pay special attention to the large colonnaded structure along the southern wall. This is the Royal Portico, or basilica **20**, in which various services were provided for pilgrims, such as money changing and the sale of animals for sacrifices. Those of us who have already been in the Western Wall tunnels may recall that in the model of the Temple Mount there, the Royal Portico is situated further inside,

within the Temple Mount plaza, and that this model also differs in other respects from the one found at the Holyland Hotel. These two models represent different interpretations of the description of the compound as it appears in the sources.

The western Huldah Gates

THE TEMPLE MOUNT, which we are facing, was reconstructed mainly on the basis of the Tractate *Middot* in the Mishnah. The gate in the eastern wall of the Temple Mount is called Shushan Gate, since, according to *Middot* (1:3) "there was a representation of the capital city of Shushan over it." The Temple Mount plaza is encompassed by stoas whose capitals are gold plated. The stone-paved plaza could contain the masses of people who thronged to the Temple on the three pilgrimage festivals (its area equals that of 12 soccer fields!). Opposite the Shushan Gate, the Sanctuary 22, clad with marble slabs, towers in the west. There are two pink granite columns in its facade. These columns stand in place of the two columns that flanked the entrance of the Sanctuary in the First Temple and were called Yachin and Boaz. The Bronze Altar, on which the sacrifices were offered,

Second Temple

stood in front of the Sanctuary. This narrow area was known as the Court of the Israelites. Anyone who was not a priest was permitted to enter this area, in order to be present when his sacrifice was offered. The Court of the Israelites is bounded on the east by two bronze doors that were donated by a person named Nicanor. An ancient Hebrew source tells of a miracle that befell these doors:

When Nicanor brought them from Alexandria in Egypt, a gale in the sea threatened to sink them. They took one of them and cast it into the sea. They sought to cast the other one, but he [Nicanor] would not allow them.... He was aggrieved until he arrived at the port of Jaffa. When he arrived at the port of Jaffa... a creature in the sea... spat out [the door] and cast it onto the dry land (*Tosefta, Yoma* 2:4).

At the foot of the brass doors are the fifteen steps (*ma'alot*) arranged in a semicircle, on which the Levites would stand when they sang the "Song of Ascents [*Ma'alot*]" (Psalms 120-134).

The open space in front of these stairs is the Women's Court, each of whose four corners contained a chamber used for storing the wood which was needed as fuel for the altar, for the purification of lepers, etc.

The Temple was surrounded by the Soreg, a fence with stone inscriptions in Greek and Latin, warning Gentiles not to enter the sacred precinct, and threatening offenders with death. Two such inscriptions were discovered in archaeological excavations in the city.

THE INFLUX OF TENS OF THOUSANDS of pilgrims to the Temple Mount on the three pilgrimage festivals created a sensitive situation in the city of which the authorities were ever wary. Instigators and agitators against the government were always likely to take advantage of the charged atmosphere, the inflamed spirits, and the spiritual elevation engendered by the holidays. This was probably the reason why Herod built to the north of the Temple Mount the Antonia Fortress, named after his friend **Mark Antony**, one of the three rulers of Rome at the time. The fortress, which made possible the surveillance of everything happening on the Temple Mount, was built on the site where the Hasmonean Citadel (*birah*) had previously stood. A Roman garrison would later be stationed here.

Mark Antony (83-30 BCE) ruled in Rome as a member of a triumvirate, together with Lepidus and Octavian. He is known especially for his love affair with Cleopatra queen of Egypt, an episode which was described by Shakespeare in the play *Antony and Cleopatra*. In the power struggle between Antony and Octavian, after the deposition of Lepidus, Octavian was victorious; he named himself Augustus (= the divine), and established himself as the sole ruler in Rome.

Scholars are currently of the opinion that the fortress was smaller than its representation in the model. Its size may not have exceeded that of one of the towers in the reconstructed fortress. According to a prevalent tradition, it was here that the Roman procurator Pontias Pilate judged Jesus, and it was from here that Jesus went forth bearing the cross to the site of the Crucifixion. According to another view, the Roman procurator resided in the area of Herod's palace, and Jesus' trial was conducted there and not in the Antonia Fortress.

Close to the northern wall we also see a large reservoir 24 into which floodwater from the area drained. This pool was known in recent generations by its Arabic names, as the "Pool of the Tribes" or the "Pool of Israel". Until shortly after the Six-Day War, its remains were still visible near the Lions' Gate.

Antonia Fortress

Another pool is situated not far from here, in the Bezetha quarter. This pool, which is called Bethesda or the "Sheep Pool," 25 still exists in the courtyard of the Church of St. Anne. This site apparently housed a pagan temple and medical installations (see Tour 8).

To the north of the pool is the funerary monument of the Hasmonean king Alexander Yannai (103–76 BCE) 26. Our walk around the model is completed.

We will now go down to the road to the south which leads to the Jerusalem Shopping Mall **27**, about a fifteen-minute walk from the model.

The Shopping Mall, which was opened in 1993, is one of the largest and most modern ones in Israel and a major shopping and entertainment center in the city. We can stop here for a short rest. As we enter the Mall, pay special attention to the glass wall on the southern side, adjoining the Food Court, which affords us a breathtaking view of the Gilo neighborhood and the park with pine trees to its south.

After resting in the Shopping Mall we can visit a number of other sites in the vicinity which are not connected with the Second Temple period. The afforested slope at the foot of which issues forth the En Ya'el spring **28** (known in Arabic as Ein Yalo) is covered by a series of agricultural terraces. Remains of agricultural installations and farms were found in this area, and in the vicinity of the **Manahat (Malha)** neighborhood and the Biblical Zoo opposite it, attesting to agricultural activity around ancient Jerusalem from the third millennium BCE to the present.

The En Ya'el Active Museum was established on the site of a farm from the Roman-Byzantine period. It contains a farmhouse whose floor is decorated with a breathtaking mosaic depicting a number of figures from Greek mythology.

Close to the farmhouse we see the conduit roofed with stone slabs, which still leads the water of En Ya'el to the nearby storage pools. A bathhouse, which was an integral part of Roman culture, is also to be found here. You are invited to walk about the site and along its green paths, following the map available at the museum. If you come at the right time, you will see groups of visitors on the terraces engaging in various ancient labors, under the guidance of the site's staff members (call in advance to join any of the workshops).

After our visit to the museum, we will return to the road, in the direction of the Shopping Mall, and turn left at the first traffic light to the new Biblical Zoo **29** located on the northern slopes of Refa'im Valley. The Zoo moved here in 1994 from its previous home in the Romemah neighborhood. In addition to the animals we can see archaeological excavations containing remains of ancient farms from the Middle Bronze Age (first half of the second millennium BCE).

The Arab village of **Malha** was conquered by the Israel Defense Forces on 14 July 1948. Its name was changed to Manahat, after the biblical settlement that, it is conjectured, had formerly occupied this site (I Chronicles 8:6). In the 1950s new immigrants from North Africa were settled in the houses of the village. In the 1990s construction began of the new neighborhood of **Manahat,** close to the abandoned village. The old houses were renovated and property values rose. Malha was incorporated in the development of the entire area (the Shopping Mall, the stadium, the industrial area, etc.).

A scene in the Biblical Zoo

The Western Wall Excavations and Tunnel

IN THE LATE SECOND TEMPLE period Jerusalem reached the peak of its greatness under the rule of King Herod (37–4 BCE). In this relatively short period Jerusalem changed its appearance, being transformed from a small city on the fringes of the Roman Empire to an architectural jewel that competed with the magnificence of Athens, Rome, and Alexandria. The Roman historian Pliny the Elder (23–79 CE), who described the civilized world of the time in his book, singled out Jerusalem, noting that it was "the most renowned of the cities of the East."

Herod's construction projects left their mark throughout the land, from Masada in the south to Banias in the north, and even beyond the boundaries of the kingdom – in Damascus, Beirut, Rhodes and elsewhere. The Temple stood in Jerusalem, Herod's capital, and the national and religious life of the entire nation centered around the sanctuary.

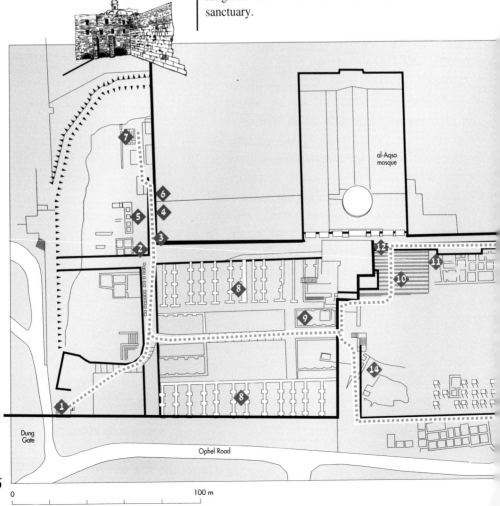

Great efforts and much money were invested to beautify the Temple Mount and the precinct that encompassed it.

On our tour we will see the remains of the monumental construction around the Temple Mount, and we will take a close look at the still majestic walls, the gigantic arches, the stone-paved streets, the broad staircases, and the cisterns cut in the bedrock. We will also learn of the customs and practices associated with pilgrimage to the Temple. We will see the continuation of the public building projects along the Western Wall tunnels, and we will conclude by walking through the water channel from the time of the Hasmonean dynasty.

The route: the route begins at the Western Wall excavations close to the Dung Gate, passes through the excavation areas and continues to the Western Wall tunnels. The tour ends at the Western Wall plaza.

Duration of the tour: about three and a half hours.

Public transportation: buses nos. 1, 2 to the Western Wall, or no. 38 (minibus) to the Jewish Quarter (from there one walks down to the Dung Gate)

By private car: the parking lot at the foot of Dung Gate, outside the Old City walls.

Visiting hours: Western Wall excavations: Sun–Thur: 9:00 a.m.–4:00 p.m., Friday: 9:00 a.m.–2:00 p.m.
Entrance fee.
Western Wall tunnel: the tour must be coordinated about two weeks in advance in the office of the Western Wall Heritage Foundation (tel. 6271333). The entrance fee includes a guided tour by the Foundation.

Note: modest dress is required. Due to ongoing preservation and restoration works in the Western Wall excavations, there may be some changes in the walking tour route at the site.

N

The Entrance

IMMEDIATELY FOLLOWING THE SIX-DAY WAR, an Israeli archaeological expedition was organized for the purpose of realizing the dream of all those to whom Jerusalem was precious: to uncover its past at the foot of the Temple Mount. Many archaeologists and hundreds of volunteers joined in the work, and hundreds of thousands of cubic meters of earth and debris were removed from the site, at times with the aid of bulldozers and heavy earth-moving equipment.

Warren excavating near Robinson's Arch

Research by archaeologists was not always so simple and technically possible. The first scholars to arrive at the site, in the late nineteenth century, who were interested in the extensive area to the south and west of the Temple Mount, encountered difficulties created by the Ottoman authorities. One of these researchers was Charles Warren, a British officer of the Royal Engineers, who came to Jerusalem in 1867 and also excavated in the City of David. He discovered the ancient waterworks which ever since have borne his name (see Tour 1). Warren, like his colleagues Wilson, Conder, and others, was primarily guided by scientific curiosity, but did not ignore the great military value of the information he gathered about the city and its rulers. The Ottoman authorities, who possibly suspected his motives, or perhaps only wanted to extract the traditional *bakshish* (bribes), would not grant him permission to excavate in proximity to the Temple Mount walls. Warren decided to adopt a ruse. His expedition dug vertical pits at a distance of dozens of meters from the walls, to a depth of about 25 meters. Each pit was about one meter wide. At the bottom of the shaft, they dug a horizontal tunnel in the direction of the walls in order to study them. Even though only small sections of the walls were uncovered by this method, Warren's expedition made a major contribution to the research of the area. When walking around in the excavations areas, we should recall the brave British captain and his stratagems.

We will enter the site by walking along the path. The walls standing to our left ❷, which were reconstructed from debris found at the site, were part of the complex of magnificent palaces erected here in the Muslim Ummayad period, in the eighth century (see Tour 11).

THE FIRST TEMPLE was built on the summit of the Temple Mount by King Solomon in the tenth century BCE. This sanctuary was burnt down when the Babylonians conquered Jerusalem in 586 BCE, and was replaced by the less magnificent Second Temple which was built by those returning to Zion (516 BCE). This Temple still stood in the time of the Hasmoneans and remained in use until Herod's day. The dimensions of the precinct surrounding the Temple, however, could not hold the myriads who thronged to the Temple on the three pilgrimage festivals, nor did it correspond to the vision of Herod, who planned the transformation of the capital into a city with spacious marketplaces, theaters, palaces, and fortresses. Herod accordingly ordered his engineers to build four tremendous retaining walls around the Temple Mount, one of which is the Western Wall. In the space between the walls and the Mount he added fill and

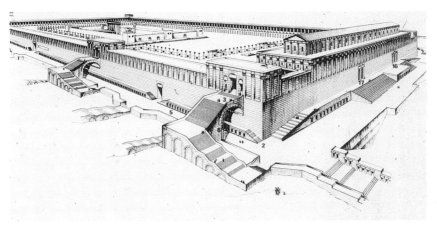

Proposed reconstruction of the Temple Mount in the Second Temple period

erected vaults, above which was built a paved plaza with an area of 144,000 square meters, about the size of 12 modern soccer fields. This was the largest sacred precinct in the entire Roman Empire. The plaza was bordered by magnificent stoas, with an especially large one, known as the "Royal Portico," on the southern side. This and the other stoas were occupied by money changers and merchants, including those who sold animals for use as sacrifices, etc. In place of the existing Temple, Herod erected a new edifice, which was ornamented with marble and gold. For its construction, which took a year and a half, one thousand priest-masons were specially trained, and ten thousand select laborers were employed in the work on the plaza, along with one thousand wagons for hauling stones.

A listing of only a few of the dimensions of this building project will convince us that one of the purposes of this undertaking was to impress visitors from all parts of the Roman Empire and leave them speechless. The length of the western wall is 485 meters, the eastern wall, 460 meters, the northern wall, 315 meters, and the southern wall, 280 meters. The walls soared to a height of 30 meters

Why did Herod's masons use such gigantic **ashlars** (blocks of stone), which were so difficult to transport from where they had been quarried and hoist up to the desired course? The use of such monumental stones enabled them to engage in "dry" construction, without cement, since the weight of the stones provided stability. With no need for cement, the builders could save the wood used as fuel in the production of lime, which was required for the preparation of cement. Additional advantages of this method are the outstanding durability of the walls, their uniquely esthetic form, and the tremendous impression they leave on anyone who sees them.

above the streets (the height of a ten-story building), and the foundations were always laid on the bedrock, even if this meant that the builders had to dig to a depth of 20 meters. The smallest **ashlars** weigh between two and five tons (the weight of a medium-sized elephant), and some are much larger than the stones of the Egyptian pyramids. A course of especially large stones (termed the "Master Course") encompasses the Temple Mount like a belt. It was meant to apply pressure and stabilize the underlying stones, and to constitute a firm base for the courses above it. From where we are standing, we can see that each course of the wall is recessed about three centimeters from the one below it. This was intended to correct the optical illusion that the wall, when viewed from below, seems about to topple over. Anyone who has ever stood at the base of a modern skyscraper knows how unnerving such an illusion can be...

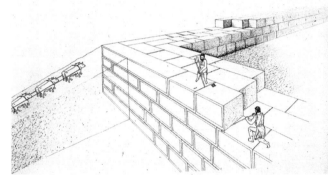

Reconstruction of techniques for the hoisting and transporting of ston

Herod's builders gave the stones a finish characteristic of all the Herodian construction. The margin of the stone is recessed and well smoothed, while the rest of it protrudes slightly. In the bright Jerusalem sunlight, this dressing gives rise to plays of light and shade that enhance the beauty of the Western Wall. The grandeur of the precinct turns it into the "eighth wonder" of the ancient world.

The following questions arise: how were the building stones transported to the site from the quarry, and how were they hoisted and placed in position? The sketches on this page offer a few answers.

At the foot of the corner of the Western Wall the excavators discovered among the ruins a large stone bearing the inscription: "To the place of trumpeting *le-hakh*...". The continuation is missing. It has been proposed to complete the phrase: "To the place of trumpeting to pr[oclaim]." According to the excavators, this ashlar was the top cornerstone of the Mount's southwestern corner, at a point where the priests would announce with trumpet blasts the beginning of the Sabbath, as Josephus relates (*War of the Jews* 4:9:12). It is presently on display in the Israel Museum.

THE ROW OF STONES protruding from the wall above our heads is a remnant of a giant vault that projected from the Western Wall, the other end of which rested on stone pillars on the other side of the path, at a distance of about 13 m from the Wall ⑤. The vault was first identified by the biblical scholar Edward Robinson in 1838. He thought that this was the beginning of an arched bridge that connected the Temple Mount with the

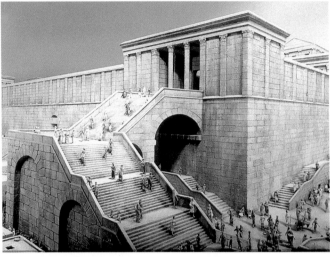

Reconstruction of the Robinson's Arch "interchange"

Upper City on the hill to the west. When, however, the bases of additional arches were found, extending southward instead of westward, it became evident that this was not a bridge, but rather a series of vaults descending to the level of the Second Temple period street that passed underneath, upon which we are now standing. The staircase supported by the vaults was about 15 meters wide (about the width of a modern six-lane highway).

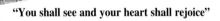

"You shall see and your heart shall rejoice"

From the street, one could ascend the steps of the vault and enter the Royal Portico in the southern part of the Temple Mount. Pedestrian traffic on the staircase did not interfere with the crossflow of pedestrians on the street below, and so Robinson's Arch was the first "interchange" in history. The architects incorporated chambers, which were used as shops, at the base of the system of the vault's pillars. The excavations there uncovered stone vessels, including a fragment bearing the inscription "sacrifice," weights, and coins.

We will now proceed northward, alongside the Western Wall. To our right we see a stone ⑥ bearing the inscription carved in Hebrew letters: "You shall see and your heart shall rejoice, their limbs like grass...". This is a quotation (with a slight change) from the prophecy of consolation of Isaiah (66:14). According to one opinion, the inscription was engraved in the fourth century CE, possibly as an expression of the expectations of the Jews for redemption in the time of the emperor **Julian the Apostate**.

◆ The emperor **Julian the Apostate** (331-363 CE) was raised as a Christian, but was drawn to Greek culture and paganism, which he sought to restore throughout the Roman Empire. The sources maintain that Julian sought to rebuild the ruined Temple in Jerusalem, but this plan was shelved, probably because of his death in battle.

Other scholars date the inscription to the Early Islamic or to the Crusader period.

Below and to our left we see the remains of the Herodian street 7 which is covered by rubble from the Temple Mount that was destroyed in 70 CE. A drainage system was discovered underneath the street. This street is part of the layout of broad streets that encompassed the Temple Mount precinct, in which there were marketplaces, shops, and squares. On entering the Western Wall tunnel, later in this tour, we will walk on the pavement of the northern part of this street.

We will return by ascending the steps, walking to the south, and then turning to the east. The path takes us away from the southern wall and leads us through later ruins. To the right and left we see the walls and courtyards of an 8th-century CE Ummayad palace 8 and houses from the Byzantine period 9 with basements, cisterns, and rooms, the walls of which are coated with ornamented plaster. We will exit through the small gate breached by the archaeologists, and find ourselves outside the walls of the Old City, but still within the bounds of Herodian Jerusalem.

10   THE HULDAH GATES

The Stairs to the South of the Huldah Gates

T HE AREA WHERE WE ARE STANDING was called the "Ophel" in the First Temple period, from the Hebrew root "to ascend," because those coming from the City of David in the south passed through it to reach the Temple. This tradition was so rooted that Herod also established the series of entrance and exit gates for the Mount on the south, even though in his time the urban center had already moved to the Upper City, to the west of the Temple Mount. Those coming to the Temple were thus compelled to climb up to the holy place that towered above

Proposed reconstruction of the western Huldah Gate tunnel

them, as was only fitting. **The staircase** on which we are standing (most of which has been restored) led to the Temple Mount gates. The ritual baths ⓫ in which pilgrims immersed before entering the sacred precincts were uncovered to the east of these stairs.

Above the staircase we can discern the arch of a gate, which is blocked at present ⓬. The arch is from the early Muslim period. During the Second Temple period, a double gate stood here, which was apparently used as an exit from the Temple Mount. About 70 meters east of this gate we see a blocked triple gate ⓭. This was the entrance gate to the Mount. Its original shape is unknown, but it too may have been a triple gate. The present gate is Muslim, but its threshold and western doorpost stone are remnants from the Herodian construction.

The Mishnah calls these gates the "Huldah Gates," and relates:

All who entered the Temple Mount entered by the right and went around [to the right], and went out by the left, except for the person to whom something unseemly had occurred, who entered and went around to the left. [He was asked,] "Why do you go around to the left?" [and he replied,] "Because I am a mourner." "May the One who dwells in this House console you"; "Because I am excommunicated" – "May the One who dwells in this House cause them to befriend you" (*Middot* 2:2).

We learn from this of the worthy practice according to which the mourner would enter and exit in the direction opposite to other people, so that strangers would recognize him as such and console him.

What is the source of the strange name of the gates? In the past it was thought that the tomb of Huldah the prophetess, a contemporary of the prophet Jeremiah, may have stood in the vicinity, but no tomb which could be identified with that of Huldah was found in the excavations. The name (*huldah* = rat) may possibly refer to the special manner in which the gates lead to the Temple Mount: the level of the gates is about 14 meters lower than that of the Temple Mount plaza. Accordingly, long and sloping tunnels were built which brought those entering the gates up to the level of the plaza. These tunnels are reminiscent of the underground burrows of various rodents, which may be the source of the name. At present, these tunnels are closed to the public at large.

Only some of the original domes that roofed the entrance tunnel, with ornamentations engraved in the stone, are preserved. We can envisage the excitement of the pilgrim who came from his village in Galilee or Judea as he slowly made his way along the torchlit tunnel and gazed in awe at the breathtaking domes above his head. When he exited from the tunnel and emerged into the dazzling sunlight, he suddenly saw before him the colossal paved precinct, the tall surrounding porticoes, and the myriads of pilgrims in their holiday finery. There was a great tumult all around, the smell of the sacrifices hung in the air, and facing him – the magnificent Temple, clad with marble and

The breadth of the **stairs** varies in width. This was to prevent those leaving the Mount from running in the holy place, as they hurried to their homes. A similar problem was solved in the Acropolis in Athens by building steps which are half a meter high, thus forcing the visitor to walk slowly. It seems that the planners in Jerusalem devised a more sophisticated solution, which required less effort.

crowned with glittering gold ornamentation. This must have been a unique moment for the pilgrim, and Herod's building project undoubtedly contributed to transforming it into the unforgettable experience of a lifetime.

Before we leave the excavation area, it is well worth a moment to look at the Second Temple period cisterns cut in the bedrock to our south ⑭ and at a large structure attributed to the First Temple period that was discovered at the edge of the excavation area ⑮. On leaving it, we will turn northward, to the Western Wall plaza. The entrance to the Western Wall tunnel is located at the northern end of the plaza.

Section of the western Huldah Gate

16   THE WESTERN WALL TUNNEL

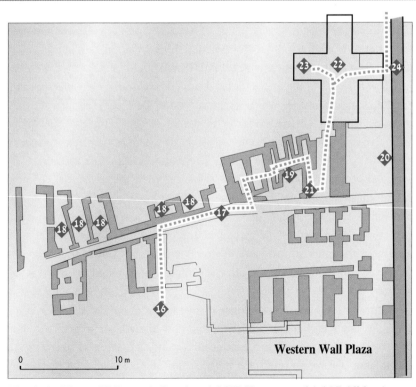

Western Wall Plaza

0   10 m

Map 2: the Western Wall tunnels (based on *Ariel* 57-58, courtesy of Ariel Publishers)

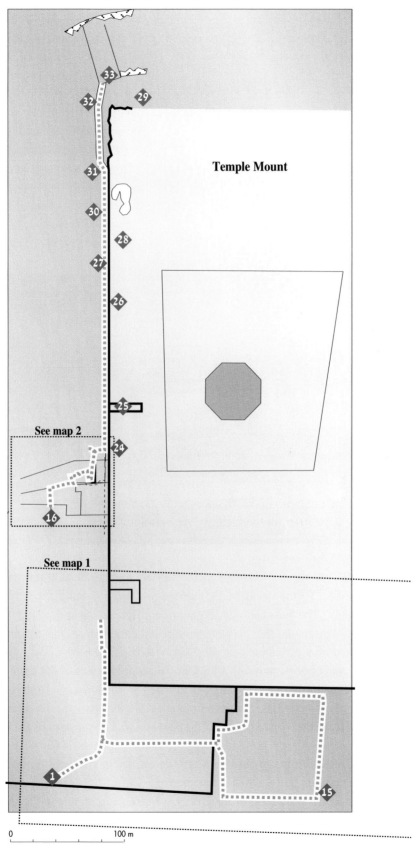

Temple Mount

See map 2

See map 1

0   100 m

Map 3: the Western Wall tunnels (based on *Ariel* 57-58, courtesy of Ariel Publishers)

In the Mamluk period, arches and vaults were built adjacent to the Western Wall (except for the Jewish prayer area), and both public and private structures were erected over them. This raised the city level to the height of the Temple Mount plaza, in order to establish a vital and continuous link between the sacred precinct and its immediate surroundings. This massive construction has covered and hidden the facade of the Wall ever since, while the substructures were used in part as storerooms and cisterns; over the course of time, some of them were filled with debris and earth. In the wake of the wave of excitement and emotion following the Six-Day War, the Ministry of Religious Affairs decided to dig a narrow tunnel along the Western Wall that would expose it for its entire length (485 meters). The tunnel, which was dug under extremely difficult conditions, passes through the basement and cisterns. As we walk through it, however, we should recall that a wide street, which was under the open sky, ran along this course in the Second Temple period.

The Western Wall tunnels

We will go into the entrance to the tunnels and continue toward the vaulted passage ⑰. To the north of the passage are two adjoining series of east-west arches ⑱. The passage was already identified in the nineteenth century by Charles Warren as the "secret passage" mentioned in the writings of the fifteenth-century Muslim historian Mujir al-Din. It probably was built in the Middle Ages, but its purpose is unclear (Mujir al-Din was of the opinion that the secret passage was used by King David when he wanted to go from his palace to the Temple Mount). The two series of arches are the continuation of the arch that projects from the Western Wall. These arches were also most likely built in the Middle Ages. As we proceed along the narrow tunnels, we will note a small opening on our right ⑲ through which we can see in the depths a basement with a single column, that we will reach shortly.

An impressive arch ⑳ named Wilson's Arch towers above the inner prayer space for men. In the Second Temple period, a gigantic arch stood here, the first in a series that supported the bridge connecting the Upper City and the Temple

Drawing of Wilson's Arch, 1871, by William Simpson

Mount. The aqueduct that brought water from Solomon's Pools to the Temple area also was borne on these arches (see Tour 7). The current arch most likely dates from the Middle Ages (possibly from the early Muslim period), and on top of it runs the street leading to the Chain Gate on the Temple Mount.

We will retrace our steps to the hall ❷ in which an audiovisual show on the site is screened, and descend through the gate on the southern side to the hall with a single column, which we looked upon earlier. Those with vivid imaginations will probably expect to hear that this was a medieval dungeon, in which unfortunate princes were chained to the column in its center; the archaeological truth is different, but no less fascinating. The hall was built during the reign of Herod (or possibly even earlier, in the time of the Hasmonean dynasty) and was most likely part of the complex of public structures constructed close to the Temple Mount. Some authorities identify it with the "Council House" mentioned

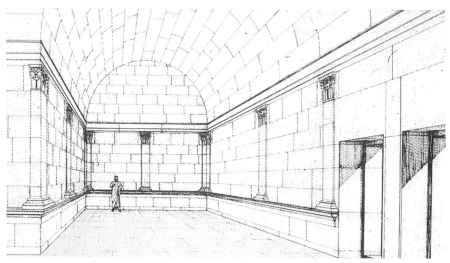

Proposed reconstruction of the Hasmonean hall

in Josephus' writings. The sessions of the municipal council were held here. The council's responsibilities included supervision of the markets and prices, sanitation and order, and the well-being of pilgrims. According to another opinion, this may have been the municipal archives. At any rate, this is the first public structure from the Second Temple period discovered in Jerusalem. The smooth ashlars, the finely carved columns protruding from the wall, and the one surviving capital which bears an engraved rosette pattern, are all very impressive. The central column does not belong to the original hall, and was brought here in a later period. Examinations have shown that other halls, which have not yet been excavated, are concealed beyond the walls, and many secrets are just waiting to be revealed.

We will ascend the stairs and continue to the large cruciform hall **22** which was built in the Mamluk period on earlier foundations as a supporting structure for the madrasa (Muslim religious school) that was constructed over it. In the western wing of this hall **23** is an electrically powered model of the Temple Mount and the Western Wall in the Second Temple period and today. This reconstruction of the interior of the Temple Mount differs in a number of details from the model next to the Holyland Hotel (see Tour 3).

24 THE WESTERN WALL'S LARGEST STONE

W E HAVE COME to the entrance of the tunnel cleared by the Ministry of Religious Affairs. The ashlar opposite us belongs to the "Master Course" that we mentioned at the beginning of the tour. Walk alongside this stone, and try to imagine where it ends. The surveyors found that it is 13.6 meters long, 3.3 meters high, and 4.6 meters thick. This may possibly be the largest building stone in antiquity, and its weight is estimated at 570 tons – the equivalent of eight tanks. How was the stone brought here, and how was it set in place? We are unable to offer any satisfactory explanation and can only admire and wonder at the amazing capabilities of Herod and his engineers.

Thick plaster coats the stones of an inner wall of a pool, built here apparently in the Byzantine period. The large rectangular holes within the stones of the Western Wall, that look like large mailboxes, were probably hewn to ensure better attachment of the pool's walls, with the aid of pegs which are visible.

A stone in the Western Wall weighing 570 tons

T HE BLOCKED GATE BEFORE US was also visited by Charles Warren a century before the excavators of the Ministry of Religious Affairs. Warren, however, examined the inner side of the gateway, within the Temple Mount, whereas we see its outer face. The gate in its current vaulted form dates from the eleventh century, and was built over the ruins of a gate from the Second Temple period, which was one of the **four gates** that led to the Herodian plaza. It is conjectured that the "Cave Synagogue," which is mentioned in documents from the Cairo Genizah, may have been located in this gatehouse in the Middle Ages. The gate is blocked at present, to prevent passage to the Temple Mount.

> Josephus relates that in the Second Temple period there were **four gates** in the Western Wall, which corresponds with the archaeological finds. The Mishnah (*Middot* 1:3), however, mentions only a single gate on the west. The discrepancy between the sources may possibly be due to the fact the Mishnah refers to the Temple Mount gates in the Hasmonean period, while Josephus describes the gates of the precinct after Herod's extension of the Temple Mount.

We will proceed northward, observing in the wall to our right the familiar Herodian dressing and the gradual regression of each successive course. The bedrock along the wall is quite low in the south, but gradually rises as we advance northward, reaching the level of the Herodian street **26**. Herod's engineers decided at a certain stage not to bother with the removal of the bedrock. Instead, they smoothed its facade, with the intent of incorporating it in the built wall. From this point on the street, which rested in the south on fill, rests on the bedrock on which we are treading.

We have come to a large stone **27** whose upper part is rounded. Its function is not clear; according to one opinion, it was positioned at this spot as a safety parapet alongside an ancient cistern that was here.

It is conjectured that we are standing close to the northern boundary of the Hasmonean Temple Mount, to the north of which stood the Baris fortress **28**. This fortress was demolished, and its area was included by Herod in the enlarged Temple Mount precinct. To the north of the extended precinct Herod erected a new fortress, the Antonia **29**, named after his patron, the Roman ruler Mark Antony.

Rounded stone barrier

W E HAVE ENTERED a small plaza with the original Herodian paving. Two columns with Doric capitals bound it on the west. This may have been a public square or the entrance to some structure to the west. The bedrock at the base of the Western Wall is very high at this point; in some places, the builders began to smooth and dress it as if it were ashlar masonry, but this work was stopped here. It seems as if time stood still, and only a few minutes have passed since the banging of the hammers died down and the builders went off for their lunch break. Paving stones which were intended for the northern continuation of the street still lean against the wall. They have been waiting two thousand years

The Herodian Plaza

for the builders, who will never return. This evidence indicates that the mammoth building project was halted and the construction of the Western Wall never completed, perhaps because of the death of Herod, who was the moving force behind the entire enterprise. It is interesting that these facts are inconsistent with the testimony of Josephus, who writes that the construction work was completed, leaving unemployed the thousands of workers who had been engaged in the paving of the city streets. As we continue along the corridor, we see to our left a quarry with partly hewn stones that are still attached to the bedrock.

We will now pass through the iron gate and ascend the stairs.

WE ARE STANDING at the entrance to an ancient water channel which apparently was hewn during the time of the Hasmoneans. It brought water from the area of the present-day Damascus Gate area to the cisterns of the Baris fortress. When Herod extended the Temple Mount, the Western Wall bisected the channel, and it was no longer usable. This water installation was cut in the bedrock as an open channel, and was roofed with the large stone slabs we see over our heads. We will carefully advance some seventy meters in the direction of the Western Wall through the channel and pass a small dam 32 built by Herod's engineers to block the passage of rainwater that seeped into the channel. Twenty meters further on we come to a large chamber with a stone vault for a ceiling 33. This is the southern part of the Strouthion Pool (see Tour 8) mentioned in Josephus' writings. The northern part of the pool is located beyond the wall opposite us, in the basements of the Sisters of Zion Convent. The pool was dug in the time of Herod within the moat protecting the Antonia fortress. It cuts

through the channel, thus providing additional proof that the channel predated Herod. This concludes our subterranean tour of Second Temple period Jerusalem. We will turn to the modern tunnel on our right and go out to the Via Dolorosa, through the exit which was breached late in 1996.

The Hasmonean channel

The Herodian Quarter and the Kidron Valley Tombs

T HE EXCAVATIONS ON THE SITE of the Herodian Quarter, which were conducted in the Jewish Quarter of the Old City, reveal to us a part of the Second Temple period Upper City. We will visit the houses of the wealthy neighborhood that existed here during the time of Herod and his descendants, and which was inhabited by four generations of residents over a period of about a century (37 BCE–70 CE). We will gaze at the remains of the "mansions" of that time, and learn of the inhabitants' taste in art, the styles they were fond of, the objets d'art that pleased them, the furniture they introduced into their homes, and even their bathing habits. The archaeological finds paint for us a detailed and colorful picture of the life enjoyed by Jerusalem's wealthy class in the late Second Temple period.

The second half of the walking tour will bring us to the Kidron Valley, at the foot of the Mount of Olives, where we will encounter the monumental tombs that affluent individuals of the Second Temple period built for themselves as an abode for eternity. The city of the living in the Upper City and the city of the dead in the Kidron Valley are linked artistically and architecturally, and the worldview of their builders was expressed in their structures. All this enriches our understanding of the period. As an introduction to this part of the tour, we recommend reading about the burial practices of the Second Temple period (see Tour 6).

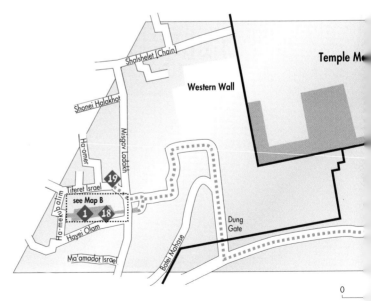

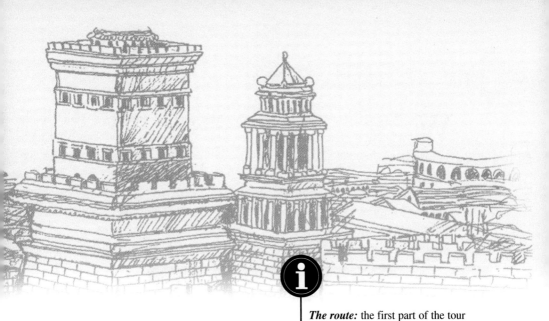

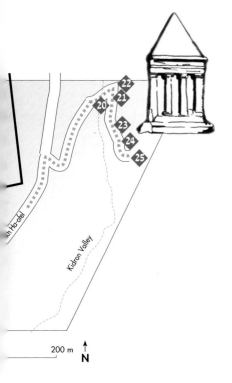

The route: the first part of the tour
begins at the excavations of the
Herodian Quarter in the Jewish Quarter
(Ha-Karaim Street) and continues to the
Burnt House. The second half of the tour
is in the Kidron Valley, to the east of the
Temple Mount.

Duration of the tour: about three hours.

Public transportation: bus no. 38
(minibus) to the Jewish Quarter; nos. 1,
2 to the Western Wall (from there one
walks up to the Jewish Quarter).

By private car: the parking lot of the
Jewish Quarter.

Visiting hours: the Herodian
Quarter: Sun–Thur: 9:00 a.m–5:00 p.m.,
Friday and eves of holidays: 9:00 a.m.–
1 p.m. Entrance fee.

The Burnt House: Sun–Thur: 9:00 a.m.–
5:00 p.m., Friday and eves of holidays:
9:00 a.m.–1 p.m. Entrance fee. An
audiovisual show is screened every half
hour, in various languages.

200 m ↑ N

W E WILL ENTER THE Herodian Quarter and go down the stairs to the excavation area. At the bottom of the staircase, a large sign informs us that we have descended three meters below the level of the Jewish Quarter, and have gone back in time two thousand years. The large quantities of earth and debris from different periods that accumulated here over the centuries buried the remains from the Second Temple period city. These debris were removed for the first time only after the Six-Day War, when a plan was drawn up to restore and rebuild the houses of the ruined Jewish Quarter, along with the excavation of

The Western House

extensive areas before the latter would be covered once again, this time by the modern construction. And so the restoration and rebuilding of the Jewish Quarter was conducted concurrently with the uncovering of Jewish life in the same place two thousand years ago. In most instances, the important finds were covered after their

exposure with a protective layer of sand and earth, prior to the casting of the concrete columns which would serve as the foundations of the modern buildings. When the construction work was concluded, the finds were uncovered a second time, restored, and opened to the public as subterranean sites. The ceiling of the hall to which we have descended is therefore the floor of the modern building that stands above us.

We will continue along our route to the column with illustrations and holograms, to the east of the excavations ❷. The remains facing us are the basement of a house in the Herodian Quarter, which, due to its location, has been named the "Western House." No one lived in the basement level, and only service facilities, such as storerooms, cisterns, ritual baths, and bathing installations, were found in it. The upper floors, in which the inhabitants lived, have not survived, leaving only a trace in the form of the small staircase ❸ that led to the second floor. At the western end of the house ❹ we see a fine bathroom, with a small bath and an adjoining mosaic floor. In contrast with the storage rooms, whose floors were made of packed earth, the bathrooms were paved with mosaics, to prevent mud from being tracked around. To the east of this pavement is another mosaic pavement ❺ with a (partially destroyed) pattern

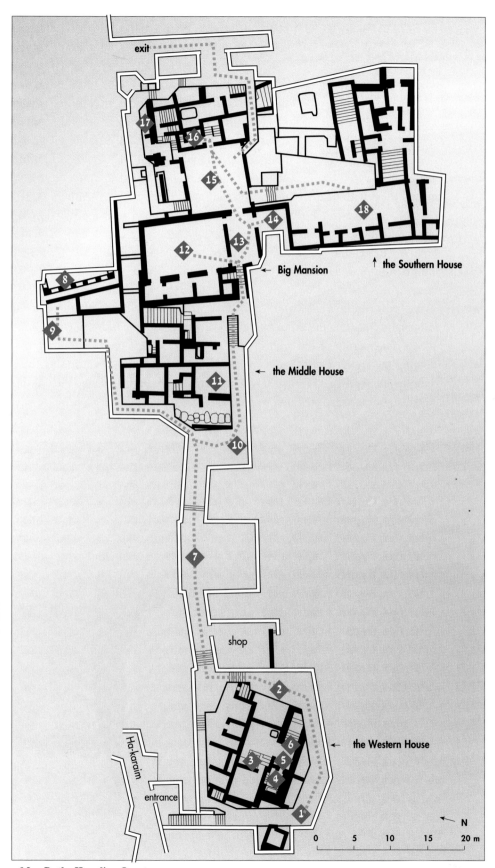

Map B: the Herodian Quarter

exit

17

16

15

14

13

12

← Big Mansion

8

↑ the Southern House

18

9

← the Middle House

11

10

7

shop

2

Ha-karaim

6

← the Western House

3
5
4

entrance

1

← N

0   5   10   15   20 m

of rosette leaflets in different colors at its center, and a small **spindle-shaped bottle** in the lower corner.

The geometric and floral patterns in the mosaics reflect an important rule in Jewish art of those days: the strict observance of the prohibition against making graven images. Mosaics in Pompeii, the famous city of the period in Italy, depict scenes with human and animal figures. The Jews of Jerusalem adopted the external trappings of these styles, but infused them with content more in keeping with their religious worldview.

At the entrance to the ritual bath ⬦6 is a stone bowl with a projection in it, which may have been used for washing one's feet before entering the bath. This might have been the "footbath" mentioned in the Mishnah (*Yadayim* 4:1). Washing one's feet prior to entering the bath helped to maintain the cleanliness of the bath water, which could not be changed frequently, especially in the summer.

We will continue eastward, to the corridor ⬦7 with photographs which graphically illustrate the different phases of the restoration of the Jewish Quarter and the uncovering of the archaeological finds. On the opposite wall are maps showing the location of the remains of the Herodian Quarter within the Second Temple period city, and further down the corridor are finds from the First Temple and Hasmonean periods which were discovered here.

8   THE PERISTYLE HOUSE

THE COLUMNS BEFORE US, most of which have been restored, are part of the series of columns that encompassed the courtyard of a house. Such a colonnade is known as a "peristyle." The columns are fluted, and appear to have been carved from a single stone block, but a close examination reveals the deception. Actually, they were built from a number of drums which were assembled one above the other and coated with stucco, to create the impression that this is a marble column. Herod's builders employed a similar technique in the Northern Palace at Masada. Herod understood that it was wasteful to invest in real marble when impressive results could be obtained by using an inexpensive substitute.

The plan of the house hanging on the wall indicates that we are viewing only the courtyard and part of another room in the house. The area between the columns and the place where we are standing is paved with colorful stones which form a fine geometric pattern. This style, which is called *opus sectile*, was very fashionable throughout the Roman Empire in the first century CE. In a contemporary

Doric capital

Ionic capital

villa in Pompeii, we would almost certainly find a statue in the center of the peristyle courtyard; in Jerusalem, the general style was adopted, but without the accompanying pagan content.

Architectural decorations found in the excavations are on display close to the Peristyle House ⑨. Among them are Doric, Ionic, and Corinthian column capitals, along with ornamental patterns which were popular in Jewish art of that time, such as egg-and-dart, acanthus leaves, trailing vine twigs, rosettes, and other designs. In Hellenistic-Roman art, these patterns were used as frame ornamentation around scenes with images at their center. The Jews, who refrained from depictions of images, transformed these frame ornamentations into the main decorative element. According to one view, this final product is a distortion and degeneration of the original style, while others regard this as an independent, and no less beautiful, work of art.

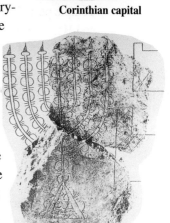
Corinthian capital

We will return to the display windows ⑩ that contain everyday items, such as a sundial (*even sha'ot*, literally, "stone of the hours," in Mishnaic language), stone table tops, and bronze, ceramic, and glass vessels. Stone vessels were extremely common in Jerusalem at the time, even though they were more expensive than ceramic vessels and more difficult to produce. They were so widely distributed because, according to Jewish religious law, stone vessels do not acquire ritual impurity, and therefore their use, in the long run, is more worthwhile. The stone vessel industry ceased when the Temple was destroyed, therefore the presence of such vessels in structures aids in the dating of the latter.

Temple Candelabrum engraved on plaster

Another unique find on display further along the wall is a depiction of the Temple Candelabrum (*menorah*), engraved in plaster on the wall of one of the houses (a reproduction is on display here). This is one of the earliest extant detailed depictions of the Temple Candelabrum. We may safely assume that the anonymous engraver had seen the Candelabrum with his own eyes. Was this a priest who served in the Temple,

Temple Candelabrum on reliefs of Arch of Titus

or perhaps the young son of a priest, who had returned from a visit to his father's place of work with such profound impressions that he permitted himself to engrave on the wall of his room what he had seen? The engraved Candelabrum has a tripodal base. This form differs from the base of the Temple Candelabrum known to us from the triumphal arch built by Titus in Rome after he defeated the Jews. The reason for the difference between the two depictions is unknown, and various explanations have been offered.

11   THE MIDDLE HOUSE

T HE DRAINAGE CHANNEL that crosses the western part of the house and is roofed with stone slabs was dug after the destruction of the Temple, probably in the Byzantine period. To its east is the **triclinium** (dining room) of the house, with a mosaic floor. In the reconstruction of the floor we can see the technique used in laying the mosaic: first, the outline of the desired pattern was engraved in the plaster base, and then it was filled with tesserae. This house is the middle one of the three uncovered at the site. The triclinium was reconstructed with characteristic furniture, the first items of furniture from the Second Temple period to be discovered in archaeological excavations. In the corner of the room, the reconstructors placed a stone dining table supported by a stone leg. Fragments of similar tables were found in excavations, with engraved marginal ornamentation featuring geometric and floral patterns. The placement of large stone jars next to the table is based on portrayals appearing on contemporary Roman reliefs.

The term **triclinium**, meaning a dining room with couches along three sides of its table, derives from the Greek *tri* (three) and *cliné* (couch). The couches were positioned around the center of the room, in the shape of a U. The guests would recline on the couches and spend their time in pleasant conversation and eating.

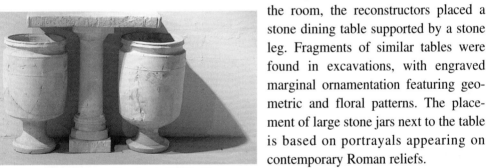

Stone table and jars in the Middle House

12   THE BIG MANSION

W E HAVE ENTERED the reception hall of the largest and most impressive house at the site, which undoubtedly aroused the envy of the neighbors. It covered an area of 600 square meters, and the reception hall is 11 meters long. The hall was open along its entire length and lacked the modern columns which it currently contains.

The walls of the reception hall were coated with stucco fashioned to resemble ashlar. This decorative style, known to scholars as the "First Pompeian Style," was popular in Italy until the first century BCE, when it was replaced by the

"Second Pompeian Style," which was characterized by paintings executed on the plaster of the walls before it had dried (frescoes). It appears that the inhabitants of the house chose to decorate the walls of their home in a style that had gone out of fashion decades previously. We will enter the side rooms, where we note the walls coated with stucco to resemble ashlars, beneath which are visible traces of an earlier fresco. In other words, in these rooms the Second Pompeian Style preceded the First Style. How did this come about? Was this a caprice of the owner of the building? Perhaps this indicates that the "old" Roman fashion was quite long-lived in Eretz Israel, and was part of the local catalog of interior decorating styles for many years after it had been abandoned in Italy? Like many other archaeological mysteries, this enigma must remain unanswered.

Reconstruction of the Big Mansion in model

Fine vessels which were found in the house are displayed in the reception hall. The most outstanding among them is a set of vessels coated with red slip (*terra sigillata* ware), which were regarded as prestigious in the East at the time. A rare glass jar made by the master glassblower Ennion of Sidon (in Lebanon) was found in the rubble; only three other jars of this kind are known to have survived. This jar bears the seal of the artisan in Greek: "Ennion made it," like signatures on modern works of art. There is a photograph of the jar on the southern wall of the courtyard which we will soon enter. We will go into the room to the south of the reception hall ⬦13. On the floor is a charred cypress beam which fell from the ceiling, testimony to the burning of the house by the Romans in 70 CE. South of this room is another room ⬦14 with a colorful fresco of the highest quality on its wall. When the archaeologists removed the soot that covered the walls, none of the paint came off.

We will turn to the large courtyard in the center of the house ⬦15, from which doorways lead to the various wings. In the courtyard, which stands over a huge

Ritual bath in the Herodian Quarter

What was the reason for the large number of **ritual baths** and water installations discovered in the Upper City? It has been suggested that many of the families living in the Herodian quarter belonged to the wealthy priestly class, whose members performed various functions in the Temple, which called for scrupulous maintenance of ritual purity and immersion. Some of the ritual baths might have been used for the cleansing of vessels or by domestic servants, while others may have been at the disposal of guests, such as those participating in the priestly watches who came from outside Jerusalem and stayed in the city for specific periods of time while fulfilling their duties in the Temple. The bathing installations are indicative of an awareness of the need for bodily hygiene, and may also express the influence of Roman culture, in which the bathhouse played an important role.

rock-cut cistern, is a stone model with a reconstruction of the Big Mansion. Nothing remains of the ground floor rooms to the east of the courtyard, with the exception of an intimate bathing corner ⓰ with a bench and a bathtub recessed in the floor. The basement story to the east of the courtyard contained storerooms, cisterns, as well as ritual baths. The vaulted **ritual bath** ⓱ has a double entrance. It is conjectured that this made possible the separation of the impure who descended to immerse themselves from the pure who came up from the bath. The water for these installations came from the cisterns of the houses, to which rainwater was drained through gutters, and not from the aqueducts which supplied the city with water from the Hebron and Bethlehem areas and intended primarily for public consumption.

On the way to the exit, we will take a look at the ruins of another house, to the south of this site ⓲, which reflects the state of the remains as they were uncovered, before the archaeologists began the work of restoration. We will leave the Herodian Quarter and go up to the Burnt House ⓳, where an audio-visual presentation is screened about the house and its owners, who apparently were priests from the Kathros family which is mentioned in the Talmud (Babylonian Talmud, *Pesahim* 57a). We will now go back down to the Dung Gate, and turn eastward on the road to the Kidron Valley.

20   THE KIDRON VALLEY

THE KIDRON VALLEY (also called the Valley of Jehoshaphat) was the natural eastern boundary of Jerusalem in antiquity. The prophets of Israel proclaimed that in this place God would judge the nations in the End of Days. This fact, along with its proximity to the Temple Mount, made it an attractive burial site for the elite of Jerusalem society in the Second Temple period (and even earlier, in the First Temple period). The Kidron Valley was not the only burial site of the city at the time, and we know of hundreds of additional tombs which formed a "burial belt" around the city. The monumental tombs, which were constructed in the valley in the Second Temple period, generally lack inscriptions that would aid us in identifying those interred, since their identity was known to all in their and following generations. This knowledge was lost after the destruction of the Temple, and traditions slowly developed that attributed the tombs to biblical characters, such as David's son Absalom, the prophets Isaiah and Zechariah, Kings Uzziah and Jehoshaphat, and others. Islamic tradition attributes these tombs to the family of Pharaoh; thus, for example, the Tomb of the Sons of Hezir is called the "Tomb of Pharaoh's Wife," and Absalom's Tomb, " of Pharaoh's Hat." Christian tradition attributes the tomb of Jehoshaphat to Joseph, the husband of Mary, Jesus' mother, and to others.

ABSALOM'S MONUMENT 21

THE NAME YAD AVSHALOM (Absalom's Monument) originated in the biblical narrative about David's son Absalom: "Now Absalom, in his lifetime, had taken the pillar which is in the Valley of the King and set it up for himself; for he said, 'I have no son to keep my name alive.' He had named the pillar after himself, and it has been called Absalom's Monument [**Yad** Avshalom] to this day" (II Samuel 18:18). Some authorities identified "the Valley of the King" with the Kidron Valley, and regarded the magnificent tomb before us as that of the prince who rebelled against his father David. As time passed, a Jerusalem practice developed in the wake of this identification: a father would bring his rebellious son to this place and stone the tomb, in order to graphically illustrate to him what fate would befall a son who rises against his father. The fact that archaeologists who examined the site found the base of the structure covered with a pile of stones attests to the enthusiasm with which this educational practice was conducted.

The word **yad** has two meanings in Hebrew: "hand" and "monument." Some people, apparently because of the confusion between the different meanings, thought that an engraved hand appeared on Yad Avshalom. A Jerusalem legend relates that this hand was lopped off by a shell fired from one of Napoleon's cannons when he arrived in Eretz Israel.

The structure, which is dated to the early first century CE, is the latest of the funereal monuments we will encounter on the tour. Its facade reflects a mixture of stylistic influences. The capitals of the facade columns are Ionic, like those we saw in the Herodian Quarter. The columns bear an architrave above which is a Doric frieze. Above the frieze is a protruding cornice, clearly Egyptian in style. Above the cornice is a square structure bearing a drum and a concave cone topped by a lotus flower with six petals. The facades of Second Temple period houses in Jerusalem have not survived, but we may learn of the architectural elements that appeared in them from the style of the funereal monuments.

The shape of Absalom's Monument is firmly anchored in the building tradition of the Hellenistic-Roman world, and it has many parallels. In most cases, the cone topping such monuments is separated from the lower part of the structure by columns. The absence of such columns from Absalom's Monument imparts to it

remains of lotus flower

concave cone

nefesh built of stone

rope-like ornamentation

Egyptian cornice
Doric frieze
architrave
Ionic capital

rock-cut tomb

engaged column

base

entrance to burial cave

later openin into burial chamber

Absalom's Monument

a more "dwarfish" appearance. The reason for this change may lie in the desire of the tomb's owners to avoid creating an overly pagan effect.

The structure consists of two main parts. The lower part (up to the top of the Egyptian cornice) is entirely cut in the bedrock, while the upper part is built of ashlars. This differential gave architectural expression to an idea prevalent in the Hellenistic world: that a distinction is to be drawn between the body and the soul after death – the chamber in which the corpse is interred is the tomb for the body; in addition, a special monument, the *nefesh* (literally, soul), was built for the soul of the deceased. The nefesh could have been a simple stone or a magnificent structure, either adjoining the tomb or apart from it. In Absalom's Monument, the nefesh is built directly over the rock-cut tomb. The entrance to the tomb is high above us, in the course built above the cornice, on the south side. Access to the entrance was most probably provided by a small wooden bridge, which led up from the cliff on the south. Stairs descend from the entrance into the burial chamber, with its rock-cut shelves on which the corpses were laid. In the Byzantine period, Christian monks entered the tomb in order to withdraw from the world; they breached another entrance in the side of the tomb, below the original one.

Concealed behind Absalom's Monument, like a bashful child hiding behind its mother's skirt, is another tomb from this period, named Jehoshaphat's Tomb 22. The rock-cut gable above the closed entrance is ornamented with floral designs, such as acanthus leaves, clusters of grapes, and other fruit. The tomb contains rock-cut loculi with vaulted ceilings.

THE TOMB OF THE SONS OF HEZIR — 23

A FTER SEEING ABSALOM'S MONUMENT, we may be somewhat disappointed by the appearance of the Tomb of the Sons of Hezir, which is simple and stylistically uniform. The style of the tomb is clearly Doric, with no Eastern influence, which may possibly attest to its antiquity. It may be assumed that many years passed before the local style became more decorative and richer, as a result of the increasing cultural encounter between the East and the West. The tomb is dated to the second half of the second century BCE. It too is rock-cut, but does not stand apart from the rock and is hewn into it. Two baseless columns stand in its facade. In structures built of stone, such columns support the ceiling, but here they have a purely esthetic function. Above the Doric capitals is the architrave, and above it is an ornamented frieze, similar to the one we saw in Absalom's Tomb. The sharp-eyed visitor will spot a Hebrew inscription engraved in the architrave. The inscription, which probably dates to the Hasmonean period, reads: "This is the tomb and the nefesh of Eleazar, Haniah, Joezer, Judah, Simeon, Johanan, the sons of Joseph son of Obed, Joseph and Eleazar the sons of Haniah, priests from the sons of Hezir." This therefore was a family tomb, which was used by a few generations of one of the wealthy priestly families in

Jerusalem able to afford prestigious burial in the Kidron Valley. We know of a priestly family by the name of Hezir from the Bible (Nehemiah 10:21; I Chronicles 24:15), centuries before the time of this inscription, but we have no way of determining whether this family was connected with the deceased listed in the inscription.

Only the names of men appear in the inscription. Where were the women buried? We should not rashly conclude from this that it was the practice to bury women separately. It is more likely that they were buried together with the men, but the inscription listed only the (male) heads of the family.

The inscription explicitly mentions the existence of a nefesh on the tomb, but no trace of such an element has been found. The archaeologists surmise that in the past such a nefesh stood on the rock-cut area to the north of the tomb but was destroyed in the course of time. To the south of the tomb's facade is a metal staircase leading to the central hall, from which doorways offer access to the burial chambers in which the corpses were placed in rock-cut loculi. We can enter the tomb and examine the chambers.

Boris Schatz (sitting), Izhak Ben-Zvi and others at the Tomb of the Sons of Hezir (1922)

24 ◢ ZECHARIAH'S TOMB

E VEN IF WE WALK all the way around Zechariah's Tomb, we will not find an entrance to the burial chamber, because there is no tomb here. The structure, which is cut in the bedrock from the base to the top, apparently is the nefesh of a nearby tomb which has not survived. As in the case of Absalom's Monument, the architecture bears influences from both East and West. The tomb is encompassed by columns with Ionic capitals, under which is a band with ornamentation resembling eggs-and-darts and surrounded by acanthus leaves. Above the columns is an Egyptian style cornice, and the structure is completed by a pyramidal roof. On the basis of its style and a comparison with other tombs, Zechariah's Tomb is dated to the second half of the first century BCE.

A Jewish tradition from the thirteenth century holds that this is the funereal monument of Zechariah son of Jehoiada the priest (according to another version: the prophet Zechariah son of Berechiah) who, the Bible tells us, launched a forceful attack against idolatry in the time of King Jehoash:

Zechariah's Tomb

Then the spirit of God enveloped Zechariah son of Jehoiada the priest; he stood above the people and said to them, "Thus God said: Why do you transgress the commandments of the Lord when you cannot succeed? Since you have forsaken the Lord, He has forsaken you." They conspired against him and pelted him with stones in the court of the House of the Lord, by order of the king (II Chronicles 24:20-21).

According to the sages, who were shocked by this narrative of murder in the Temple, in this single act the people committed seven sins: "They killed a priest, a prophet, and a judge, they spilled innocent blood, they defiled the Temple Court, and this took place on the Sabbath and Yom Kippur" (Jerusalem Talmud, *Ta'anit* 4:8). An ancient Jewish source relates that when the Babylonians conquered Jerusalem and burned the Temple, Nebuzaradan, the captain of the Babylonian guards, saw Zechariah's blood seething and bubbling in the Temple Court:

He asked what it was. They said: "It is the blood of the sacrifices which has been poured there." He had some blood brought, but it was different from the other. He then said to them: "If you tell me [the truth], well and good, but if not, I will tear your flesh with combs of iron." They said: "What can we say to you? There was a prophet among us who used to reprove us regarding the word of Heaven, and we rose up against him and killed him, and for many years his blood has not rested." He said to them: "I will appease him." He brought the Great Sanhedrin and the Small Sanhedrin and killed them over him, but the blood did not cease. He then slaughtered young men and women, but the blood did not cease. He brought schoolchildren and slaughtered them over it, but the blood did not cease. So he said: "Zechariah, Zechariah, I have slain the best of them; do you want me to destroy them all?" When he said this to him, it stopped (Babylonian Talmud, *Gittin* 57b).

South of Zechariah's Tomb is another burial site ㉕, which was not completed. The facade of this cave resembles, in general lines, that of the Tomb of the Sons of Hezir.

This brings the tour to an end. We will retrace our steps and go back to the Dung Gate.

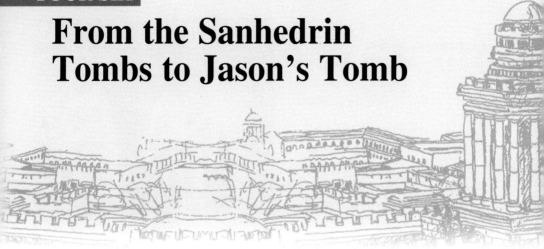

From the Sanhedrin Tombs to Jason's Tomb

WHETHER PROPHETS OR KINGS, heads of the Sanhedrin or priests, the high and mighty or the common people, from the First and Second Temple periods – all are buried under the houses of modern Jerusalem outside the city walls. As the modern city expands, more tombs are being discovered, giving a new meaning to the terms "Upper City" and "Lower City." On this tour we will visit some Second Temple period tombs.

As we have already seen in our visit to the Kidron Valley funerary monuments (Tour 5), here too we will observe how the Hellenistic culture that penetrated into Palestine in the late fourth century BCE influenced the fashioning of tombs in the city. Unlike the tour of the Kidron Valley, however, which focused mainly on the characteristic features of the monuments built next to the tombs, in this tour we will examine the tombs themselves, their structure, the burial practices observed, and the worldview reflected by these customs.

Our visit to the necropolis of the Second Temple period requires us to go beyond the city bounds of the time. This reflects what would nowadays be termed a "municipal bylaw" and was in effect at the time, as the Mishnah attests: "Carrion, tombs, and tanning yards must be kept fifty cubits from a town" *(Bava Batra 2:9)*. The dead were not buried within the city walls in order to maintain the proper level of public sanitation.

Along with this legislation, which applied to every Jewish town and city, an additional limitation was imposed in Jerusalem because of its status as a sacred city. The Temple called for the utmost observance of the purity laws. We may assume that tombs were kept away from the city for fear of corpse impurity, which is regarded as the gravest type of impurity. As Jerusalem expanded during the course of the Second Temple period, the city reached previously uninhabited areas that had been used for burial in earlier times. How could the neecessities of the growing city be accommodated to the graveyards that stood in its way? The city's residents apparently adopted a very practical solution: the contents of the early tombs were removed and transferred to more distant areas. An echo of this procedure is to be found in early Jewish sources: All tombs may be removed, except for the tomb of the king and the tomb of the prophet *(Tosefta, Bava Batra 1:9).*

Today, the burial caves of the Second Temple period are no more than archaeological sites that perpetuate a dead past that was and is no more. On the other hand, during the tour we will also visit a tomb that is exceptional in this respect, the cave of Simeon the Just. It is an example of the transformation of ancient burial caves into vibrant sites that are connected with ancient traditions associated with exemplary individuals in Jewish history. These sites attract large numbers of people who come there to pray and celebrate.

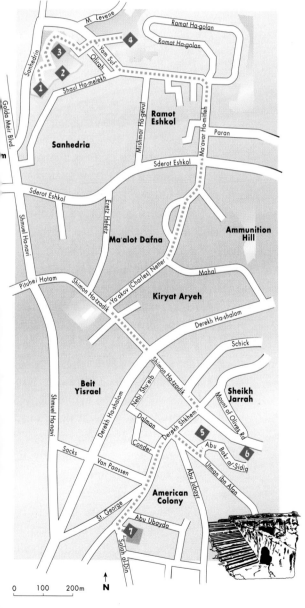

The route: the tour begins at the Sanhedrin Tombs, passes through the Eshkolot Cave and the tomb of Simeon the Just, and we continue from there by bus to Jason's Tomb in Rehaviah.

Duration of the tour: about four hours.

Public transportation: buses nos. 9, 28, 35, 36 to the Shmuel Ha-navi–Bar Ilan intersection, and from there proceed about 200 meters northward to Sanhedrin Park, to the right of the street.

By private car: leave your car in the small parking lot next to Sanhedrin Park. You may return to the parking lot after the visit to the Eshkolot Cave, and continue the tour by car.

Visiting hours: Tombs of the Kings: Mon–Sat: 8:00 a.m.–12:00 noon; 2:00 p.m.–5:00 p.m. Entrance fee. Tomb of Simeon the Just: daylight hours.

Note: modest dress and a flashlight are required.

ABOUT TWO HUNDRED METERS north of the intersection of Bar Ilan and Shmuel Ha-navi streets is the municipal "Sanhedrin Park," that contains a group of tombs from the late Second Temple period. Like many other localities to the north of the Old City walls, this area also served as a quarry from which masonry was dragged to building sites on a lower level within the city. The rock that could easily be quarried for building purposes also lent itself to the hewing of tombs, and therefore many burial caves are located in areas that were used in different periods as quarries, as we shall see in the tomb of Simeon the Just and the Eshkolot Cave.

Sarcophagus

On entering the Park through its southern entrance (to the north of the small parking lot), we see in front of us a rock face containing the entrances to three simple, unornamented burial caves. The cave on the left was found to contain two rock-cut sarcophagi. A sarcophagus is a stone either freestanding or cut out of the bedrock, in which the corpse would be placed for initial burial for a period of twelve months. The meaning of the Greek word *sarkophagos* is "flesh eater," which attests to its function: the corpse was laid here until the flesh was consumed. When the flesh had decomposed, the bones were gathered and placed

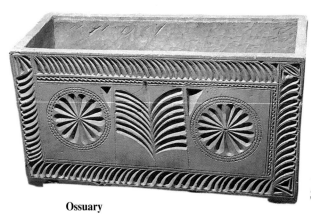

in a small rock-cut loculus, or within an ossuary, for secondary burial. An ossuary is a stone chest that had to be at least as long as the femur (the thighbone, the longest bone in the human body), and at least as wide as that of the pelvis (the widest human bone). Ossuaries were used primarily in Judea and in Jerusalem in the late Second Temple period.

Ossuary

The collection of the bones from each corpse into a separate loculus or ossuary in the late Second Temple period differed from the occasional practice, in the First Temple period, of gathering all the remains of the deceased members of a family into a communal charnel in which the bones from different bodies would likely be mixed together. According to one opinion, this change attests to the development among Jews in the Second Temple period of the belief in the **resurrection of the dead.** According to this theory the belief that the body of a person would regain its flesh in the End of Days required that his or her bones be kept separately.

The sages regard the day on which the bones are collected as a day of mourning, because of the handling of the bones of the deceased. The following day, however, was a joyous occasion, because the end of the decomposition process of the flesh was considered to conclude the period in which the deceased suffered punishment for the sins he/she had committed in this world.

It is interesting that prior to the Second Temple period it had been the practice to bury in ossuaries only in the Chalcolithic Age, in the fourth millennium BCE. Is there some connection between these similar customs, separated by more than three thousand years, or did they originate independently?

We will continue on the path to the right, going up the small hill. After about thirty meters we see the entrance of another burial cave, with a single column in its facade.

One example of the belief in the **resurrection of the dead** during the Second Temple period is found in the statements of the martyrs and their mother in the horrifying narrative of a mother and her seven sons who were ordered by Antiochus to violate the tenets of their religion: "You wicked one, you release us from this world, but the King of the Universe will awaken us from the dead... I received these [the tongue and the hands] from Heaven, and from it I hope to receive them back again... for we will be raised again by Him, but you [Antiochus] will have no resurrection to life." And the mother to her sons: "the Creator of the world... will give you back again life and breath in His mercy" (II Maccabees 7:9-23).

THE COLONNADE TOMB   2

IN MODERN TIMES, when the family of the deceased visits the grave on the anniversary of the death, the members assemble at the entrance to the cemetery, continuing from there to the grave, which is situated among many others. In most instances, there are no benches in the area on which visitors can sit. The planners of the family tombs in the Second Temple period would often devote thought to the comfort of the visitors, and we find in front of tombs, such as the one before us, a forecourt cut in the bedrock and flanked by stone benches for visitors. Those attending the funeral may have sat on these very benches as they awaited the interment ceremony. Such forecourts were also hewn in later periods, as is known, for example, from the cemetery in Beth She'arim in Galilee, from the period of the Mishnah.

In the past, two rock-cut columns stood at the facade entrance, only one of which, topped by a Doric capital, has survived. Facades of similar style are known to us from various temples and other structures in the Hellenistic world. It can be assumed that the planners of tombs probably used the ornamentations and styles with which they were familiar from everyday life At times it is only from the appearance of the tombs that we can learn of the form of the city's houses, which unfortunately have not survived to a height that would enable us to reconstruct the appearance of their facades in all their glory.

The facade of the cave before us is fairly modest, possibly reflecting the financial status of the family that ordered its construction. The wealthy inhabitants of Jerusalem left after them burial caves and monumental tombs, while less well-to-do families contented themselves with more simple interment. It may be safely assumed that the majority of the city's population had to make do with burial in pits in the ground, most of which have left no trace.

We will descend from the hill toward the road, continuing to the right along the path parallel to the road until the northern end of the park.

3   THE TOMB OF THE GREAT SANHEDRIN

W E HAVE COME to the largest and most ornately decorated tomb in the park, which gives it its name. Here too a forecourt flanked by rock-cut benches extends in front of the tomb. The opening is surrounded by a frame carved in the stone, above which is a carved gable with attractive vine and acanthus leaf decorations. Acroteria are carved on both sides of the gable and at its top. At present the tomb is securely locked, but if we look through the entrance, we see on the right a deep shaft at the bottom of which are two burial chambers. At the far end of the entrance hall we see a more recessed entrance, fashioned similar to the outer one. Since we cannot go inside, in our mind's eye we will accompany the child and his Uncle Kalman, the heroes of the story "The Found Article" by David Shahar:

Sanhedrin Tomb

Sanhedrin Tomb (detail)

He was walking in front of me, and he went down the steep path that descends from the top of the hill concealing in its innards the cave, to its depths, the place where the mouth of the cave is revealed, like the entrance to an ancient building. As I skipped after him, my dread grew heavier. Continuing into the hidden recesses of the cave, I was enveloped by the fear of its dark interior, the cold and musty atmosphere of the ancient stone, and the heaviness of ancient, preserved air.... The two of us breathed deeply, as one, of the oppressive, breathtaking air that was about to smother us the very instant that it would fill the chamber of our lungs. Once we held our breath, we were saved from suffocation, and in its stead came a bit of rest. The murkiness was no longer hostile. It surrounded me all around, like the sheltering comforter of Father's existence, imparting security and tranquility (*The Pope's Moustache*, p. 184).

In the next photograph we see some of the loculi located within the cave.

Interior of the Sanhedrin Tomb

Pay special attention to the unique arrangement of the loculi in two tiers, with vaults above them. This is an interesting precedent for the concept of tiered burial that has been proposed in recent years to overcome the problem of a shortage of space for cemeteries in Israel. There are between 70 and 80 loculi in the cave, and from the Middle Ages certain people associated this number with the 71 members of the Great **Sanhedrin** in Jerusalem and identified this cave as the place of their burial. This popular assumption is patently groundless.

> The **Sanhedrin** was an assembly of 71 sages, the supreme religious body in Eretz Israel in the Second Temple period and in the first centuries following the destruction of the Temple. The Sanhedrin constituted the spiritual leadership of the nation and was the final arbiter of religious issues. Smaller judicial bodies, with 23 members, were called a "small Sanhedrin," and they were authorized to try capital cases.

The first to mention this cave was Rabbi Jacob, the emissary of Rabbi Jehiel of Paris in the mid-thirteenth century, who tells of "a cave within a cave, which is a very fine building, where many sages are buried." The site is mentioned in more explicit fashion by Rabbi Obadiah of Bertinoro, who arrived in the Land of Israel in 1488; he speaks of "the cave of the seventy elders."

We will ascend the stairs to the north of the cave, passing on the way a broad and impressive cliff containing the entrances to other burial caves. The caves which have been revealed are apparently only part of a much more extensive cemetery that existed here. We will now turn left to Ofirah Street, and descend the stairs between numbers 8 and 10 to Yam Suf Street. Here we turn to the right, cross the street, and go down the stairs into Weiller Park. We will continue along the path until it splits, taking the right fork to the end.

Doris Weiller Park

THE FACADE OF THE Eshkolot Cave is one of the most highly decorated of all the tombs in Jerusalem. Around the entrance is a carved frame that gives it the appearance of a majestic gate, with a carved gable over the entrance. Within the gable are grape clusters (*eshkolot* in Hebrew), that give the tomb its name, intertwined with vine shoots. The name of the neighborhood in which the cave is located is "Ramot Eshkol," but there is no connection between it and the cave; the neighborhood is named after Israel's third prime minister, Levi Eshkol.

The facade of this tomb, like those of the other tombs we have seen or will see during the course of this tour, clearly demonstrates the absence of images from tomb ornamentations, sarcophagi, and ossuaries in Second Temple period

Eshkolot Cave

Jerusalem. The mosaic floors from this period also do not contain any human or animal representations, and their place is taken by geometrical patterns and floral forms. The influence of Hellenistic culture finds expression in the adoption of ornamental frames, such as the gable form or the various column orders, while eliminating the mythological and pagan motifs common in Greek-Hellenistic decorative art and replacing them with other content.

As we stand under the lintel of the entrance and look upwards, we see the wonderful floral decorations on its underside. The ornamentations are enclosed by a square frame. If we look inwards, stopping for a moment to accustom our eyes to the darkness, we will see in the four corners of the entrance hall carefully fashioned column

Eshkolot Cave (details)

reliefs which "support" the cornice of its ceiling.

Facing us is another, inner entrance that leads to the main chamber from which the loculi chambers branch off. The Eshkolot Cave was also situated in a former stone quarry, traces of which can be seen in the exposed rock near the cave.

Tomb of the Small Sanhedrin

We emerge from the Weiller Park into Yam Suf Street, and continue until the next stop, adjoining the Sheikh Jarrah neighborhood. Those coming by private car may return to the parking lot next to Sanhedrin Park and drive to the next stop.

To the left of the narrow street leading to the tomb of Simeon the Just is the entrance of a burial cave covered by an iron grille ⑤. This cave was formerly called the Tomb of the Small Sanhedrin, but the source of this name is unclear. In 1918 this site was renovated, by order of the Zionist Commission, as we learn from the inscription next to the entrance.

THE TOMB OF SIMEON THE JUST   6

Abu Bakr al-Sidiq Street

WHO WAS SIMEON THE JUST, whom Jewish tradition identifies with this tomb? Simeon the Just, who lived in the fourth century BCE, is mentioned in the Mishnah (*Avot* 1:2) as an early sage who was "one of the remnants of the Great Assembly," the Jewish leadership institution that most likely was active after the Return to Zion and before the establishment of the Sanhedrin. Many legends have sprung up around the vague figure of Simeon the Just. One of them, which is mentioned in the Talmud (and with a few variations by Josephus), tells of his fateful encounter with Alexander the Great, the conqueror of Eretz Israel, when the Samaritans sought Alexander's permission to destroy the Jewish Temple:

[On] the day on which the Cutheans [the Samaritans] demanded the House of God from Alexander the Macedonian in order to destroy it, and he had given them the permission, some people came and told Simeon the Just. What did he do? He put on his priestly garments, robed himself in priestly garments, and some of the noblemen of Israel went with him carrying fiery torches in their hands. They walked all night, they [the Jews] walking on one side and the others [Alexander's army] walking on the other side, until the dawn broke. When dawn had broken, Alexander asked them [the Cutheans], "Who are these?" They replied, "The Jews who rebelled against you."... When [Alexander] saw Simeon the Just, he descended from his chariot and bowed down before him. They asked him [Alexander]: "A great king such as yourself should bow down before this Jew?" He replied, "It is his image that wins all my battles for me." He asked them [the Jews], "Why have you come?" They answered, "Is it possible that idol worshipers should mislead you to destroy the House in which prayers are recited for you and your kingdom, that it never be destroyed?" He asked them, "Who are these [who seek to destroy me]?" "These Cutheans standing before you." He said to them, "They are delivered into your hand." They immediately perforated their heels, tied them to the tails of their horses, and dragged them over thorns and thistles... and that day they made a festival" (Babylonian Talmud, Yoma 69a).

When we descend the stairs into the cave, which is used for study and prayer, we see in front of us a cloth curtain, on which it is written that this was the location of Simeon the Just's ritual bath. If we carefully lift the curtain and look inside, using a flashlight, we see a large rock-cut chamber containing the remains of three burial vaults. The tomb may possibly have already been hewn in the Second Temple period and continued in use in the Roman-Byzantine period. A

barely legible inscription mentioning a "Julia Sabina," who might have been the wife or the daughter of a Roman military commander, was discovered at the site in 1871.

The tomb of Simeon the Just has long been a pilgrimage site for the Jews of Jerusalem. The best time for a visit is on Lag ba-Omer, when the *halakah* ceremony is conducted – the first

Tomb of Simeon the Just

haircut for three-year-old boys. This practice, which is familiar to many from the tomb of Rabbi Simeon bar Yohai in Meron, has also become established here. Possibly the similarity between the names (Simeon bar Yohai and Simeon the Just) and the difficulty of traveling to distant Galilee brought the custom to Jerusalem.

Like the Sanhedrin Tombs, the tomb of Simeon the Just has also lent its name to two nearby Jewish neighborhoods: Shimon Ha-tzadik and Nahalat Shimon, which were built in 1891–92 and were inhabited until the outbreak of the Arab revolt (1936–39), when their residents were evacuated.

We will return to the main road, turning left at the intersection onto Derekh Shkhem, as we pass by the minaret of the **Sheikh Jarrah** neighborhood and the American Colony (see Tour 21).

◆ **Sheikh Jarrah** was the
◆ name of Saladin's
◆ personal physician (*j*
◆ means "surgeon" in
◆ Arabic), who was giv
◆ this area as a landho
◆ after the Arab conqu
◆ the land from the
◆ Crusaders. Another
◆ Jerusalem neighborh
◆ named after one of
◆ Saladin's men is Abu
◆ in the southern part c
◆ city, which was given
◆ warrior who rode a k
◆ (*abu tor* is "father of
◆ bull" in Arabic).

46 Salah al-Din Street

W E ENTER THE GATE and go down the massive rock-cut staircase, which is nine meters wide and thirty meters long. The descent via the monumental stairs removes us from the hustle and bustle of the street, and each additional step seems to take us back in time to the days when this burial site, undoubtedly one of the most magnificent in the city, was hewn in the bedrock.

To our right we see two drainage channels cut in the side of the bedrock and linking up with the gutters running the width of the staircase. Rainwater falling on the stairs was thus drained to a small cistern on the right and to a much larger cistern in front of us, which were used as ritual baths. We will go down to the bottom of the staircase and enter the gate to our left. An expansive courtyard, entirely cut from the bedrock, spreads before us. Cut to a depth of about eight meters, some twenty thousand tons of rock were removed during this operation. The facade of the cave situated in the wall of the courtyard may prove to be somewhat disappointing, since the hand of man and the ravages of time have damaged its ornamentations. We can discern a stone block protruding down-wards from the lintel, between the two iron columns placed at the facade of the cave for support. This block apparently is all that remains of one of the two columns that stood in the facade, which was similar to that of the Colonnade Tomb in Sanhedrin Park. On the basis of the surviving ornamentation fragments and the parts of decorations found in the courtyard during archae-ological excavations (some of which have been assembled behind the small fence to the right of the entrance way), we are able to reconstruct around the entrance a sort of leafy braid, topped by a

Proposed reconstruction of the Tombs of the Kings

Theodor Herzl visiting the Tombs of the Kings

cornice, parts of which have survived in situ. The lower part of the cornice was divided into decorated square areas, known as metopes, separated by groups of three vertical lines (triglyphs). The names of these decorations clearly point to their Greek origin. According to the description by Josephus (*Antiquities* 20:4:3), above the cave were three "pyramids."

From the archaeological finds we learn that at least one of these "pyramids" resembled the concave cone standing above Absalom's Tomb in the Kidron Valley. These were most probably monuments in memory of the deceased, known as the nefesh (literally, "soul" – see Tour 5).

Josephus' description of the Third Wall, that encompassed northern Jerusalem in the late Second Temple period (*War of the Jews* 5:4:2), enables us to identify the place where we are standing as the burial site of Queen Helena of Adiabene and the members of her family. Helena's sons Izates and Monobaz ruled the kingdom of Adiabene, which was located in what is now Iraq, on the banks of the Tigris River. Helena and her two sons converted to Judaism, and she even came to Jerusalem in the thirties of the first century CE and lived in the city for a while. The charitable acts and other good works she and her sons performed on behalf of the city's inhabitants are mentioned by Josephus and the Talmud. Helena and her family built for themselves palaces to the south of the Temple Mount, and their burial site is probably located here. When Izates and Helena died, King Monobaz sent their bones to Jerusalem, where they found their final rest.

During the nineteenth century, the first modern explorers of Jerusalem expressed a great deal of interest in this cave, which, due to its magnificent style, they erroneously identified as the tomb of the kings of Judah from the First Temple period. In 1863 the French researcher de Saulcy began to excavate the cave, in the hope of finding the treasures of the kings of Judah. During the course of the excavations, the bones of those buried in the site were scattered. When this became known, it greatly agitated and angered some residents of the city, especially the Jews, who believed that Kalba Savua, Rabbi Akiva's father-in-law, was buried here. Joseph Rivlin described these events in a letter to the public published in the *Ha-maggid* newspaper. His description is so vivid that the reader might think that it relates to the recent altercations that have taken place in modern Israel over the excavation of tombs by archaeologists:

Before our very eyes, the bones of the great ones of Israel, that have lain in the earth for more than two thousand years, have been taken out. Woe to the eyes that see such a sight! ... First, they removed the myriads of large and small stones that had accumulated there during many years... and they cleaned the floor of the cave... then they saw crypts in the sides of the cave, they broke into the wall and found large stone coffins... and one coffin they brought out whole... and within the coffin they saw bones. This terrible thing provoked and agitated the heart of every Israelite... our hearts were broken by worry when we heard that they would undoubtedly further excavate the graves of prophets and the righteous, may their merit protect us, Amen. Woe and woe! After two thousand years, the bones of these holy righteous ones, the fathers of Israel, including their prophets and their princes, will be moved and will suffer severe shaking, disgrace, and shame.

And on Sunday, the eighth day of Hanukkah, the rabbis and synagogue officials assembled...to draw up a public letter to the great Pasha, the governor of Jerusalem... to cry out and plead against this wicked thing, that he hand over the bones to the Israelites, to bring them to proper interment, and our people be given permission to place individuals to keep an eye on the excavators, so that they will not touch any grave, nor move any more bones, God forbid ... (*Hamaggid*, 6 Tevet 5624 [1864]).

Interior of the Tombs of the Kings

The excavations caused such an outcry that a French Jewess by the name of Bertha Bertrand decided to purchase the site, for eternal possession by the Jewish people. In 1886 the son of Mrs. Bertrand's heirs, Henri Péroire, donated the burial site to the French government, which has retained ownership of it to the present.

We will proceed to the entrance chamber in the facade of the cave, which contains a plaque in memory of the Péroire family, that, according to its wording, gave over the "tombs of the kings of Judah" to the government of France.

To the left is a small entrance leading into the cave. This entrance was closed by the rolling stone that is still located in the groove hewn in the bedrock to its left. A sophisticated defense mechanism which has not survived, was apparently used to protect the entrance and prevent the entry of unwanted intruders.

We must stoop to enter. We find ourselves within a large hall with surrounding stone benches. The precise hewing into the bedrock is quite impressive. A number of entrances lead from this hall to the burial chambers, into whose walls loculi and arcosolia are hewn. One of the chambers is on a lower level, below the floor of the entrance hall.

De Saulcy found a few sarcophagi here, including one that is decorated with rosette patterns, similar to those we saw on the underside of the lintel in the Eshkolot Tomb, and has a convex lid. The name "Tzadah Malkatah" and "Tzadan Malkata" was engraved on the cover of another sarcophagus, whose discovery caused great excitement. De Saulcy was certain that he was holding in his hands the remains of the wife of King Zedekiah of Judah. It would seem, however, that this is the coffin of one of the daughters from the family of Queen Helena, or possibly of Helena herself. All the finds from the tomb were brought to the Louvre Museum in Paris.

We will leave the tomb and return to Salah al-Din Street, where we take bus no. 23 or 27 to the city center. If we want to go on, we can take bus no. 9 to the Rehaviah neighborhood and enter Alfasi Street (Rehaviah is included in the map for Tour 27), where another interesting burial cave is located.

8 — JASON'S TOMB

10 Alfasi Street

AMONG THE WEALTHY RESIDENTS of the Rehaviah neighborhood in twentieth-century Jerusalem, an affluent Jerusalemite from the late Hasmonean period, by the name of Jason, has found eternal repose.

The tomb appears to be located at a remote site, far from any Second Temple period structure or tomb, but this is not actually the case. The Rehaviah neighborhood, especially the axis formed by the parallel Gaza Road and Ramban Street, is probably built over a burial complex from the Second Temple period. The most likely reason for the concentration of tombs in this area was the access provided by the road that led southward from Jerusalem to the city of Gaza. This practice of burial along the sides of the roads leading to a city is also known from other places (such as Rome), and is reflected in a midrashic narrative:

[This is like] a father and son who were walking along the way, when the son became tired. He said to his father: "Where is the city?" He replied: "My son, let this be a sign for you: If you see a cemetery before you, know that you are near the city." Thus the Holy One, blessed be He, said to Israel: "If you see that troubles are enveloping you, at that moment you will be redeemed" (*Midrash Shoher Tov* on Psalm 20).

Jason's Tomb is closed to visitors, but through the bars we can see the tomb structure that was reconstructed following archaeological excavations. Access to

Jason's Tomb

the chamber is by means of an entranceway and two court-yards, while a single column stands at its entrance. The pyramid we see on top of the tomb is reminiscent of the monument of Zechariah's Tomb in the Kidron Valley and the pyramids that most likely topped the Tombs of the Kings. The reconstructed pyramid before us incorporates some of the original masonry found during the excavations.

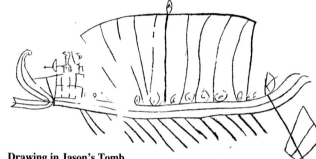

Drawing in Jason's Tomb

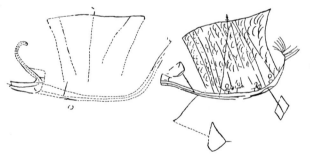

The tomb contains a number of inscriptions, one of which mentions an individual by the name of **Jason,** and an interesting wall drawing depicting a ship with a man standing on its deck (possibly one of those buried in the tomb), which is sailing behind two merchant ships or fishing boats.

The tomb, which dates from the late Hasmonean period, was destroyed in an earthquake, but was probably restored afterwards and used for burials at least until the destruction of the Second Temple.

In 1995 another burial cave was discovered on Diskin Street in Rehaviah. Engraved on one of the ossuaries in it is the name "Jason" in Greek and Hebrew, possibly a relative of the Jason in this tomb.

◆ According to one opinion, the maritime scene depicted here indicates that **Jason** or one of the other deceased in this tomb was a sailor or a merchant who possessed a fleet of ships. Other authorities maintain that it portrays a sea chase, and therefore this might possibly not be the tomb of an honest merchant, but rather that of a daring Hebrew pirate.

From the East Talpiot Water Tunnel to Mamilla Pool

SECOND TEMPLE PERIOD JERUSALEM was a city of purity, a city of sanctity, a royal city, and a vibrant, living city. Each of these identities was expressed in the city's water consumption. In this city of purity, every priest who officiated in the Temple and frequently entered it was required to be pure, and every pilgrim or individual offering a sacrifice who went up to the Temple Mount had to immerse himself in water. In this city of sanctity, the Temple area, which stood at the heart of the city, had to be washed at frequent intervals to remove the blood of sacrifices. The many pilgrims who thronged to the city consumed large quantities of drinking water. Jerusalem was also the royal city, the capital of the kingdom. The splendid Hasmonean palaces and the fountains in Herod's palace, of which Josephus speaks, also required a large supply of water. And most importantly, Jerusalem was a living city. Its population, which continually increased during the Second Temple period, needed considerable amounts of water for drinking, laundering, bathing, and the maintenance of a proper level of sanitation.

The Gihon Spring and En Rogel, together with the pools and cisterns that Jerusalem relied on, in the First and early Second Temple periods were no longer capable of supplying the ever-increasing needs of the city during the days of the Hasmoneans, and especially during the reign of Herod. Two aqueducts were therefore built to bring water to the city from springs located many kilometers from Jerusalem and at a higher elevation. During this tour we will follow the remains of one of them – the Lower Aqueduct, which brought water to the Temple area. We will learn of the engineering sophistication required to construct this installation. This waterworks continued to function, while undergoing renovations and repairs, for more than two thousand years. The tour will end at the Mamilla Pool, which may have been an important component of the other aqueduct that conveyed water to Jerusalem – the Upper Aqueduct, which supplied the Upper City area.

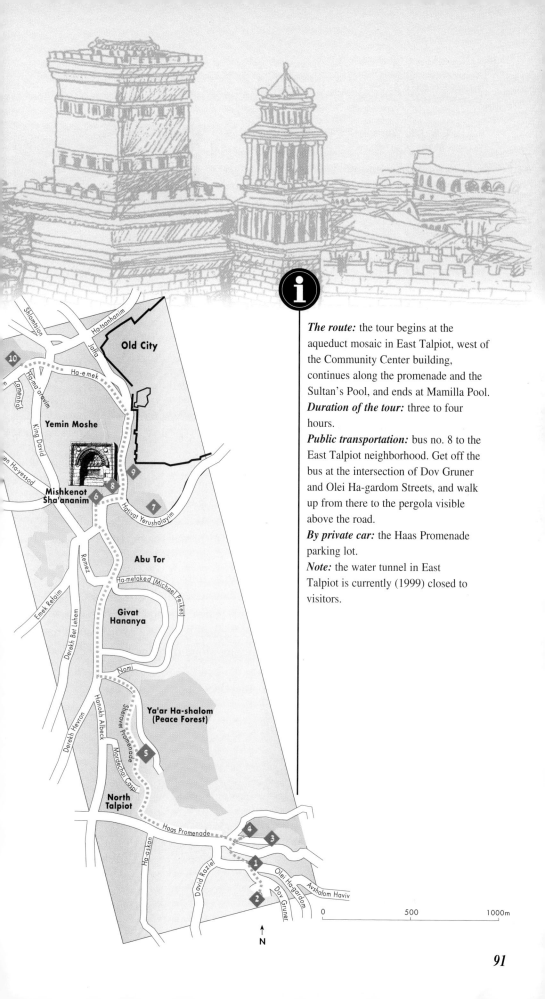

Old City

Shlomtsion

Ha-tsanhanim

Jaffa

Ha-emek

Yemin Moshe

Ha-ma'aravim

Yomenhof

King David

Ben Ha-yessod

Mishkenot
Sha'ananim

Hativat Yerushalayim

Abu Tor

Remez

Emek Refaim

Derekh Bet Lehem

Ha-metaked (Michael Feikes)

Givat
Hananya

Nomi

Derekh Hevron

Hanokh Albeck

Sherover Promenade

Mordechai Gispi

Ya'ar Ha-shalom
(Peace Forest)

North
Talpiot

Haas Promenade

Ha-astan

David Raziel

Olei Ha-gardom

Dov Gruner

Avshalom Haviv

0   500   1000m

N

The route: the tour begins at the aqueduct mosaic in East Talpiot, west of the Community Center building, continues along the promenade and the Sultan's Pool, and ends at Mamilla Pool.
Duration of the tour: three to four hours.
Public transportation: bus no. 8 to the East Talpiot neighborhood. Get off the bus at the intersection of Dov Gruner and Olei Ha-gardom Streets, and walk up from there to the pergola visible above the road.
By private car: the Haas Promenade parking lot.
Note: the water tunnel in East Talpiot is currently (1999) closed to visitors.

WE ARE STANDING on the periphery of the East Talpiot neighborhood commonly known as Armon Ha-natziv (Government House), named after the nearby official residency of the British High Commissioner in the Mandate period (1918–48). This is one of the neighborhoods ringing the city that were planned following the Six-Day War. In the vicinity are the Arab villages of Jabl Mukabar, Arab al-Sawahra, and Sur Bahr. Some of the interesting archaeological finds that were revealed here were incorporated in the neighborhood.

The aqueduct mosaic was placed here as part of an excavation and restoration project relating to sections of the Lower Aqueduct. The mosaic shows the course of the Lower and Arrub Aqueducts, and we must therefore

Mosaic of Lower and Arrub aqueducts

also refer to the schematic diagram on this page which displays four aqueducts.

One view, which is no longer accepted, associates the aqueducts with King Solomon. The sages were of the opinion that the laver that Solomon installed at the entrance of the First Temple for the immersion of the priests was supplied with water from Etan, near **Solomon's Pools.** These pools were so named on the basis of a verse from Ecclesiastes (the authorship of which is traditionally ascribed to King Solomon): "I constructed pools of water, enough to irrigate a forest shooting up with trees." (Ecclesiastes 2:6).

This diagram clearly shows that the heart of Jerusalem's water supply system was **Solomon's Pools,** south of Bethlehem. The Arrub Aqueduct from Ein Kuweiziba and Ein Arrub to the south of the Etzion Bloc, and the Biyar Aqueduct from the springs of Wadi Biyar led water to Solomon's Pools, like veins bringing blood to the heart. From Solomon's Pools emerge a winding aqueduct – the "Lower Aqueduct," and a straighter aqueduct at a higher level – the "Upper Aqueduct." These two channels resemble the arteries conveying blood from the heart to the limbs and organs.

The Upper Aqueduct issues from the upper pool of

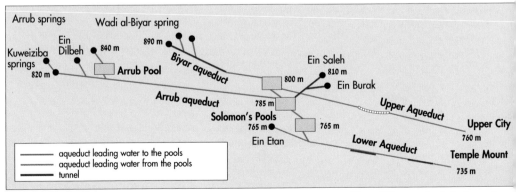

Plan of the aqueducts to Jerusalem

Solomon's Pools and follows the watershed line. One part of it consisted of a stone pipe, segments of which were found in the Bethlehem area. The aqueduct passes near the Mar Elias monastery, runs to the west of kibbutz Ramat Rahel, and continues from there along the line of Hebron Road to its final destination in the Upper City. Latin inscriptions bearing the names of commanders of the Roman Tenth Legion that were found on stone pipe segments, are evidence that this aqueduct was built no later than the second century CE. It is not inconceivable that an earlier aqueduct followed this course in the time of King Herod.

Roman leveling instrument (chorobates)

The Lower Aqueduct, which is at the center of this tour, leaves the lowest of Solomon's Pools at an elevation of 765 m above sea level, crosses Bethlehem, continues north and crosses Jabl Mukabar, the site of the East Talpiot neighborhood, passes through the Abu Tor neighborhood and that of Mishkenot Sha'ananim, goes around the Sultan's Pool, and bypasses Mount Zion on the south before heading for its final destination on the Temple Mount, at an elevation of 735 m. The length of the aqueduct is 21 km, while the rectilinear distance between its starting and ending points is about 10 km. This differential is due to the fact that the Lower Aqueduct bypasses many obstacles, while maintaining the slight gradient that causes the water to flow in the proper path. In two instances, the Lower Aqueduct passes through mountains via tunnels, rather than circumventing them. The tunnel in Bethlehem is estimated to be 360 m long, while the one in Jabl Mukabar, right below our feet, is 395 m long. The hewing of a tunnel here saved a circumvention of about 4 kilometers. The mosaic next to us is built around one of six vertical **shafts** that the builders of the aqueduct dug from ground level to the tunnel. This shaft descends to a depth of 35m. The shafts were probably dug in order to provide ventilation while the tunnel was being dug, remove waste material from it, and enable routine maintenance. The moderate slope of the Lower Aqueduct (0.14%) raises the question: how did the planners manage to maintain such a gradient over a distance of more than 20 km? On the left side of the mosaic you can see an instrument with four arms that revolve around a central axis, with a plumb suspended from each arm.

The archaeologists who cleared the entire length of the tunnel to make it accessible to visitors relate that in the process of their work they came across religious objects, such as Torah scroll parchments, defective phylacteries, and other such items. It seems that in recent times some Jerusalemites have used the **shafts** along the tunnel as a genizah, a repository for worn-out or defective religious books and objects.

Roman leveling instrument (groma)

This important instrument, called a *groma* in Latin, was used in the Roman period to ensure the proper level of aqueducts. A second question is, when during the Second Temple period was the Lower Aqueduct constructed? During the course of the tour, we will suggest an answer.

We will descend to Dov Gruner Street, and continue down the stairs of the park to the right of the street to the structure alongside the archaeological excavations.

2 THE EAST TALPIOT TUNNEL

AT THIS POINT the Lower Aqueduct enters the tunnel hewn through Jabl Mukabar. If we look at the excavations, we will see on the left the original channel of the aqueduct. This was an open and plastered U-shaped trench, approximately 0.5 meters wide. A ceramic pipe was laid in the channel in the seventeenth century. The Turks encased the pipe with cement to protect it, but it was soon blocked by alluvium. In order to clear it, from time to time round holes were drilled in the cement, big enough for a worker to insert his hand and remove the sediment. We will follow the aqueduct toward the iron door at the entrance to the tunnel. We find ourselves inside a small pool, which can easily be identified by its thick plaster coating. The alluvium carried

Entrance to the East Talpiot tunnel

along in the water would sink in this settling tank, thus helping to prevent blockage in the tunnel. Pay special attention to the extreme height of the tunnel, which is connected with an interesting story from the more recent history of the aqueduct. At the beginning of the twentieth century, the Ottoman authorities decided to "improve" the functioning of the ancient aqueduct, and to convert the East Talpiot tunnel into a sausage-shaped reservoir. They accordingly deepened the tunnel by 2.70 m and plastered its sides. An iron pipeline was installed from the tunnel at Bethlehem to the entrance of this tunnel. Another iron pipeline was installed from the exit of this tunnel which led water to the Temple Mount through the Dung Gate and a secondary pipe branching off from it to the *sabil* (water fountain) at the Sultan's Pool. In 1902, upon the completion of the project, the authorities held a grand ceremony to inaugurate the waterworks, but it soon became evident that the celebrations had been premature: the new method did not function efficiently and the flow of water even decreased, possibly due to blockages. The investment proved to have been in vain. The water tunnel is currently (1999) closed, but there are plans for opening it to visitors in the future. We will return to stop 1 on this tour and go up to the road north of it. To the east is the United Nations Truce Supervision Observers' headquarters ③, which was constructed in the 1930s as the residency of the British High Commissioner. Another of the six shafts of the aqueduct tunnel is visible in the cypress grove in front of us ④.

We will continue to the **Haas Promenade**. From here we have a spectacular view of Jerusalem. The golden Dome of the Rock marks the final destination of the water carried by the Lower Aqueduct. If you want to see the exit of the water tunnel and the aqueduct leading from it, go down the steps to the path below the cafe and continue to descend to the right on the winding route, until the tunnel becomes visible to the left. An observation point in the style of an ancient theater, which will be reached by those walking through the tunnel, is planned for this area.

We will continue to the west on the Haas Promenade and descend northward along the **Sherover Promenade**. We will go down from the stone plaza of the Promenade to the lawn to our right, to an additional section of the aqueduct.

Sherover Promenade

The **Haas Promenade** (1986) is partly built on arches, which give it the appearance from a distance of an aqueduct. This monumental promenade runs in a straight line and provides a panoramic view of the city looking to the north. The **Sherover Promenade** (1989) differs in style from the Haas Promenade: it winds, its several levels are integrated into the hilly terrain, and it is entirely surrounded by greenery.

THE AQUEDUCT IN THE SHEROVER PROMENADE ⟨5⟩

THE SECTION OF ceramic pipe in the aqueduct apparently is an Ottoman "implant" from the seventeenth century, when efforts were made to improve Jerusalem's water supply. This method of conducting water through ceramic pipes built of segments was already described in the writings of the Roman engineer **Vitruvius**, who lived in the first century BCE. According to him, the advantage of a ceramic pipe is that since it is closed (unlike an open

Vitruvius was an engineer in Julius Caesar's army, who planned several important structures in the Roman world. In 25 BCE he wrote *De architectura*, dedicated to Augustus, in which he provided a detailed and comprehensive description of the building techniques and materials of his day. The eighth part of that book deals with water supply. This work was known during the Middle Ages, and became a basic textbook in architecture in the early Renaissance period.

aqueduct, in which the flowing water is exposed), it is both inexpensive and has no deleterious effect upon the water (unlike that of a lead pipe). When asked about the greater durability of a lead pipe as compared to a ceramic one, Vitruvius replied that the latter's construction of segments facilitates its maintenance and the making of repairs.

We will now return to the Promenade and continue walking until we exit to Hebron Road. We will continue through the intersection, in the direction of the Mishkenot Sha'ananim quarter.

We will now enter the access path to the neighborhood (past the western ascent to the pedestrian bridge) and continue to the observation platform at its end.

Aqueduct near the Sherover Promenade

6   THE SULTAN'S POOL

Observation Platform below Mishkenot Sha'ananim

A FINE SECTION OF THE Lower Aqueduct is preserved at the foot of the observation platform. The unique feature of this section is the stone slabs that covered the aqueduct and protected the water against contamination and evaporation in the hot Jerusalem sun. Such stone slabs are high-quality building material, the availability of which tempted every farmer or builder who lived or passed nearby to steal them. There were also other dangers that threatened the vital artery of the aqueduct. This is obvious from the concern expressed by the authorities for the smooth operation of the aqueduct, as is attested by a Greek inscription from the Byzantine period that was found in the Bethlehem area:

Flavius Anias Silentrius [proclaims] to the owners, the sharecroppers, and the farmers: Know that the divine and pious king has commanded that no man is permitted to plant or sow within a distance of 15 feet from the aqueduct. And if anyone shall attempt to transgress the decree, he shall be punished by death and his property will be confiscated. The measure of the foot is drawn at the bottom [of this inscription].

The prohibition was most likely instituted for fear of the damage to the aqueduct that would be caused by plant roots. Now look up to Mount Zion ⑦ and the road that skirts it on the south, where the continuation of the aqueduct is located. In order to reach Mount Zion, the aqueduct had to cross the Hinnom

Valley (below us), and this was achieved by means of a bridge supported by arches that passed slightly to the north of the Sultan's Pool. In the 1920s, a tour guide of Palestine and the nearby countries was jointly authored by the archaeologist Eliezer Lipa Sukenik (the father of archaeologist and Chief of the General Staff

Aqueduct near Mishkenot Sha'ananim

Yigael Yadin) and the teacher and author Hayyim Aryeh Zuta. When dealing with the Sultan's Pool they wrote that "the water pipe on the bridge brings water from Solomon's Pools to the Temple area," thus attesting to the fact that the bridge was still in existence at that time. No trace of it remains today, since it is entirely covered with earth.

Before we leave this area, we should say something about the history of the Sultan's Pool , which forms part of the Hinnom Valley flanking Mount Zion on the west and the south. This pool most likely had its beginnings in the time of Herod, and some authorities identify it with the Snake Pool mentioned by Josephus (*War of the Jews* 5:3:2). Herod, who built his palace south of the Citadel area (which we can see above us to our left), ensured that it would have a reservoir nearby. The pool was formed by building a dam across the Hinnom Valley to the south, along which the road below us now passes. In this it

resembles other ancient pools in Jerusalem which made use of natural water courses. The Hinnom Valley actually begins in the vicinity of Zion Square, in the center of modern Jerusalem, where it is almost unnoticeable, but the section before us is quite deep and thus probably obviated the need for further quarrying. An interesting hypothesis recently put forward is that the Sultan's Pool was the site of the hippodrome that existed in Second Temple period Jerusalem, according to Josephus. The pool was renovated

Sabil (water fountain) at the Sultan's Pool

in 1176, during the Crusader period, by Germanus, and therefore was called Lacus Germani (the Pool of Germanus) at the time. The Crusaders used the pool to bathe their horses. In 1398 the Mamluk sultan Barquq gave the pool its present dimensions and depth. The sabil on the rim of the dam was built by Sultan

Suleiman the Magnificent in the early sixteenth century (1536) following the Ottoman conquest. The drawbacks of the pool are obvious: its distance from the city, and the difficult access to it, obligating those bringing water to the city to first descend and then climb back up to the city walls with their full vessels. A livestock market existed in the northern part of the pool until the end of the British Mandate, and below us to the left, in the corner of the pool, was a veterinary hospital that functioned during the Mandate. The Jerusalem Foundation has recently adapted the pool for use as an open-air theater.

We will go back down to Hebron Road and descend to Hativat Yerushalayim Street. To our right we see the entrances of First Temple period burial caves (some of which were still in use during the Second Temple period), that were sealed with square stone structures. Near these caves is another section of the aqueduct, which reaches this point after crossing the valley north of the Sultan's Pool. Here too we can identify a broken section of the Ottoman ceramic pipe.

9 THE LOWER AQUEDUCT

W E ARE COMING to the end of the tour and have not answered the question when the Lower Aqueduct was constructed. Unfortunately, there is no surviving inscription or any other means that would enable us to definitively date the aqueduct. Our only option is to attempt to determine its age indirectly.

The **Pharisees** and the **Sadducees** were two Jewish groups first mentioned in the Hasmonean period. The Pharisees are identified with rabbinic Judaism, whose teachings were later formulated in the Mishnah and Talmud. The Sadducees were connected with the wealthy priestly class. The two groups differed with regard to certain issues, such as man's free choice, the eternity of the soul, and the influence of Divine Providence.

A well-known passage in Tractate *Yadayim*, which deals with the laws of purity, tells of a discussion between the **Pharisees** and the **Sadducees** in the Second Temple period concerning the impurity of liquids:

The Sadducees say: We complain against you, Pharisees, since you declare an uninterrupted flow of liquid to be pure. The Pharisees say: Do we complain against you, Sadducees, for declaring the aqueduct [that comes] from a cemetery to be pure? (Mishnah, *Yadayim* 4:7).

We learn from this dialogue that the water that flows in an aqueduct passing through a cemetery is pure (even though a corpse imparts impurity). An analysis of this passage indicates that it reflects a law established in the time of the Hasmoneans, when the Sanhedrin was dominated by the Sadducees. According to one hypothesis, this discussion alludes to the Lower Aqueduct which, as we have seen, passes through a cemetery. If this assumption is correct, then we may establish that the aqueduct was already in existence in the Hasmonean period. This conclusion is supported by the discovery of aqueducts built by the Hasmoneans in their desert fortresses (Jericho, Sartaba, Hyrcania), in which they used a building technique and plaster similar to those of the Lower Aqueduct.

We will go up the road and turn left into Ha-emek Street, walking by the David's Village neighborhood to our last stop on the tour.

THE MAMILLA POOL 10

THE MAMILLA POOL is situated within Independence Park, in the area of the Muslim cemetery which was in use from the thirteenth century to 1927 (see Tour 26). This seems to have been the final destination for the water that flowed through the Upper Aqueduct. Mamilla pool has a storage capacity of about 32,000 cubic meters of water. Its height enabled water to flow from it to the area of the Citadel, near Jaffa Gate. The water passed through a channel about 750 m long that extended from the eastern wall of the pool to another reservoir near Jaffa Gate, the Pool of the Towers,

Mamilla Pool

popularly known as Hezekiah's Pool (see Tour 3). The entrance of the channel is presently blocked, but portions of it were uncovered recently when ground was broken for the construction of the David's Village neighborhood. The **Mamilla** Pool still served as a municipal reservoir during the British Mandate period. The area is to be restored as part of the Independence Park renewal project. Waterfalls and a garden have recently been constructed here. Our tour ends here. If you want to continue, you can proceed toward Jaffa Gate, enter the Petra Hotel to the left of the entrance to David Street (the markets), and ascend the stairwell which affords an impressive view of the Pool of the Towers, completely surrounded by residential structures.

♦ **Mamilla** is the name of the adjacent Muslim
♦ cemetery. The name may be a corruption of the
♦ Arabic concept *mu'min Allah* (the believer in
♦ God), possibly alluding to the belief in the
♦ resurrection of the dead. It has also been
♦ conjectured that it derives from the phrase *ma-min*
♦ *Allah* [water from God], referring to the Mamilla
♦ Pool located within the cemetery. The pool is
♦ mentioned in the writings of Mujir al-Din, a
♦ Jerusalem judge and historian of the fifteenth
♦ century, and is still visible today.

Pool of the Towers

The destruction of Jerusalem and the Temple in 70 CE brought an end to the Second Temple period, but Roman control of Eretz Israel continued. The Roman Tenth Legion, which had participated in the conquest, remained in the deserted and ruined city. The Jewish spiritual leadership moved to Galilee (the period of the Tannaim and the formulation of the Mishnah). Jerusalem, whose population grew once again as time passed, was also inhabited by Syrians and Greeks. The Roman soldiers were permitted to marry and raise families, and the early Christians, who had been expelled from the city on the eve of the great revolt, also returned. In 130 the emperor Hadrian passed through Eretz Israel on his way to Egypt. He decided to raise the city from its ruins and to rebuild it as a pagan city – Aelia Capitolina. This intention was one of the reasons leading to the outbreak of the Bar Kokhba revolt. The Jewish uprising was brutally suppressed, and Hadrian's plans were implemented. The establishment of the city was commemorated by the striking of a coin, one side showing the emperor plowing the borders of Jerusalem with a pair of oxen. The layout of the city's streets at that time has been maintained, in large degree, to the present. The city was most likely not encompassed by a wall in this phase, the time of Pax Romana – when peace reigned throughout the Roman Empire. Jews were forbidden to reside in the city, and the Romans built squares, triumphal arches, and pagan temples, one of which was erected on the Temple Mount.

In the early fourth century the Roman emperor Constantine the Great also took control of the eastern parts of the Empire, and transferred his capital from Rome to the city of Byzantium (renamed Constantinople after him). Constantine (died 337) granted Christianity the status of preferred religion throughout the Empire. This opened a new chapter in the history of Jerusalem, the Byzantine period, which would end about three centuries later, in 638, with the Muslim conquest. Politically, the Byzantine period was a continuation of the Roman era in Eretz Israel, with a smooth transition from one to the other. From the religious aspect, however, a great change occurred in the city, and Jerusalem was transformed from a pagan into a Christian city. The centrality of Jerusalem in the history of Christianity and in its sacred writings turned the city into a pilgrimage site. Churches were erected in the city that would become sites sacred to Christianity. The focal point shifted from the Temple Mount to the Church of the Holy Sepulcher built by Constantine. Large-scale construction was conducted throughout the city, and its walls were restored in the fifth century. There are a large number of extant finds from this period, as well as many historical testimonies by churchmen, such as the Church Father Eusebius, the historian Procopius, descriptions by pilgrims, and, most importantly, the Madaba Map – the mosaic map of Eretz Israel and Jerusalem found in Transjordan.

Although the ban on Jewish residence in the city was not renewed, it appears that Jews did not live there in this period. The Jewish spiritual endeavor continued outside Jerusalem – in Galilee, where the redaction of the Jerusalem Talmud was concluded (ca. 400), and primarily in Babylonia, where the Babylonian Talmud was completed (ca. 500). The city's size approached that in the late Second Temple period, except for its northern part, which was bounded approximately by the line of the northern section of the present-day city wall.

The Byzantine period was one of prosperity and construction throughout Eretz Israel, including Jerusalem. The city attained its floruit during the reign of the emperor Justinian (527–565), who built many structures in Jerusalem, including the Nea Church.

In 614 Eretz Israel, including Jerusalem, was conquered by the Persians who destroyed the city's churches and massacred its Christian inhabitants. In 629 the Byzantine emperor Heraclius succeeded in ridding the empire of the Persians and returned triumphantly to Jerusalem. Christian control of the city, however, would last for only nine years, and in 638 Jerusalem fell to the new rising star on the stage of history – the Muslims.

For a map of Jerusalem in this period, see p. 209

Ancient arch beneath Alexander Nevsky Church ⟶

ROMAN-BYZANTINE
PERIOD

From the Lions' Gate along the Via Dolorosa

O N THIS TOUR we will visit most of the Stations of the Cross on the Via Dolorosa, the way of suffering of Jesus on his way to the Crucifixion, an event that occurred in the late Second Temple period, on the eve of the Roman-Byzantine period. As on several other tours, during this one we will learn how the threads of the past are woven together into a typical Jerusalem fabric, both complex and confusing. But rest assured – during the tour we will try to unravel the historical and archaeological maze.

We will encounter a route that began in another place in Byzantine Jerusalem and whose present course developed in the Middle Ages, following the events of the Second Temple period and legends from the Byzantine period. The tour focuses mainly on major archaeological sites, mostly from the late Second Temple and Roman periods, that were revealed from the nineteenth century on – pools, squares,

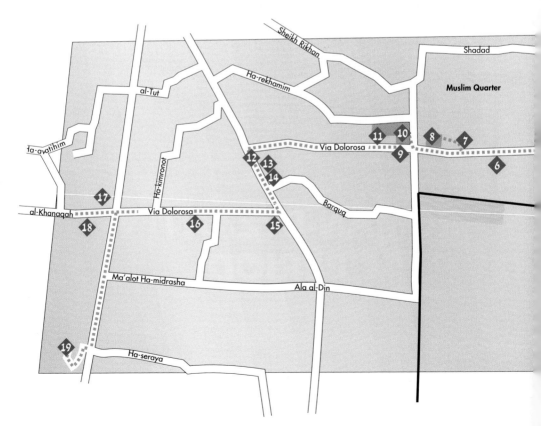

marketplaces and magnificent triumphal arches. Some of these sites, which were believed by the excavators to be connected with events in the New Testament, will give us an insight into the fascinating relationship between science (as expressed in archaeological excavations) and faith, which at times seeks its support.

Those of us who are interested in Jerusalem's water supply in the Second Temple period, which was the subject of Tour 7, will learn more about the water systems to the north of the Temple Mount.

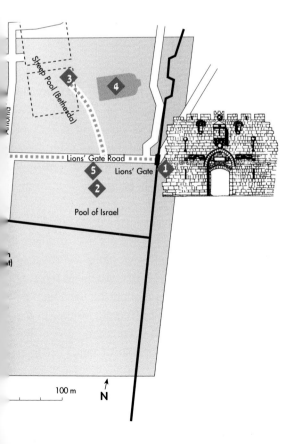

The route: the tour begins at the Lions' Gate, continues with the Monastery of St. Anne and the Sisters of Zion Convent, and ends at the Alexander Nevsky Church in the Christian Quarter. On the way we pass by Stations I–VIII of the Via Dolorosa.

Duration of the tour: about three hours.

Public transportation: bus no. 99, which circles the city (once per hour, 11:00 a.m.-3:00 p.m.). You can also take buses nos. 23, 26, or 27 to Damascus Gate, and walk from there along al-Wad Street to the Lions' Gate.

By private car: there is no orderly parking available. Park outside the Lions' Gate.

Visiting hours: Monastery of St. Anne: Mon–Sat: 8:00 a.m.–12:00 noon, 2:00 p.m.–5:00 p.m. (until 6:00 p.m. in the summer). Entrance fee.

Church of the Condemnation and Imposition of the Cross: October–March (entire week): 8:00 a.m.–12:00 noon, 1:00 p.m.–5:00 p.m.; April–September (entire week): 8:00 a.m.–12:00 noon, 1:00 p.m.–6:00 p.m.

Franciscan Museum: entire week: 9:00 a.m.–11:30 a.m. Entrance fee (up to twenty people).

Sisters of Zion Convent: Mon–Sat: 8:30 a.m.–12:30 p.m. 2:00 p.m.–5:00 p.m. Entrance fee.

Ecce Homo Arch: Mon–Sat: 8:30 a.m.–12:30 p.m., 2:00 p.m.–4:00 p.m.

Alexander Nevsky Church: Mon–Sat: 9:00 a.m.–1:00 p.m., 3:00 p.m.–5:00 p.m. Entrance free.

Note: modest dress is required.

ALTHOUGH THE LIONS' GATE is not associated with the period which is the theme of this tour, we cannot ignore its great significance in the history of modern Jerusalem. It was through this gate that Israeli paratroopers broke into the Old City in the Six-Day War (another force, from the Jerusalem Brigade, breached the Dung Gate at the same time), continuing from here to the Temple Mount. This is the only open gate in the eastern wall, and one of the original gates of the sixteenth-century wall encompassing the Old City. It was called by many names in the past: Gate of the Tribes, Bab Sitt Maryam (Lady Mary's Gate) by the Arabs, Gate of Jehoshaphat, and St. Stephen's Gate (by the Eastern Church). From the mid-nineteenth century the Jews called it the Lions' Gate after the two pairs of flanking carved lions (actually, leopards) in its facade – the symbol of the Mamluk sultan Baybars, who conquered Eretz Israel in 1260. Some authorities are of the opinion that these stone leopards were taken from one of the structures built by Baybars, and are in secondary use here.

The leopards on the Lions' Gate

A Jerusalem legend provides another explanation for the presence of the lions/leopards here. Before Jerusalem was encompassed by a wall, the Ottoman sultan Suleiman the Magnificent had a recurring dream in which he saw tremendously powerful lions about to tear him apart as punishment for not properly protecting the holy city. The sultan understood that this was a sign from Heaven, whereupon he ordered the erection of the wall that encircles the Old City to the present day. He also decreed that images of the lions he had seen in his dream were to be placed in the facade of the eastern gate.

We pass through the gate. Today, entry through the gate is direct, to enable the passage of motor vehicles, but initially it was not along a straight line, similar to Zion Gate which has retained its original plan. We will walk along the street to the large entrance on our right with a wooden door that leads into the Monastery of St. Anne. Before entering, look at the parking lot to the left (on the south) of the monastery ❷ and beyond it the northern wall of the Temple Mount. In the Second Temple period, the area of the parking lot was occupied by one of the larger reservoirs of the city, which the Arabs call "the Pool of Israel" (Birkat Isra'il).

Lions' Gate Street

three apses of Byzantine church

apse of Crusader church

Roman healing baths (concealed)

eastern wall of Old City

Church of St. Anne

southern pool

covered mosaic of Byzantine church

Roman pool

Byzantine church

dam separating the pools

Excavations at the Monastery of St. Anne

ENTER THE COURTYARD of the monastery, which is also known as the Monastery of the White Fathers because of the white robes worn during religious ceremonies by the members of the French Catholic order that owns the site.

We will cross the courtyard, passing by the church (on our right) that we will shortly enter, and stop at the excavations site. Since the wide range of archaeological finds is confusing at first glance, we should go around the excavations from the right and ascend to the observation point. From here we can consult the photograph of the excavations, reproduced on this page, where the finds from different periods are identified.

We are standing before two large reservoirs which, according to the accepted explanation, were hewn in the Second Temple period. Archaeologists have recently uncovered evidence that the northern reservoir may have been installed as early as the First Temple period. The pools, measuring 100 x 100m, with a depth of about 15m, have only been partially excavated. A dam separates them.

The pools are identified with the **Bethesda** (variant reading:

◆ The miraculous healing
◆ performed by Jesus in this pool
◆ is reflected in Christian hospitals
◆ bearing the name **Bethesda.**

Bezetha) pool mentioned in the New Testament as the place where Jesus performed one of his miracles, close to the Sheep Gate (in Greek: *probatice*, meaning "of sheep"). The New Testament contains the following narrative:

Now there is in Jerusalem by the Sheep Gate a pool, in Hebrew called Bethesda, which has five porticoes. In these lay a multitude of invalids, blind, lame, paralyzed, waiting for the moving of the water; for an angel of the Lord went down in certain seasons into the pool, and troubled the water: whoever stepped in first after the troubling of the water was healed of whatever disease he had. One man was there, who had been ill for thirty-eight years. When Jesus saw him and knew that he had been lying there a long time, he said to him, "Do you want to be healed?" The sick man answered him, "Sir, I have no man to put me into the pool when the water is troubled, and while I am going another steps down before me." Jesus said to him, "Rise, take up your pallet, and walk." And at once the man was healed, and he took up his pallet and walked (John 5:29).

During the Second Temple period the pool area was outside the city wall, and was included in the city only at the end of the period, upon the erection of the Third Wall. No trace has been found of the porticoes mentioned in the New Testament account, but stepped ritual baths were uncovered that attest to its use by Jews.

To the east of the pools we see a system of channels which apparently were part of the healing complex that existed here from the Hellenistic period to the fourth century CE. The excavators of the site are of the opinion that this was a therapeutic complex with an adjacent temple to the god of medicine **Aesculapius**. The excavations uncovered a relief depicting the facade of a building, next to which is an offering of ears of wheat and a snake. Evidence of another custom associated with healing in this period is provided by a marble leg dedicated by a woman named Pompeia Lucilia. The presentation to the deity of an offering fashioned in the shape of an ailing limb, accompanied by appropriate vows, in the hope of a cure, was a common practice and continued afterwards in the Christian Church.

We know of about two hundred sites in the Roman world dedicated to **Aesculapius**. The new temples were generally inaugurated by bringing one of the god's holy serpents from his temple in Epidaurus. The baths connected with these healing sites were entered as preparation for receiving a cure. The patients would generally lie on a *klin* (Greek: couch, bed), which is the source of the modern term clinic.

The tradition of the sacred pools of healing led to the construction of the Church of St. Mary of the Probatice in the fifth century. Visible today are re-

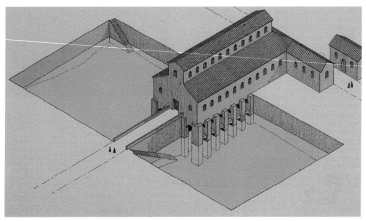

Proposed reconstruction of the Byzantine church

mains of its apses, the mosaic floor, and a few walls. The church, which measured 28 x 70m, was built over the central dam of the pools, its foundations descending to a depth of 13m. It was supported along its length by pillars, one of which was revealed in the western part of the excavation area. This sketch, on the opposite page, presents a reconstruction of the Byzantine church in relation to the pools. The builders of the church founded its eastern walls on the pagan temple of healing, which they probably intended to destroy. Following the Crusader conquest of Jerusalem, a new church, smaller in size, was built at the site on the foundations of the Byzantine church. The apse of this later church is clearly visible in the excavations. You can proceed along the footpath and descend into the depths of the impressive excavation, whose main elements bear explanatory plaques.

We will leave the excavations and go to the Church of St. Anne ◀4▶. On the way, we pass on our right a tombstone leaning against the wall, opposite the church entrance. The stone bears the Greek inscription: "The private grave of Amos, priest of the Probatice." Amos was one of those officiating in the Byzantine church. The Church of St. Anne was erected in the twelfth century by the Crusaders, who named it after Anne (Hannah), the mother of Mary, mother of Jesus. According to one tradition, Anne dwelled with her husband Jehoiachin in the vicinity, and Mary was born here. Note the simple lines of the building. An Arabic inscription from the Ayyubid period is carved in a stone of the facade, above the lintel of the main door. It commemorates the Ayyubids' conversion of the church into an Islamic *madrasa* (school) named Salahiyya, after Salah-al-Din, who wrested control of the city from the Crusaders. Only in 1878 was the

church once again used as a Christian house of worship, when it was given over to the custody of the White Fathers.

We will enter the basilica-shaped church. Its simple design dominates the interior as well. The windows are placed in the upper part of the thick walls which remind us of a fortress. This type of construction is very typical of the European Romanesque style. In the southern aisle, we can see stairs descending to an ancient crypt which may possibly have commemorated the birthplace of Mary. You have no doubt noted the exceptionally good acoustics in the church. It is worth waiting here for one of the many groups of Christian pilgrims and listen to their chanting, which will be an unforgetable musical experience.

We will leave the Church of St. Anne, going back through the Lions' Gate, and turn to the right. To our left we pass by a small square ◀5▶, where Christian pilgrims assemble on Fridays before

Procession of the Cross along the Via Dolorosa

retracing Jesus' steps along the Via Dolorosa. We will continue to walk up the street to an arch, to the left of which is a wide staircase leading to the Omariyya school ⬦. The compound to our left, which is adjacent to the northern side of the Temple Mount, contained the Antonia Fortress, built by Herod to replace the earlier fortress from the Hasmonean period, named the Baris. The area of the Hasmonean fortress was incorporated in the Temple Mount when the latter was extended by Herod. In the period preceding the destruction of the Second Temple, the fortress was manned by a Roman garrison which supervised all activity in the Temple Mount plaza. The plaza was likely to have constituted a focal point for anti-Roman agitation, especially on the three pilgrimage festivals, when tens of thousands of Jews thronged to Jerusalem from all parts of Eretz Israel and the Jewish Diaspora. Later in the tour, we will see the remains of the deep rock-cut moat that defended the Antonia Fortress on the north. Christian tradition identifies this spot as the place where Jesus was judged by Pontius Pilate (Matthew 27:26), and from where he was taken to the site of the Crucifixion, Golgotha (which is identified with the Church of the Holy Sepulcher). This is Station I of the Cross on the Via Dolorosa. The tradition identifying this as the Via Dolorosa is a relatively late one, from the thirteenth century. It was preceded by an earlier tradition from the Byzantine period, according to which the faithful walked from the Kidron Valley to Mount Zion (where Jesus was imprisoned), continuing to the Church of St. Sophia (whose location has not been determined), and from there to Golgotha. Modern scholarly research tends toward the view that the trial did not take place here, but rather near the present-day Jaffa Gate and Herod's palace, which apparently served as the residency of the Roman procurator when he was in Jerusalem. Further along in the tour we will encounter some of the other Stations of the Cross.

Now, pass through the entrance to the right, which leads to the courtyard of Station II of the Cross on the Via Dolorosa.

7 CHURCH OF THE IMPOSITION OF THE CROSS

Via Dolorosa

T WO CHURCHES ARE SITUATED at Station II of the Cross. To our right (the east) is the Franciscan **Church of the Flagellation**, which marks the Roman soldiers' abuse of Jesus after he was condemned to death. Pay special attention to the thorn-like geometric ornamentation in the facade of the church, alluding to the crown of thorns that the Romans placed on Jesus' head to humiliate him (John 19:15). The church was founded in 1927, based on the design by the architect

It is related that when the site of the **Church of the Flagellation** passed into the hands of the Ottomans in 1618, the son of the pasha decided to convert the church into a stable for his horses. One morning when he came to visit his horses, he discovered that all had died. He immediately ordered that other horses be placed in the stable, but these suffered a similar fate. The Ottoman noble realized that the sanctity of the place was the source of his troubles, and he removed all his horses from there. The site thus remained a ruin from that day until 1927, because people feared to make any use of it.

Barluzzi, over the ruins of an early church from the Middle Ages. To the left of the Church of the Flagellation are a series of doors; one of them leads to the Franciscan Museum, that contains archaeological finds from the excavations of the Franciscan Faculty for Biblical and Archaeological Studies, also located within this compound.

Now we will turn our attention to the second (western) church ⟨8⟩, which marks the place where the cross was imposed on Jesus (John 19:17). A few archaeological finds are on display to the right of the church entrance, along with an old model of late Second Temple period Jerusalem. Many details in this model are no longer accepted by modern scholars. The present church is the result of the restoration conducted by the Franciscans in 1903, based on the remains of the Byzantine church that had stood here in the past. Within the church we see sculptured and painted

Church of the Condemnation and Imposition of the Cross

scenes depicting the events related in the New Testament: Pontius Pilate sending Jesus to be crucified, acceding to the people's wishes, as he washes his hands to symbolize his clearing himself of responsibility for the act; alongside this is a portrayal of the imposition of the cross on Jesus.

Of primary interest to us in this church is a small section of the floor close to its western wall. The paving stones are large and flat, and some feature parallel grooves. Such stones were used to pave streets in the Roman period. The grooves, perpendicular to the direction of walking on the street, helped to prevent pedestrians from slipping on the smooth pavement. We will soon see the continuation of the pavement later in the tour, in the Sisters of Zion Convent, where we will learn of its significance.

We will leave the church and return to the Via Dolorosa. Slightly beyond the intersection with Ha-nezirot Street ⟨9⟩ we see above the Via Dolorosa the vaulted arch known as Ecce Homo (Latin for "Behold the man"). In Christian tradition, this arch marks the place where Pilate presented Jesus to the people with the words "Behold the man," prior to delivering the verdict of death by crucifixion (John 19:5). Fix in your mind's eye the image of the arch, to which we will return shortly.

We will now enter the Sisters of Zion Convent through the door on Ha-nezirot Street.

Ecce Homo Arch

Via Dolorosa

W E ARE NOW WITHIN the Sisters of Zion Convent. The construction of the convent was completed in 1869, on land purchased by the converted Jew **Alphonse Ratisbonne**. In the entrance hall take a copy of the map of the site. We can sit and look at the models and drawings presenting late Second Temple period Jerusalem, the Antonia Fortress, and the water supply to these areas at the time.

Alphonse Marie Ratisbonne (1814–84) was a member of the Regensburg family, an important Jewish family in Strasbourg, France. He was a lawyer and banker, and an anti-Christian, who strove to help his fellow Jews. On a visit to Rome in 1842 he converted to Christianity, as his brother Theodore had already done. The two brothers adopted the name Marie, and changed their family name to Ratisbonne (the French name for the city of Regensburg). The two were active in disseminating Christianity, in the establishment of monasteries in Jerusalem and founding of the Christian societies of Notre Dame de Sion and the Fathers of Zion.

Follow the arrows in the archaeological display. We will descend the steep stairs and find ourselves in a large hall, the high point of our entire visit to the convent – a gigantic pool hewn in the bedrock, with an area of 60 x 15m. We can see only about three-quarters of the pool, because the wall supported by arches to our left conceals the rest of it. The stone wall opposite us in the southern part of the pool is from the nineteenth century. It blocks the entrance to the Hasmonean water tunnel that continues to the Temple Mount, which we saw in the tour of the Western Wall tunnels (see Tour 4). What is this pool, and when was it built?

The pool is situated to the north of the Antonia Fortress and forms part of its moat. This fact led some scholars to assume that it had been built as part of the fortifications of the Herodian fortress. Josephus refers to a pool near the Antonia Fortress during the great revolt against the Romans, which hampered the Romans laying siege to this stronghold:

Strouthion Pool

Now as the Romans began to raise their banks on the twelfth day of the month Artemius [Iyyar] ... for there were now four great banks raised, one of which was at the Antonia Fortress; this was raised by the V Legion, over against the middle of that pool which was called Strouthion (*War of the Jews* 5:11:4).

This pool can therefore be identified with the Strouthion Pool. This Greek word means "lark," in an apparent reference to the fact that it was the smallest of the public pools in Jerusalem.

The pool was open to the sky when it served as the reservoir for the Antonia Fortress. The vault covering it today was only added in the time of the emperor Hadrian, after 135 CE, when Jerusalem became the pagan city Aelia Capitolina.

A large stone plaza, to which we will now ascend, rested on the vault. We will continue walking on the wooden bridge, leave the pool, go up through the corridor, and pass by the archaeological exhibition and other excavations. We have arrived at the stone plaza on which stand modern columns bearing a low ceiling. This plaza is actually the roof over the vault of the pool's eastern wing. If we look through the opening in the floor in one of the corners on the right of the plaza, we can even see the reflection of the water below. Pay special attention to the large and impressive pavement on which we are standing: its grooved part, on the southern side farthest from us, reminds us of the pavement we saw in the Church of the Condemnation and Imposition of the Cross, and indeed, this is the continuation of the Roman street. The stones without grooves are part of the square that existed here, adjacent to the street. An interesting story is connected with this pavement, one that brings together religious belief and archaeology.

In the past, scholars associated this pavement with the **Lithostrotos** ("The Pavement"), which is mentioned in the New Testament as the place to which Pilate brought Jesus after his trial (John 19:13). This opinion was reinforced by the assumption accepted by researchers at the time that the Antonia was a huge fortress whose area also included the present-day Sisters of Zion Convent. On the basis of this assumption, it was suggested that the pavement had been an inner square within the fortress. Another element in the identification of the site as the Lithostratos was the incisions visible on the paving stones, one of which contains a schematic drawing of a crown and the Greek letter ß. The nuns of the order thought that this letter alludes to the Greek word *basilius* (king), and that this is a sketch of the "king game" played by the Roman legionnaires, as reflected in the New Testament:

◆ The Greek term *Lithostrotos* is
◆ composed of two words: *lithos*
◆ (stone) and *strotos* (lying, prone).

Then the soldiers of the governor took Jesus into the praetorium, and they gathered the whole battalion before him. And they stripped him and put a scarlet robe upon him, and plaiting a crown of thorns they put it on his head ... And kneeling before him they mocked him, saying, "Hail, King of the Jews!" (Matthew 27: 27-29).

The excavations also uncovered bone dice used for playing games. The new excavations conducted here in the 1980s changed our understanding of the site. The pavement laid on top of the vaults from the time of Hadrian postdates the time of

Engravings in the Lithostrotos

Jesus, and therefore its identification with the Lithostrotos is no longer accepted. Nor does it belong to the Antonia Fortress, because, according to the new findings, this fortress was much smaller than had been thought in the past, and did not include the area of the Sisters of Zion Convent. The pavement was part of a large plaza, a sort of market square (forum), similar to those found in Rome and other cities of the Empire. While the nuns of the Sisters of Zion agree with the later archaeological dating of the pavement, they do not regard this as contradicting the tradition they accept. In their opinion, it may be assumed that the paving stones of the square were laid here by Hadrian, who took them from the nearby ruins of the Antonia Fortress. Accordingly, they maintain, Jesus may have walked on these stones, but not in their new location. The nuns are willing to accept the argument that the games engraved on the pavement may postdate Jesus; nonetheless, they are likely to recall the atmosphere and the events described in the New Testament.

We will continue to follow the map we received in the entrance, and ascend the metal steps that take us outside, back to the Via Dolorosa. We will turn to our right (westward), and enter the second door on the right ⓫. We are still within the bounds of the Sisters of Zion Convent, and its church is visible through the glass window. In the eastern wall facing us, we see a small arch, and to its right, the beginning of a larger one. This is part of the Ecce Homo arch that we saw on the street before we entered the convent. These arches are a remnant of a

Unearthing of the Ecce Homo Arch

triumphal arch in all proba-bility built by Hadrian in the forum. It consisted of three arches, in the accepted style of a Roman triumphal arch, more than 600 of which are known in the Roman world. This photograph from the nineteen-th century shows the unearth-ing of the arch, prior to the construction of the convent. It was taken from an angle similar to the one that we view the arch, thus helping us to understand the connection between the arch in the street and the one in the church. Roman Jerusalem boasted three other such triumphal arches: at Damascus Gate, north of Damascus Gate, and also close to the Church of the Holy Sepulcher, where we will end this tour.

We will return to the Via Dolorosa, continuing until it meets al-Wad Street ⓬

Ancient paving on al-Wad Street

Station III of the Cross on the Via Dolorosa

Here we are stepping on the paving stones of the eastern Roman Cardo of Jerusalem which, like the central Cardo (Cardo Maximus), began at Damascus Gate, to our north (see Tour 9). The paving stones were found at a depth of several meters below Ha-gai Street, and were raised to the present level.

To our left we see two fragments of ancient columns  marking Station III of the Cross on the Via Dolorosa, where Jesus fell for the first time under the weight of the cross. Note the modern relief on the wall depicting this event. Immediately after it, on the left, is another relief , denoting Station IV, where Jesus met his mother on the way to the Crucifixion. As we walk along, we will see other Stations of the Cross, which can be identified by the prominent Roman numerals on the signs, and by the special paving stones forming a semicircle at the foot of some of the stations, emphasizing their location. At the turn to the right we will pass by Station V , where the legionnaires forced a passerby named Simon of Cyrene (Cyrene is located in present-day Libya) to bear Jesus' cross (Luke 23:26); and by Station VI , where a woman named **Veronica** wiped Jesus' face with her cloth. Where the Via Dolorosa meets Khan al-Zait Street, we see Station VII . According to tradition, this was the site of the *praetorium*, the gate of judgment through which Jesus was taken from the city to the hill of Golgotha, which is identified with the nearby Church of the Holy Sepulcher. The column fragment to the left, which marks this Station, probably belonged to the central Cardo, which followed the line of Khan al-Zait Street. To see Station VIII , you will have to stray somewhat from our route, walk up on al-Khanaqah Street (count sixteen steps), and look for a stone on the left with an engraved cross. This is where Jesus told the daughters of Jerusalem who were bemoaning his fate not to weep for him, but rather for themselves and for their children (Luke 23:28). This is the last Station of

◆ Some of the Stations of the
◆ Cross on the Via Dolorosa
◆ relate to events mentioned
◆ in the New Testament
◆ (Station I, for example),
◆ while others are associated
◆ with events which appear
◆ only in later Christian trad-
◆ itions, such as the one
◆ regarding **Veronica.** This
◆ symbolic name is com-
◆ posed of two Latin words:
◆ *verus* (true) and *icon* (an
◆ image) and refers to the
◆ true image of Jesus' face,
◆ which was imprinted on the
◆ cloth of Veronica.

Station VI of the Cross on the Via Dolorosa

the Cross that we will see today. Stations IX–XIV are located within the Church of the Holy Sepulcher and on its roof (see Tour 12).

We will return to picturesque and colorful Khan al-Zait Street, and procede southward. Turn right at the first corner and walk along the massive reddish structure until we come to its entrance, on Shuk Ha-tsabaim Street. This is the Alexander Nevsky Church, that adjoins the Church of the Holy Sepulcher. Ring the bell (be patient, sometimes it takes many minutes before the door is opened) and go inside. Within the church, we will descend the steps to the lower hall.

19 ALEXANDER NEVSKY CHURCH

Shuk Ha-tsabaim Street

THE RUSSIAN CHURCH we have just entered was built in 1896, and is owned by the Holy Places Department of the Orthodox Palestine Society. It is named after the medieval Russian military commander Alexander Nevsky, who extended his country's borders and established its rule in the northwest, all the way to where St. Petersburg would later be built. Alexander Nevsky was the patron saint of Czar Alexander III, who founded the Orthodox Palestine Society in the nineteenth century; every Thursday a prayer service is held in memory of the Czar. The archaeological finds that were revealed during the building of the church are on display in the lower hall.

·We will pass through the arched entrance, which is supported on one side by a pillar and on the other by a column braced by metal hoops. Roman Jerusalem boasted market-

Ancient remains in the Alexander Nevsky Church

places and magnificent triumphal arches. This arch is most likely the southernmost of the three that formed a triumphal arch built by the emperor Hadrian on the eastern side of the city's main forum, close to the temple of the goddess Aphrodite; this temple was located where the Church of the Holy Sepulcher now stands. In the fourth century this triumphal arch was incorporated into the Church of the Holy Sepulcher built by Constantine. The arch adjoins thick walls built of ashlars in the Herodian style, which continue north of the modern wide, reddish staircase. It was suggested in the past that these walls are part of the Second Wall of Second Temple period Jerusalem, and that the threshold between the walls, as well as the pavement in front of it, belongs to a gate in that wall. In accordance with this view, the owners of the site exhibit the finds before us as the Judgment Gate, through which Jesus was led from the city to the hill of the Crucifixion, as can be seen in the painted recon-struction hanging on the wall. Accor-ding to another opinion, these walls were built later, as part of the entrance complex of the Church of the Holy Sepulcher, the Herodian stones being put to secondary use. Pay special attention to the small holes that were cut in some of the stones in order to attach a marble overlay surface. Above the modern stairs (to our north) we see a course of masonry higher than the

Alexander Nevsky Church

level on which we are standing. We do not know for a fact the purpose of this height differential: was this elevation meant to bring those coming from the street up to the level of the Byzantine Church of the Holy Sepulcher? This is a distinct possibility, because the Madaba Map, from the Byzantine period, clearly shows that a large staircase provided access to the church from the east. However, one should also bear in mind that this might be the raised foundation of a ritual precinct connected with the Roman temple of Aphrodite, predating the erection of the church.

The street on which we are standing opposite the entrance complex is the Byzantine Cardo (see Tour 9). When it was constructed it was decorated with flanking stone colonnades. The planners of the Cardo apparently sought to emphasize and give prominence to the entrance of the Church of the Holy Sepulcher, and accordingly chose to erect near it columns of a color different to those along the street. You can see two such columns, which are black in color, if you continue along the street to the north and enter the entrance on the right to a small room. The elevated Church of the Holy Sepulcher and the series of black columns marking its entrance must have been an impressive sight, contrasting with the hustle and bustle of daily life below, in the Cardo.

Our tour ends here. Upon leaving the church we will turn right, and then left, to Euthymos Street. From here we will go up David Street to Jaffa Gate.

From Damascus Gate to the Nea Church

OUR TOUR BEGINS with pagan Roman Jerusalem – a city of temples to Aphrodite and Zeus, magnificent triumphal arches, and typical Roman urban planning. But slowly, as we progress along the main street, the Cardo, we will find ourselves advancing in time and crossing the imaginary boundary that separates the Roman city from that of the Cross – Byzantine Jerusalem, in which the pagan temples are replaced by magnificent churches.

We will be accompanied on our way by the inhabitants of the city from this period. Merchants and peddlers will offer us their wares from a distance of sixteen hundred years of history; the historian Procopius will draw our attention with his marvelous stories about the construction of the Nea Church; and if we concentrate and exercise our imagination to the limits, we will hear the echoes of the bells and see the fleeting figures participating in the festive procession making its way from the Church of the Resurrection to the Nea, through the pageant of sounds, colors, and smells of the Oriental markets through which we will walk.

Map labels

Damascus Gate Square

Muslim Quarter

Via Dolorosa

al-Khanaqah

Ha-knessiyot

Ma'alot Ha-midrasha

Christian Quarter

Haseraya

Shuk Ha-tsaba'im

Shuk Ha-basamim

al-Kirani

Muristan

Shuk Ha-qatsavim

Shuk Ha-tsorfim

al-Hagan

David

Chain

St. Mark

Jewish Quarter Cardo

Assyrian Monastery

Western Wall

Armenian Quarter

Habad

Misgav Ladach

Or Ha-hayyim

Ha-malakh

Beit-El

Hayyei Olam

Mishmerot Ha-kehunah

Batei Mahase Square

Barkay

Batei Mahase

Tiferet Yerushalayim (Square)

Ma'ale Ha-shalom

0   100   200 m

N

Info box

The route: the tour begins at Damascus Gate. From there we walk along Khan al-Zait Street and the Cardo, before ending at the ruins of the Nea Church in the Jewish Quarter.

Duration of the tour: about two hours.

Public transportation: bus no. 23 to Damascus Gate. You can also come on foot via Ha-nevi'im Street or Ha-tsanhanim Street.

By private car: the parking lot opposite Damascus Gate, or the small parking lot west of the gate, along the city wall.

Visiting hours: the Roman gate at Damascus Gate: Sat–Thur: 9:00 a.m.– 4:00 p.m., Friday: 9:00 a.m.–2:00 p.m. Entrance fee.

The Cardo (covered portion): all week: 8:30–sunset; the apse of the Nea Church: all week: 9:00 a.m.–5:00 p.m.

Note: the vaulted cisterns of the Nea Church are currently (1999) closed to visitors.

WE ARE STANDING before the most beautiful gate in the city wall. The ornamented gate was built in the Ottoman period. According to the dedicatory inscription, it was built by command of the sultan Suleiman the Magnificent, the restorer of Jerusalem's walls, in 1538.

For many years this gate, perhaps the most central one in the Old City, was neglected, and a taxi stand located in front of it. In the 1980s the plaza was restored and given a tiered form, so that the Ottoman gate would occupy center stage.

Dentil ornamentation above the Ottoman Damascus Gate

In the Roman period (and certainly until the departure of the Tenth Legion from the city) Jerusalem was not encompassed by a wall. The Romans did build a number of impressive and characteristic triumphal arches, including two near

Mount of Olives   Muslim Quarter   Dome of the Rock   Al-Aqsa mosque   Street begin Damascus C

Panoramic view to the east of Damascus Gate (photographed in 1906)

Left gate of the Roman triumphal arch

where we are standing. One, whose remains are no longer visible, stood to the north of Damascus Gate; the other, whose magnificent remains have survived and may very well be the most outstanding of the Roman triumphal arches known in Eretz Israel, is on the side of Damascus Gate. These remains were revealed during the British Mandate, and are now excavated and restored in their entirety.

We will turn to the path on the right of the plaza, go down the stairs to the left, pass under the bridge leading from the plaza to the Ottoman gate, and stop in front of the vaulted stone gate ❷. Here stood a Roman triumphal arch com-prising three vaulted gates: a high central one flanked by two smaller ones. The central one was located on the spot currently occupied by the Ottoman gate, and we are facing the surviving eastern (left) gate.

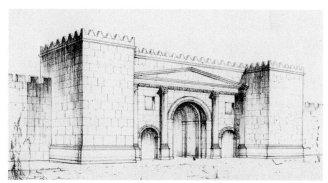
Damascus Gate in the Roman period – proposed reconstruction

The reconstruction on this page shows how this gate was incorporated in the original triumphal arch. To its left is a prominent tower structure built of ashlars which remind us of Herodian masonry. It appears that the Romans made **secondary use** of the Herodian stones in the construction of the tower. Its lower section is decorated with a stone cornice. The tower is not

The Herodian stones have characteristic fine drafted margins forming a sort of frame around the stone. In some of the ashlars incorporated in the tower we can see that the frame has been removed on one side, evidence that the original stone was cut to fit its **secondary use** in another place.

t Israel jogue · Hurvah synagogue (in the Jewish Quarter) · Church of the Redeemer · Church of the Holy Sepulcher (in the Christian Quarter) · Mosque of Omar · The Citadel (David's Tower)

preserved to its full height, and its present-day upper part dates from the Mamluk or Crusader period. A similar tower is partially preserved to the right of the western gate, but the gate itself has not survived.

Look at the bottom of the first stone above the gate. Tax your eyes a bit, and you will discern the remains of the letters engraved in it: "CO.AEL.CAP.D.D." This is an abbreviation of the Latin sentence: "Colonia Aelia Capitolina decreto decurionum," which means: "Aelia Capitolina [was engraved] by order of the ten elect [the city's leaders]." Aelia Capitolina was the Roman name of the city, that it was given when it became a Roman city in the second century CE, by order of the emperor Hadrian. Note the pavement close to the gate, which is grooved to prevent the horses and carriages that passed over it from slipping. Before we enter, pay special attention to the fact that the modern bridge above us rests on the remains of older structures, most of them from the Crusader period. The Crusaders built their own gate here, with a plan different from that of the Roman structure.

We will go through the gate and turn to the left. We are now within the tower we saw from the outside, and the room built of ashlars that we have entered is the Roman guardroom. Later, in the Early Muslim period, a large oil-press was located here. From the guardroom we will ascend the Roman staircase to the city wall, which gives us a stunning view of the Old City. It is recommended to go up to the level of the dentils of the wall. The panoramic view of the Old City on the previous pages is a reproduction of a photograph taken here in 1906. Note especially the changes in the Jerusalem skyline in the decades since then.

We will go back down the stairs to the guardroom, exit via the opening by which we entered, and continue to our left, into the Roman city. We pass a mini-exhibition that presents a reconstruction of the area of Damascus Gate in various periods. We continue walking and enter a courtyard with a Roman pavement, the likes of which we already encountered in the entrance. This is part of the paved square that existed here (with grooves in the paving stones to prevent slipping). A tall column, possibly topped by a statue of the emperor Hadrian, once stood in the center of the square. The column itself was not revealed in the excavations, but we know of its existence thanks to the most important historical source for the period: a mosaic map from the sixth century CE depicting Jerusalem, that was found in the city of Madaba in Jordan. A copy of this map is displayed in the entrance room through which we have passed (we will come to know this map in much greater detail during the course of the tour). Columns in the plaza in front of a gate are known to us from other Roman cities of the period. The column was not intended merely as a decorative element and to glorify the emperor; it also had another, important, function – distances to and from the city were measured from it. Incidentally, one of the names of Damascus Gate in Arabic is Bab al-Amud, the "Gate of the Column." This name apparently preserves the memory of the Roman column that soared above the square in front of the triumphal arch. Here you can see a hologram of the column, topped by a statue, standing in the center of the paved square. Around the paved square are the stores of the small shopping center built in the 1980s. We will go back through the ancient gate, ascend the stairs to the bridge leading to the entrance of Damascus Gate, and pass through this magnificent Ottoman gate. As was customary with regard to gates in antiquity, entry is not direct: one has to first turn to the left, and then to the right. Such an approach was meant to break the momentum of an attacker seeking to burst into the city.

THE CARDO 3

LET'S STOP FOR A MOMENT and look around. The stores and coffee shops on both sides of the street, the smells of the market that waft towards us, the colors and loud Oriental music, the crowds of people bumping into one another, the three-wheeled carts, and the stands selling the Middle East's version of the bagel – this is the charm and uniqueness of the *shuk* (marketplace). This street follows the streambed, "the *gai*" (valley in Hebrew) known in the Second Temple period as the Tyropoeon, which is usually translated as the "Cheesemakers' Valley." In the Roman-Byzantine period, a wide stone-paved road passed along this route, heading southward, with sidewalks, colonnades, and shops along its length. Parts of the ancient paving were discovered below the modern pavement, and an impressive section of the road was revealed close to the Dung Gate, within and outside the later Ottoman wall. Such a central longitudinal street is called a ***Cardo.*** Al-Wad Street was, however, only one of the two main thoroughfares in

> The Latin term *Cardo* means pivot, and by extension, the street around which city life revolves. This term probably has no connection with words such as "cardiology" and others associated with the heart, as some have suggested.

Jerusalem. This Cardo was identical with the course of the present-day Khan al-Zait Street, the one to the right, along which we will now walk. Even today, Khan al-Zait Street is one of the main thoroughfares of the Old City, bisecting it from north to south. In the Roman period it probably extended only half the length of the modern street, as indicated by the archaeological finds, and only in the Byzantine per-

Roman Cardo – proposed reconstruction

iod was it extended to the south. It is difficult to distinguish remains of the Cardo in the first part of the street along which we are walking, because it was narrowed over the course of time by the shops built along it. However, the sections that have been uncovered further along, and the depiction in the Madaba Map, enable us to envisage what this street must have looked like in Roman times.

As we walk through the marketplace, we cannot help but be intoxicated by its special atmosphere. When we come to the corner of Shuk Ha-tsaba'im Street, we see to our right a building constructed of reddish stones. This is the Russian Alexander Nevsky Church ◆4◆ in which the archaeologists have exposed, inter alia, part of the main eastern entrance to the Byzantine Church of the Holy Sepulcher that faced the Cardo (see Tour 8).

At this point Bet Ha-bad Street bifurcates, as you can see on the tour map, and farther on will become three narrow, parallel markets: Shuk Ha-qatsavim (Butchers' Market), Shuk Ha-basamim (Spice-handlers' Market), and Shuk Ha-tsorfim (Gold and Silversmiths' Market). We will proceed to the three markets ◆5◆. They apparently were established in the **Crusader** period by dividing up the Roman Cardo. Their overall width, including the shops, gives us an idea of the original width of the Cardo. The names of the markets indicate the wares sold in them. Each of the different groups of artisans and merchants would be concentrated in separate streets, as is the practice in Oriental bazaars, for example in Cairo or Istanbul. The original division is still maintained in Jerusalem, especially in Shuq Ha-qatsavim, as our noses attest.

The letters T or SCA ANNA are engraved on the lintels of some of the **Crusader** shops. The first probably attests to ownership by the Order of the Templars, and the second to ownership by the Monastery of St. Anne, which was located near the Lions' Gate.

We can walk along any one of the markets, as they all eventually coalesce at the intersection of David Street, which descends from Jaffa Gate and continues to the Temple Mount.

---

6 — WHERE CARDO AND DECUMANUS MEET

Intersection of David Street and the Markets

ROMAN JERUSALEM, and the Byzantine city in its wake, were built according to the usual plan of Roman cities, with adjustments for the hilly topography. The typical Roman city had an orthogonal layout, consisting of a grid of straight streets that intersected at right angles. The main thoroughfare, the Cardo, which ran from north to south, was intersected at right angles by another main street extending from east to west. This was the *Decumanus*.

The name *Decumanus* (*decimus* means "tenth" in Latin) was given to the cross street, because, in the standard grid plan of Roman army camps, the tenth cohort of the legion was always quartered at the western end of the camp, at the beginning of the cross street. Others suggest that the name stems from the division of a city by means of symmetrical streets into a grid pattern, thus creating insulae which were obligated to pay a tithe.

The intersection of the Decumanus and the Cardo was usually marked by a *tetrapylon*, that is, four gates arranged in the form of a square (*tetra* – four, *pylon* – gate). No tetrapylon was found in Jerusalem, and it is even difficult to discern the intersection of the Cardo and the Decumanus (along which David Street presently runs), as the width of these streets was altered by later construction. The original

Decumanus descended eastward from here, to the area of the Gate of the Chain. We will proceed southward via a narrow alley, toward an iron gate that leads to the Cardo excavations. On our way, pay special attention to the coffee house and game parlor to our right ⑦. If we peek inside, we will see the ancient columns that bear vaults arranged in a square. It was thought in

Columns in the coffee house. Painting by Gustav Bauernfeind (late nineteenth century)

the past that this was the Jerusalem tetrapylon, but a more careful examination revealed that the columns are in secondary use and were placed here after the Byzantine period in order to support a later building.

Now we will enter the restored Cardo.

THE NORTHERN PART OF THE CARDO 8

W E ARE STANDING on the level of the original Byzantine Cardo, at the same elevation as the markets we have just left. Remains from all the main periods appear before us. The street is narrow – actually, slightly less than half the width of the Byzantine Cardo. We see a section of the Hasmonean city wall, in which a later cistern has been dug, and above it, Byzantine columns – and all this within a modern arched structure of concrete. A bit further along, on our left, is a stone structure with blocked shop entrances, and a bench of cast concrete in front. This is part of a Crusader shop building which was meant to divide the Cardo into two streets, in order to make more efficient use of its area. Slightly further on we can look through the windows at the top of the stone squares in the center of the street. Here we see the remains of the Hasmonean city wall (the "First Wall"), and those of the First Temple period northern city wall. When the restoration of the Cardo began, these remains were covered over, but the course

of the walls was marked on the pavement: the First Temple period wall was marked by a line of black stones, while a line of pinkish stones represents the First Wall. According to some authorities, the Gennath Gate mentioned by Josephus (*War of the Jews* 5:4:2) stood here in the Second Temple period. The illustrations and explanations hanging on the walls of the Crusader structure will give us a more complete picture of the walls and the diverse archaeological finds. We stand before a window through which we see all the different periods of the city's history.

We will continue southward to the restored section, whose eastern side opens to Jewish Quarter Road, along which stand the columns of the Cardo.

Remains from different periods in the Cardo

T O OUR RIGHT is a massive wall that was built in the Byzantine period for the evident purpose of hiding the bedrock, which prevented the construction of shops in this section of the Cardo, in contrast with the rest of the street. At this point, however, we can gain some idea of the width and shape of the Cardo. To the west of the restored colonnade, whose parts were found scattered among the ruins of the street, was a sidewalk with a **roof** of wooden beams covered by tiles.

The modern **roof** is nothing other than the floor of the courtyards of the houses built above the course of the Cardo. The restorers of the Jewish Quarter sought to build the apartments above the line of the Cardo without being delayed by excavations. They therefore installed a special structure above which they built the apartments, which were completed and occupied five years before the completion of the Cardo restoration and its opening to the public.

Note the niches cut in the wall, which once held the ends of the original beams and now support the beams laid by the restorers. The roofing of the sidewalks was very important since it prevented the wetting of merchandise in winter and provided shelter from the hot sun in summer. The column bases were placed on niches at the edge of the sidewalk, and the columns were topped by capitals. A close examination reveals that the capitals were not identical, and the construction, despite its magnificence, is not perfect (which is not exceptional

Modern shops in the Crusader market in the Cardo

in Byzantine construction). A gutter for drainage, which is clearly visible, runs along the edge of the road. The road itself is as wide as a modern four-lane highway. The east side of the street

is beyond Jewish Quarter Road (to the east), which is at a higher level. There we can see ancient arches, which actually are the entrances of Byzantine shops. Remains of columns and sidewalk sections were also found on the street's east side. The illustration of the restoration on the wall in the south will help give us an overall view of the street. In our mind's eye we can picture the inhabitants of Jerusalem striding along the sidewalks, examining the merchandise on display in front of the shops, and hear the noise of horses trotting along and chariot wheels rolling over the stone pavement.

This main thoroughfare is no less beautiful or impressive than similar streets in other Roman-Byzantine cities, such as Scythopolis or Gerasa in Transjordan. According to the Cardo's excavators, the

The Byzantine Cardo

southern part of the street, where we are now standing, was constructed in the Byzantine period, possibly during the reign of the emperor Justinian, in the sixth century. This was the continuation of the Roman Cardo, which started out from Damascus Gate but did not extend to the area of the present-day Jewish Quarter, that most probably was not inhabited at the time. It has been suggested that the southern Cardo was used for the grand processions between the two central churches of Jerusalem in the Byzantine period: the Church of the Holy Sepulcher in the north, and the Nea Church, the remains of which we will soon see, close to the southern end of the Cardo.

We will proceed and enter a small plaza in the shape of an ancient Roman theater, with a mosaic map hanging on the wall.

COPY OF THE MADABA MAP — 10

A N ANCIENT MOSAIC MAP depicting Eretz Israel, with Jerusalem at its center, was discovered in the 1880s in Madaba, Transjordan. According to the researchers, this map was drawn in the sixth century CE, and therefore provides invaluable testimony on the appearance of Byzantine Jerusalem. Among the central structures appearing in the **Madaba Map** is the central Cardo, with columns clearly visible along its length. When this area of the Jewish Quarter was excavated in the mid-1970s, the excavators recalled the magnificent Cardo that appears in the Madaba Map and assumed that they would find it during the course of their work. As Nahman Avigad, who directed the extensive archaeological excavations in the Jewish Quarter for many years, relates:

> The **Madaba Map** is composed of more than two million tesserae of different colors. Thus, for example, four shades of red and six shades of blue and green can be distinguished in the original map.

It is not uncommon for archaeological excavations to be prompted and guided by information revealed in an ancient literary source. In such instances, the excavations are intended to reveal a site or structure mentioned in the Bible, in Josephus, or in some other ancient source. But it happens only rarely that the ancient source guiding the excavator is not a literary document, but a graphic one. Our experience of this sort was possibly unique when we purposefully and knowingly sought the cardo maximus ... [which] was commemorated in the contemporary mosaic map at Madaba in Trans-Jordan....

Well aware of the possibility that an ancient street existed beneath the modern pavement, the planners [of the restoration and reconstruction of the Cardo] – Architects Peter Bugod and Esther Niv-Krendel – sought to integrate old and new. They had certainly not foreseen the extent to which the remains later uncovered would force them to alter their plan in order to accommodate the antiquities and ensure their preservation (*Discovering Jerusalem*, pp. 211-216).

Look at the portion of the map on the wall. Even though Jerusalem is depicted quite schematically from a bird's-eye view, the artist enables us to see the facades

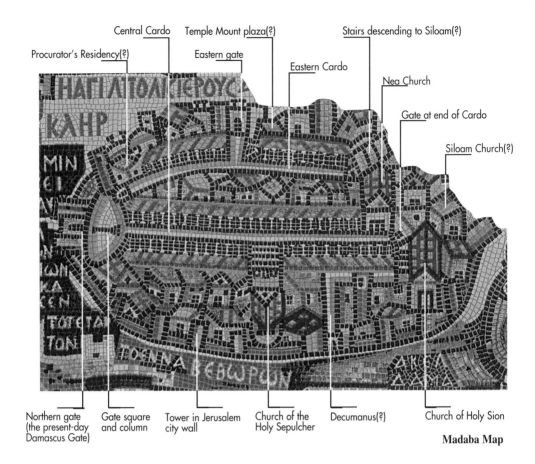

Central Cardo
Temple Mount plaza(?)
Procurator's Residency(?)
Eastern gate
Stairs descending to Siloam(?)
Eastern Cardo
Nea Church
Gate at end of Cardo
Siloam Church(?)

Northern gate (the present-day Damascus Gate)
Gate square and column
Tower in Jerusalem city wall
Church of the Holy Sepulcher
Decumanus(?)
Church of Holy Sion

Madaba Map

of the structures. Before us is a copy of the map, in which the various sites are labeled. The Church of the Holy Sepulcher stands out in the map, as do other Christian edifices, which appear out of proportion to the rest of the city. These distortions reflect the conceptual importance of these structures for those who ordered the map. The Temple Mount plaza, which had enjoyed a central position in the city until then, suffered a diminishing of its importance under Byzantine rule, and is given scanty space in the map (despite its huge dimensions). This shrinking of the Mount may possibly reflect the Christian ideology of the triumph of Christianity over Judaism.

We will continue to the open part of the Cardo ⟨11⟩. This is one of the most beautiful and best-preserved parts of the ancient thoroughfare. An entire

The Byzantine Cardo

column was unearthed here, a discovery that confirms the reconstructed height of the colonnade. Pay attention to the sidewalk, the drainage gutter below the street level, and the shops to the west of the sidewalk, one of whose arched roofs has been reconstructed. The size of the shops is not impressive, and we may assume that they were used only to store the merchandise at night, as is the practice to this day in the markets of the Old City whose stores are merely small alcoves used for overnight storage; during the day, the shopkeepers display their wares on the sidewalk or hang them on the adjoining walls, which only adds to the colorful "disorganized" appearance of the marketplace. If we take a good look at the shop to the left, which is preserved in its entirety, we see that its walls were coated with a thick layer of plaster, and that a large hole, later blocked, was cut in the vault. This teaches that when the level of the city rose in later periods and this area was buried under debris, this shop was turned into a cistern.

We will go up the stairs to Jewish Quarter Road. Looking down from the street we note the considerable height differential between the early level of the Byzantine period and that of today. We will continue, following the map, to Batei Mahase Square (see Tour 15), and cross it southward in the direction of the state religious school. Pass through the iron gate, go down the stairs, turn to the left down Nahamu Street, and enter the metal-plated entrance on the left.

THE APSE OF THE NEA CHURCH   12

Nahamu Street

THE BYZANTINE HISTORIAN Procopius, who lived in Caesarea in the sixth century CE, wrote the book *Buildings of Justinian* which, as the title alludes, describes the construction projects of that Byzantine emperor. Inter alia, he describes the marvelous act of building a church named after Mary, mother of God, known as the Nea (Greek for "new") Church, since another church named after Mary already existed in the city:

Justinian I (482-565) was a statesman and theologian. The most important building he erected was the Hagia Sophia Church in Constantinople. Justinian is known primarily for the project that was conducted in his lifetime: the codification of the laws. The Justinian Code would later exert a profound influence upon the development of law throughout Europe.

For the Emperor Justinian gave orders that it be built on the highest of the hills, specifying what the length and breadth of the building should be, as well as the other details. However, the hill did not satisfy the requirements of the project, according to the Emperor's specifications, but a fourth part of the church, facing the south and the east, was left unsupported.... Consequently, those in charge of this work... drew the foundations out as far as the limit of the even ground, and then erected a structure which rose as high as the rock... they set vaults upon the supporting walls, and joined this substructure to the other foundation of the church... the builders of this work... had to abandon all familiar methods and resort to practices which were strange and altogether unknown. So they cut out blocks of unusual size from the hills.... They built wagons, placed a single block on each of them, and had each wagon with its stone drawn by forty oxen which had been selected by the Emperor for their strength.... However, when they made the width in due proportion, they were unable to set a roof upon the building. So they searched ... every place where very tall trees grew, and found a certain dense forest which produced cedars of extraordinary height ... For the church required throughout columns ... God revealed [to Justinian] a natural supply of stone perfectly suited to this purpose in the nearby hills, one which had either lain there in concealment previously, or was created at that moment (M. Ben-Dov, *In the Shadow of the Temple*, pp. 233-235).

The search for the magnificent building described by Procopius occupied researchers for a long time. They also disagreed about the location of the church until 1970, during the excavation for the foundations of new buildings in Batei Mahase Square, when the eastern end of the church next to where we are standing was uncovered; additional remains were discovered afterwards. The location of the church corresponds to its position in the Madaba Map. As we ascend the metal stairs, we can see the large stones mentioned by Procopius, and a part of the massive (6.5 m thick) retaining wall. We cannot rule out the possibility that some of the stones, and the columns as well, were taken from ruined Second Temple period houses. Standing in the plaza, we get some idea of the plan of the

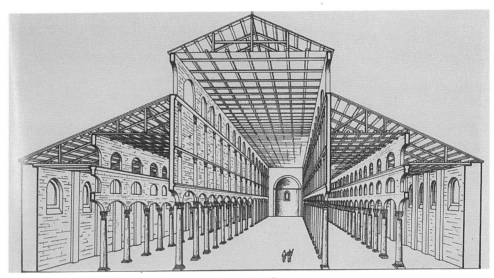

Section of the Nea Church – proposed reconstruction

church and the various phases in the excavation from the pictures and diagrams. Actually, this is not merely a church of huge dimensions, but also the compound of the adjoining monastery, parts of which we will soon see. Looking back to the east, from where we came, we see a wall built in the form of a crescent moon. This is the apse of the church, "in which the monks conduct the ritual ceremonies," in the words of Procopius. Originally, there were three apses, and the northernmost and smallest is before us. To the right was the large apse (with a diameter of 5 m), and still further to the right, on the southern side, stood a small apse, the counterpart of the one visible to us. This third apse was discovered to the south. We are located at the eastern end of the church, while its entrance was on the west, from the Cardo (next to the present-day Jewish Quarter parking lot). This was unquestionably a very large church which measured 57 x 115m. The proposed reconstruction of the Nea Church in the illustration is based on Procopius' description, the archaeological finds, and contemporary parallels.

We will leave the site, turn left, and go out to the road encompassing the Jewish Quarter. We will follow the road up to the rounded wall section visible in the excavations to the left of the road; the road runs across the continuation of this wall ◀13▶. This is the southern apse of the Nea Church. A few meters further on, we will descend the staircase to the archaeological park, Tekumah Park. At the end of the staircase we see a small section of a series of arches and vaults ◀14▶. This system, whose discovery came as a complete surprise to the excavators, is apparently the group of underground vaults described by Procopius as supporting the church. The vaults contain enormous cisterns that are connected to the church and form part of the adjoining monastery. The last remaining doubts regarding the age of the vaults and their belonging to the Nea Church were dispelled with the discovery of a Greek inscription engraved on a wall, which explicitly mentions Justinian Caesar by name, thus confirming the identity of the church.

We will continue on the path encircling the park. We see to our right, on the slopes of the Jewish Quarter, structures from the Crusader period ◀15▶, in one of which are restored large supporting columns. At the end of the path we see the reconstructed remains of a gate tower from the Ayyubid period ◀16▶ (see Tour 13). We will go up the stairs to the right, to the Jewish Quarter parking lot ◀17▶. This was most probably the site, in the Byzantine period, of a gate in the southern city wall which appears in the Madaba Map. Here ends our tour.

TOUR TEN

From the Summit of the Mount of Olives to the Tomb of Mary

THE MOUNT OF OLIVES, whose summit rises above Jerusalem to the east at an elevation of 820 meters above sea level, separates the city to the west from the Judean Desert in the east. To the north, the Mount links up with the Mount Scopus ridge on which the Arab village a-Tur is situated, and on its western slope are the houses of the villages of Silwan and Ras al-Amud. The olive groves that covered the Mount in the past gave it its names: the Mount of Olives and the Mount of Anointing.

The Mount of Olives is first mentioned in the Bible in connection with the flight of King David from his rebellious son Absalom: "David meanwhile went up the slope of the [Mount of] Olives, weeping as he went" (II Samuel 15:30). The Mount is of special religious significance because of the statements by the prophets that it will be the venue of the dramatic events that will occur in the End of Days, and the place where God will then set His feet (Ezekiel 11:23; Zechariah 14:15).

During the First Temple period, tombs for the wealthy of Jerusalem were hewn on the slopes of the Mount of Olives, a tradition continued in the Second Temple period. After this, Jewish burial on the Mount would be renewed only in the fifteenth century, leading to the creation of a cemetery with tens of thousands of graves whose white tombstones are clearly visible.

In the Second Temple period, beacons were lit on the Mount of Olives to inform the Jews of the Diaspora of the onset of a new month. Such signal fires were lit on a series of mountaintops extending all the way to distant Babylon. The red heifer was also burnt on the Mount of Olives. Its ashes were then placed in a vessel containing water, and the water mixed with the ashes was used to purify anyone who had been defiled by corpse impurity.

When the Christians gained control of Jerusalem, from the fourth century onward, new traditions associated with the Mount came into being. These related mainly to the last days in the life of Jesus, and led to the erection in the Byzantine period of twenty-four churches that adorned the Mount and established its importance for Christians. Centuries later some of these sites were destroyed by the Muslims, but were rebuilt and restored in the Crusader period. Many of these churches would be destroyed once again, ancient traditions would disappear, while others changed their venue. By the nineteenth century, only a few structures were still standing.

As the Western powers increased their activity in Jerusalem, new buildings were erected on the Mount and ancient structures were restored. The architectural shape of some of them, with their colorful minarets, domes, towers and gables, stand out against the background of the Mount. On our tour of the Mount of Olives, we will therefore

become acquainted with a wide range of traditions, structures and ruins from various periods, which we would be hard put to attribute to a specific time or a single religion. Nevertheless, this tour is included in the section on Byzantine Jerusalem, because it focuses mainly on the Christian sites on the Mount which trace their beginnings to the Byzantine period when the Mount of Olives acquired its importance for Christianity.

The route: the tour begins in the area of the Viri Galilae and the Tur Malka churches, and passes through the Ascension mosque and the Pater Noster, Dominus Flevit, Mary Magdalene, Gethsemane, and Tomb of Mary churches.

Duration of the tour: about three hours.

Public transportation: bus no. 99 (once per hour, 11:00 a.m.–3:00 p.m.) or no. 75 from Damascus Gate to the summit of the Mount of Olives.

By private car: drive from Mount Scopus or Wadi Joz, and park near the Seven Arches Hotel on the summit of the Mount of Olives.

Visiting hours: Ascension mosque: all week: 8:00 a.m.–5:00 p.m. Entrance fee.

Pater Noster Church: Mon–Sat: 8:00 a.m.–12:00 noon, 3:00 p.m.–5:00 p.m.

Tombs of the Prophets: Sun–Fri: 8:00 a.m.–3:00 p.m. (This is private property. A flashlight may be rented from the owner.)

Dominus Flevit Church: all week: 8:00 a.m.–12:00 noon, 2:30 p.m.–5:00 p.m.

Mary Magdalene Church: Tue, Thur: 10:00 a.m.–11:30 a.m.

Gethsemane Church: April–October all week: 8:00 a.m.–12:00 noon, 2:30 p.m.–6:00 p.m.; November–March all week: 8:00 a.m.–12:00 noon, 2:30 p.m.–5:00 p.m.

Visits to the Viri Galilae Church must be coordinated in advance with the Greek Orthodox Patriarchate.

Note: modest dress is required.

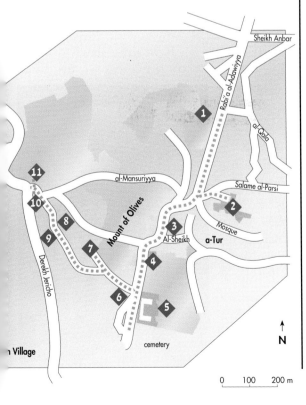

WE WILL WALK along Rabi'a al-Adawiyya street, which crosses over the summit of the Mount of Olives. To our right we see an iron gate decorated with verses from the New Testament in Greek, This is the gate of the Viri Galilae Church (Latin for "Galileans") ❶. The site derived its name from the narrative in the New Testament of the Apostles (who were from Galilee), who witnessed Jesus' ascent to Heaven from the Mount of Olives, forty days after the Resurrection (Acts of the Apostles 1:11-12). In the Middle Ages, some tour guides took advantage of the ignorance of Christian pilgrims, and told them that this place was Galilee, thereby sparing themselves the arduous trip to the north.

Slightly further along, to our left, we see a high, pointed turret ❷. This is the Russian Church of the Ascension, known as "Tur Malka" (Aramaic for "the king's mountain"). The name Tur Malka is mentioned in early Jewish sources as a place situated outside Jerusalem, bordering on Samaria, but was erroneously associated with the site before us, possibly on account of the name of the neighboring Arab village, a-Tur. This large compound is owned by the "White" Russians who identify it as the site of Jesus' ascension to Heaven, and as the place where the head of John the Baptist was discovered in the Byzantine period. John

The **Uzziah inscription,** which tells of the transferral of his bones in the Second Temple period, states (in Aramaic): "The bones of Uzziah king of Judah were brought here – do not open."

the Baptist, the harbinger of Jesus, is buried here. This monastery had in its possession the well-known **Uzziah inscription** (currently in the Israel Museum), but it is not known if it was discovered here.

We will continue walking until we see to our left a stone wall, beyond which rises the low minaret of a mosque.

3 — THE ASCENSION MOSQUE

Rabi'a al-Adawiyya Street

TO OUR RIGHT is a door providing access to the courtyard of the mosque, which is open only to worshipers. The mosque is built over a burial site, which Jewish tradition attributes to the prophetess Huldah, a contemporary of the prophet Jeremiah (II Kings 22:14). This tradition is contrary to one from the Second Temple period which maintains that Huldah was buried inside the city walls. The Christians attribute the tomb to the fifth-century nun Pelagia. Pelagia of Antioch was known for her great beauty and her life of debauchery. It is related that men killed themselves after having been rejected by her, while others committed crimes for

Ascension mosque

the purpose of winning her favors. At some stage in her life, as a result of Christian preaching that she heard, she became disgusted with her life of sin and licentiousness and declared: "I, Pelagia, am a sea of sins... I deceived myself and others, but my desire now is to rid myself of all this." She distributed her money only to the poor (and not to monks or priests), and went to live an ascetic life in Jerusalem. She arrived in Jerusalem disguised as a man, and obliterated all outward signs of her femininity to the extent that only after her death, when her body was prepared for burial, was it discovered that she was a woman. A Muslim tradition maintains that the tomb marks the burial place of Rabi'a al-Adawiyya, a female Sufi dervish who came in the ninth century from Iraq to Jerusalem, where she composed philosophical works and poetry.

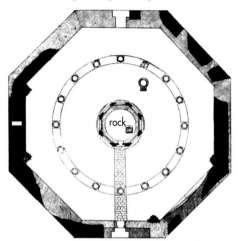

Plan of the Ascension mosque

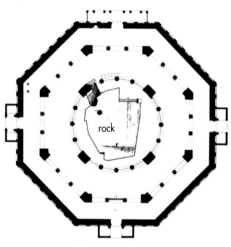

Plan of the Dome of the Rock

We will now enter the courtyard of the Ascension mosque. This is the third of the five sites on this tour that commemorate Jesus' ascension to Heaven. The name Ascension mosque is surprising – how can a Muslim mosque memorialize a Christian religious event? The answer is quite simple: the site became a mosque only after Saladin's conquest of Jerusalem; before that it had in fact been a church. The initial Christian structure commemorating the Ascension at this spot was built with a circular plan in the late fourth

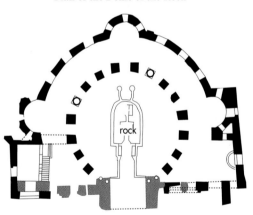

Plan of the rotunda in the Church of the Holy Sepulcher

century, and survived until the tenth century. The church was rebuilt by the Crusaders in the form that has survived to the present: outer walls encompassing an octagonal courtyard, in whose center is an *aedicula* that covers a rock from which, according to tradition, Jesus ascended to Heaven. Such a layout is known as a centralized plan, and is characteristic of Christian structures memorializing events that occurred at a specific location. Note the similarity between the plan and proportions of this church and those of the Church of the Holy Sepulcher, on the one hand, and the Muslim Dome of the Rock, on the other. The octagonal shape seems to be a product of the Crusader period (influenced by the monumental structure of the Dome of the Rock?), and is not based on the circular plan from the Byzantine period.

Column capital in Ascension mosque

As we encircle the courtyard (which was once covered, but whose roof is now in ruins), we notice the column bases adjoining the walls, three stone altars in the eastern wall, and another altar south of them. These are altars of the Syrian Orthodox, Coptic, and Armenian communities, who gather here on the festival of Ascension to conduct their religious ceremonies (with the permission of the Muslims in charge of the mosque), hanging decorative draperies on the hooks in the walls. We will now look at the aedicula and note the fine carving of the capitals and the marble columns that have survived from the Crusader period. One of the capitals is very similar to a capital on the window columns in the facade of the Church of the Holy Sepulcher, and they may have been executed by the same artisan. The walls between the columns of the aedicula are a Muslim addition, as is the dome covering it. The Crusader aedicula was open to the sky, in order to emphasize the connection between the place where Jesus stood on the rock and Heaven. We will now enter the aedicula. The Muslim prayer niche (*mihrab*) in the southern wall was added after the structure was converted into a mosque; at the same time, the rock was moved from the center of the aedicula to the mihrab. A depression is visible in the rock itself. According to Christian belief, this is **Jesus' footprint.**

One **footprint** appears in the rock. Where is the other? Some say it was removed and taken to Westminster Abbey in London; according to others, it is in Rome; it is also claimed that it is hidden in al-Aqsa mosque on the Temple Mount. According to other scholars, the generations of pilgrims took tiny pieces of it as mementos, leading to its eventual total disappearance.

We will leave the courtyard, turn left, and walk to the stone wall bearing the sign: Pater Noster. We will enter through the gate and descend the stairs to the inner courtyard.

THE PATER NOSTER CHURCH also has its roots in the Byzantine period. The column bases we see in the courtyard are remains from the Byzantine church established during the reign of the emperor Constantine the Great, in the place where Jesus had taught his disciples about what was to occur at the End of Days. The topographical conditions dictated that this structure, known as the Eleona (a corruption of the Greek *Elaia*, which means "olive tree") Church, would be built on three levels: the entrance in the west, the atrium (open courtyard) in the center, and the church, in the shape of a basilica, in the east, where we are standing. The structure was almost as large as the Church of the Nativity in Bethlehem, which was built at the same time.

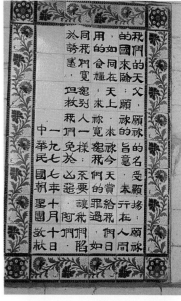
"Our Father" prayer in Chinese

When the Crusaders arrived in Jerusalem, they found ruins here above which they erected a modest house of worship. In this period the place of Jesus' Ascension had already been identified with the Church of the Ascension, which we visited earlier. This site was connected with the "Our Father" prayer, which, the New Testament relates (Luke 11:14), Jesus uttered close to or on the Mount of Olives (the church takes its name from the Latin title of the prayer: *Pater Noster*). The humble Crusader church was replaced in 1152 by a more majestic one, which was built with money given by the two Sveinsson brothers from Denmark. One of the brothers drowned during baptism in the Jordan River, and the other donated all of their belongings to the church, on condition that after his death he would be buried here, alongside his brother. The Crusader church would in its turn fall into ruins, and in the second half of the nineteenth century a modern church was built on the site. What strikes our eye in this church are the more than eighty ceramic plaques, each inscribed with the "Our Father" prayer in a different language. Some of

Corridor with inscriptions in the Pater Noster Church

these are dead languages; some others are spoken languages only, with no written alphabet, and therefore appear transliterated in Latin characters. As we pass along the inscriptions, try to find familiar words or sounds.

In the western part of the courtyard is a staircase that ends in a sort of raised prayer platform. Note especially the broken walls at the western ends of the courtyard. These are part of the frame of the Church of the Sacred Heart, whose construction began in 1920 but was never completed due to financial difficulties. Below the prayer platform is a cave hewn in the bedrock, which we will enter. Here we see a Byzantine apse on the eastern side, and an entrance to an ancient burial chamber to the west. A Christian tradition from the Byzantine period relates that in this place Jesus initiated his disciples into the secrets of the End of Days (Matthew 24:38). The bishops of Jerusalem in the Byzantine period were most likely interred in the crypt which was intended to be incorporated into the Sacred Heart church.

We will leave the cave and pass through the southern entrance of the courtyard into a side courtyard. This contains two modern tombstones erected in 1995 by the Danish people in memory of the Sveinsson brothers buried at the site. Now we will go up the stairs to the left (eastward), toward the colonnaded corridor of the Pater Noster Church. Here we find many additional ceramic plaques, bearing the "Our Father" prayer in Samaritan, Arabic, Czech, Polish, Esperanto, and other languages. To our right is a door (which is not always open) leading to an opening through which can be seen a tombstone bearing a statue of a supine woman. This is the French Princesse de la Tour d'Auvergne who came to Eretz Israel in 1866 and purchased the site of the church, which had been in ruins since the Crusader period, for the Carmelite nuns who have occupied it ever since. This noblewoman was buried here, along with the heart of her father in the nearby urn.

From the Arabic script of the prayer in **Turkish** we learn that the inscription was installed before the reforms of Kemal Ataturk in Turkey, which instituted the writing of Turkish in Latin script

Opposite the tombstone is the "Our Father" prayer in **Turkish** in Arabic script.

We will retrace out steps, leave the church, and continue down the road. After a short while, we will see on our right, beyond the fence of the road, the first graves of the Jewish cemetery on the Mount of Olives. Immediately beyond this section we see a staircase descending steeply to the west. We will pass it and continue, until we see on our left the Seven **Arches** Hotel (the former Inter-continental Hotel) 5, that was built during the period when this area was under Jordanian control. According to one opinion, the summit where we are standing is identified with the place known to Jews in the Middle Ages as "the footstool of our God" or "the dwelling place of His might and His footstool." This appellation appears in a guidebook to Eretz Israel from the eleventh century that was discovered in the Cairo Genizah. The Jews would climb up here on *Hoshana Rabba* (the seventh day of Sukkot, the Feast of the Tabernacles) and encircle the summit seven times in memory of the practice observed when the Temple was in existence.

The **arches** of the hotel allude to the Muslim tradition that in the End of Days a razor-sharp bridge will extend from the Mount of Olives to the Temple Mount. This bridge will be supported by seven arches. The righteous will walk along it unscathed, while the wicked will fall into the Valley of Jehoshaphat.

We will return to the staircase and go down the broad steps to the left, to the "Tombs of the Prophets Haggai and Malachi" 6. A burial cave from the Byzantine period (which possibly had its origins in the Second Temple period) is located here. For a small donation, the watchman who lives in the courtyard will take us through the peripheral corridor that opens onto dozens of rock-cut loculi, some of which bear the engraved Greek names of individuals from Palmyra in Syria, Beisan, and other places. The attribution of the tombs to the prophets may possibly have stemmed from Jesus' prophecy of destruction (which was most likely delivered on the Mount of Olives) concerning Jerusalem, "that kills its prophets." This same presage also mentions the prophet Zechariah (and according to another tradition, Haggai, Malachi, and Zechariah are buried here). It is unclear, however, why Haggai and Malachi are associated with this tomb, and not other prophets as well.

We will return to the road and go down to the gate of the Dominus Flevit Church. We will go in and take the right path to the structure with the arched windows.

DOMINUS FLEVIT CHURCH 7

"AND WHEN HE SAW the city he wept over it, saying... 'For the days shall come upon you, when your enemies will cast up a bank around you and surround you... and they will not leave one stone upon another in you'" (Luke 19:41–44). In these words the New Testament describes Jesus' lament over Jerusalem. But where did this take place? The description of this event in the New Testament appears before that of Jesus' entry to Jerusalem, when he came from the village of Bethpage, east of the city, to the Mount of Olives. It may be assumed that the identification of the slope of the Mount of Olives that looks out over the city to the west as the site of Jesus' weeping was based on this fact. The name of this church, Dominus Flevit ("the Lord wept" in Latin), alludes to this event. The structure next to where we are standing is built over a small excavations area, which yielded an interesting archaeological discovery: a Jewish burial complex from the Second Temple period containing about 120 ossuaries and 7 sarcophagi. Names such as Zechariah, Azariah, Jeshua, and Simon are engraved on the decorated sarcophagi. One of the ossuaries bears the Greek letters χρ the first letters of the appellation Christos (Messiah).

The Franciscans, who excavated the site, which they own, maintain that this find indicates that this was a burial site of Judeo-Christians from the late Second Temple period. However, it can be assumed that it was originally a Jewish burial site, which was put to secondary use by the Judeo-Christians in the Roman-Byzantine period.

A monastery was erected here in the Byzantine period, and its remains were revealed in the courtyard

Burial cave with ossuaries near the Dominus Flevit Church

Mosaic floor from the Byzantine period in the Dominus Flevit Church

and under the modern church building. As we continue along the path to its end, we see the remains of a winepress with a mosaic floor covered by a cement roof, and next to it a small cistern. A small Byzantine cemetery was discovered here. We will continue to walk around the courtyard until we come to a magnificent mosaic floor from the Byzantine period, behind an iron grille, next to the modern church. The mosaic contains decorations depicting flowers, fruit, leaves, two fish, and other designs. Such decorations were also common in synagogues of the time. Pay special attention to the lengthy Byzantine inscription in Greek. It mentions "Simon, the friend of Christos [the Messiah], who built and ornamented this house of worship... and dedicated it for the atonement of his sins, and for the eternal repose of his brothers Georgius the bishop and Demetius, friends of Christos." This was the site of the chapel, next to the Byzantine church. We are standing at the entrance to the modern chapel built in 1955, which was planned by the architect Antonio Barluzzi, who also designed the Church of the Flagellation on the Via Dolorosa, the Grotto of the Agony in Gethsemane, and the Italian Hospital on Ha-nevi'im Street.

The chapel is tear-shaped. As we enter, we note an unusual phenomenon: the altar is in the western wall, and not in its customary location in the eastern wall. The placement of the altar opposite the breathtaking view of Jerusalem framed by the church's western wall is intentional, intensifying the religious experience of anyone praying here.

The apse of the original Byzantine church is incorporated in the eastern wall of the modern church, at the foot of which is part of another mosaic. The hen and its chicks portrayed in the modern mosaic above the altar are reminiscent of the words of Jesus: "O Jerusalem, Jerusalem, killing the prophets and stoning those who are sent to you! How often would I have gathered your children together as a hen gathers her brood under her wings, and you would not!" (Luke 13:34). The Dominus Flevit Church, like the Church of St. Andrew (see Tour 26), has a story connected with the heart of a Scotsman: in this case, that of a nobleman named John Patrick, which, at his request, was buried in the church.

W E WILL LEAVE the church and go down the hill. We pass by the entrance to the Russian **Mary Magdalene** Church, which is conspicuous because of its onion-shaped domes, reminiscent of the style of the buildings in the Kremlin in Moscow. The church was built in 1885–88 upon the initiative of Czar Alexander III, his brother the Grand Duke Sergei, and the Duke's wife Yelizabeta Fyodorova. The Grand Duke was assassinated in 1905, and his wife suffered a similar fate thirteen years later. Her body was smuggled to Jerusalem through China in 1919. She was buried here, and in 1992 was proclaimed a saint. You can enter the courtyard with its luxuriant vegetation and spend some time walking along its paths. The church, with its very impressive exterior, is somewhat disappointing from the inside, because its ceiling does not reflect the shape of the domes. As we leave the church grounds, we see opposite the entrance a niche in a wall ⬥9⬥, with a pillar marking the spot where **Judas Iscariot** kissed Jesus, to signal to the Roman soldiers that this was the man they were to arrest (Mark 14:44).

From here we can also see to the left the roof of the next church that we will enter, the Church of All Nations. The twelve domes of the roof represent the Catholic nations who contributed to the construction of the church (1919–24). The eastern part of the church is cut into the bedrock, and around it is a drainage channel that diverts rainwater from the structure. We will go down the slope to the church.

◆ **Mary Magdalene** was the woman who went to Jesus' grave three days after his death and discovered that he had risen from the dead (John 20:1). She was later identified as the sinful woman who repented and proclaimed her belief in Jesus (Luke 7:37-50). Many churches are named after her, as are colleges in Oxford and Cambridge.

◆ Several English expressions are connected with **Judas Iscariot**: "Judas" – a traitor; "Judas colored" – red (the color of his hair, according to legend); "Judas hole" – a peephole in a door; "Judas kiss" – a kiss of betrayal; "Judas tree" – the common name of *Cercis siliquastrum*, whose leaves turned red from shame when Judas Iscariot hanged himself from its branches in remorse for his treachery.

Mary Magdalene Church

W E WILL ENTER the courtyard of the church, which is also known as the Gethsemane Church (*gat shemanin* – "oil-press" in Hebrew, based on John 18:1), where the ancient olive trees indicate the source of the name. Yet another name of the church is the "Grotto of the Agony," referring to the last events in Jesus' life that occurred here, before he was crucified. The New Testament relates that after the Last Supper, Jesus and a few of his disciples came

Ancient olive trees in Gethsemane

down to Gethsemane at night. Jesus asked three of them to remain awake and pray, while he turned aside and poured out his heart to his Maker. His disciples, however, fell asleep and left him alone. Jesus beseeched God to take from him the cup of suffering, and during this time of trying spiritual agony and profound suffering his sweat dripped like "drops of blood." He could not rely upon his sleeping disciples, and what was about to happen was crystal-clear to him. This narrative, in which Jesus is portrayed as possessing both human and divine attributes, transforms a visit to the Gethsemane Church into a climactic religious experience for the believer, who can identify with Jesus' suffering.

We will turn right on the path, go around the courtyard, and enter the modern Franciscan church, which was designed by the architect Barluzzi. The doors of the entrance are fashioned as a many-branched olive tree. When we become accustomed to the darkness, we discern the basilican plan of the church. A church with a similar plan occupied the site in the Byzantine period. The remnants of its mosaics, that were unearthed during the construction of the modern church, were placed under a glass cover and incorporated in the modern mosaics that follow the pattern of the originals. Later, in the Crusader period, a similar church was erected here, slightly to the south, but has left few remains. The Crusader church was used by the members of a Christian charitable society founded in 1112, one of whose supporters was the Crusader King of Jerusalem, Baldwin I. Coins bearing the image of Baldwin were found in the excavations of the church.

Advance toward the eastern wall. At the base of the altar we see the rock on which, Christian tradition maintains,

Jesus engaged in his solitary prayer. The rock is surrounded by metal latticework in the shape of a crown of thorns (symbolizing the one which the Romans placed on Jesus' head before the Crucifixion), and pairs of birds of prey and doves drinking from the cup of suffering. The domes are ornamented with a mosaic featuring stars against a dark blue sky, along with the emblems of the countries that contributed to the construction of the church (including Great Britain, Italy, Spain, and France).

We will leave the church and descend the stairs to the iron fence, where we can look back to the mosaic-decorated facade of the church and get a view of the Kidron Valley. The four columns supporting the arches of the facade bear statues of the four authors of the Gospels: Matthew, Mark, Luke, and John. In the large mosaic we see Jesus on bended knee gazing heavenward, and above him an angel holding a tablet with the letters AΩ – the first and last letters of the Greek alphabet, inspired by the verse: "I am the Alpha and Omega, the beginning and the ending" (Revelation of John 1:8). To the left are depictions of rulers and philosophers, and to the right, simple folk adoring Jesus. Above we see a sculpted cross and two deer, symbolizing the believers who drink thirstily: "Like a hind crying for water, my soul cries for you, O God" (Psalms 42:12).

We will leave the church, go down the road, and turn right to the sunken compound of the Tomb of Mary church.

THE TOMB OF MARY CHURCH 11

Y OU MAY NOT HAVE NOTICED, but we are now within the Kidron Valley (also known as the Valley of Jehoshaphat), that separates the Mount of Olives from the Old City. This area is frequently subject to winter floods that inundated the Tomb of Mary. The high steps in front of the church were built to solve this problem. In the Crusader period, a large reservoir was even built under the courtyard, into which the floodwater drained. The ceiling of this reservoir is supported by 143 columns.

The name of the church suggests the reason for its establishment: to commemorate the gravesite of Mary, mother of Jesus. The story behind this, however, is a bit more complicated. The New Testament is silent regarding Mary's fate, thus leading to the development of different traditions, some of which were based on allusions in the Christian scriptures. It is related that Mary did not die a

Tomb of Mary church

Page from the prayer book
of Queen Melisende

natural death, but rather fell into an everlasting sleep; after she was laid to rest she was gathered from her grave into the arms of Jesus her son in Heaven. According to one tradition, this occurred in Ephesus in Turkey, where Mary had gone to spread Christianity. Another tradition, however, maintains that these events took place in Jerusalem: Mary fell asleep on Mount Zion, was buried in the Valley of Jehoshaphat, and was gathered into the arms of her son on the Mount of Olives. Both traditions fix the date of these events as August 15, which has been celebrated ever since with an impressive ceremony as the festival of the Assumption (Mary's ascent to Heaven). Like other sites on the Mount of Olives, a church was first erected here in the Byzantine period and underwent many changes in the Crusader period.

The entrance arch of the church is of medieval Romanesque style. We will go inside through this arch and begin to descend the stairs to the dark but impressive interior of the church. After going down some eighteen steps, we see to our right an altar, which marks the tomb of the Crusader **Queen Melisende**. If we look upward, we will discern

Queen Melisende ruled the Crusader kingdom for a few years after the death of her husband Fulk of Anjou, until her son Baldwin III was crowned in 1152. The tension between the ambitious Melisende and her son led to a military conflict between the two. Melisende and her followers fortified themselves in the Citadel of Jerusalem. After a short siege, however, she was forced to cede Jerusalem and her rule was limited to Nablus, to which she retained title.

above the tomb an unlighted dome, which was unknown to researchers until the 1970s, when electric lighting was installed in the church and the dome became visible. On the other side of the stairs we see the traditional burial site of Joseph, the husband of Mary mother of Jesus. We will descend the staircase to the end and turn right.

We are now standing in the most important place in the cruciform church: the tomb of Mary, which is covered by an upper structure – an aedicula. Around us are a number of altars: to the west – a Coptic altar, in the corner of the space before the stairs and to the north of it Greek Orthodox altars, and to the west of the tomb – an Armenian altar. To the north of the tomb is an ancient burial site and an altar, which are in the possession of the Armenians and Syrians. You may have noted that no mention has been made of the Catholic communities. This is because most Catholics accept the tradition that locates Mary's burial in Ephesus, and not in Jerusalem. Nonetheless, a Catholic representative is usually present in the church. It is interesting that to the south of the

Tomb of Mary

tomb is a Muslim prayer alcove (Mary mother of the prophet Jesus is one of the figures revered by Muslims), although few come here to pray.

On the walls surrounding the Tomb of Mary are paintings depicting the sleeping Mary. The aedicula of the tomb has a Crusader character and is faced with marble, which has survived on parts of the structure; floral decorations are carved above the entrances. We will go inside to look at the tomb, also covered by engraved marble but with three round holes, exposing the bedrock in which the original tomb was hewn. This tomb seems to be part of the Jewish burial ground that covered the slopes of the Mount of Olives in the Second Temple period. Look above you at the rounded aperture in the ceiling, which serves as an outlet for the smoke from the candles, or perhaps symbolizes Mary's ascension, like the opening, that existed in Crusader times, above the rock from which Jesus ascended to Heaven that we visited at the beginning of the tour.

We will go out through the left (northern) aperture of the tomb and return to the entrance to see the ornamented Crusader lintel. The twelfth-century traveler Theodoric tells of the magnificence of the tomb in the Crusader period:

The tomb is adorned with precious decorations of marble and mosaics, and it is encompassed by twenty columns bearing arches and an architrave, with the roof above. It is written on the architrave: "From here, from the Valley of Jehoshaphat, leads the way to Heaven / Here rested in the past the maiden, the faithful servant of God, from here she ascended to the open gates of Heaven / This is the path of light for sinners, their mother who gave birth to them, and the place of their rebirth." On the roof is a round dome borne by six columns, with a ball and gilded cross above it.

We will go up the stairs and leave the church, returning to the courtyard. To our left is a passageway with a door at its end, above which is written GROTTA GETHSEMANE (the cave of Gethsemane). The door leads to a cave hewn in the bedrock that was used for burial in the Byzantine and Crusader periods, and also as a Byzantine prayer chapel. On the ceiling of the cave we can see the remains of frescoes depicting a star-studded sky, an angel, and unclear inscriptions. A tradition dating from the sixth century identified this cave as the place where Jesus was apprehended by his pursuers through the agency of Judas Iscariot. Beginning in the fourteenth century, the cave was mentioned as "the place of Jesus' agony," where he suffered in the hours preceding his detention.

Our tour ends here. We will return to the road and ascend to the right, alongside the walls, until Damascus Gate.

Jerusalem enjoyed a special status in Islam from the very onset of this faith, even though the city is not mentioned by name in the Koran. Muhammad initially decreed that Muslims would face Jerusalem while praying, but the direction of prayer was later changed toward Mecca. Over the course of time, Jerusalem became the third holiest site of Islam. In 638 it surrendered to the army of the caliph Omar ibn al-Khattab, two years after the Muslims had defeated the Byzantine forces near the Yarmuk River. It is related that when the caliph entered the city he also visited the Temple Mount, accompanied by his aide Kab al-Akhbar, a Jew who had converted to Islam. He ordered that the Mount be cleansed of the filth that had accumulated there, which revealed once again the Foundation Stone. Omar built a mosque to the south of the Foundation Stone, thus beginning a new era in the city's annals. The written sources relating to the history of Jerusalem in this period include the works of the native Jerusalemite and Muslim historian al-Maqdisi, the descriptions by Christian pilgrims, and documents discovered in the Cairo Genizah.

The population of the city waned following the Muslim conquest. Many Christians left Jerusalem for the shrinking Byzantine Empire. Jews were permitted to return to the city, and they apparently settled south of the Temple Mount.

The Byzantine character of the city did not undergo immediate change. At first, its name remained Aelia, as it had been called in the Byzantine period, and its size also did not change. During the course of the early Muslim period, Jerusalem came under the rule of three Muslim dynasties. Following the assassination of the fourth caliph, Ali, in 661, the Syrian governor residing in Damascus was appointed caliph. He founded the Umayyad dynasty, which reigned until 750. During this period extensive construction and restoration projects were carried out on the Temple Mount, which the Muslims call al-Haram al-Sharif, and its surroundings, including the erection of the Dome of the Rock, al-Aqsa mosque, and the administrative compound south of the Temple Mount. Jerusalem was transformed into an important religious center, and Jews were appointed as attendants in the Muslim structures on the Mount. It is noteworthy that, despite its sanctity, Jerusalem was not proclaimed the capital of a district.

In 750 a new dynasty rose to power, the Abbasids, who established their capital far from Jerusalem, in Baghdad. During this period Jews were no longer granted access to the Temple Mount and consequently were obliged to conduct their prayers outside the gates of the city or on the Mount of Olives. The Christians also complained of the suffering they endured under the yoke of Islam. Following their appeal to Charlemagne to exert his influence on the caliph, the attitude toward them changed, and a number of Christian edifices were erected in the city. In 841 a civil insurrection was launched by residents living around Jerusalem, who conquered the city and sowed destruction within it.

The third Muslim ruling house was the Shi'ite Fatimid dynasty, which traced its lineage to Fatima, the daughter of the prophet Muhammad. The caliph al-Mu'izz conquered Eretz Israel in 969, introducing the Fatimid rule which would continue until 1099. The Fatimid dynasty was centered in Cairo, in Egypt. During these years the Jerusalem Yeshiva (academy of Talmudic study) became the leading authority for all the Jewish communities in Eretz Israel, Syria, and Egypt. The ramified correspondence discovered in the Cairo Genizah (documents of the Jewish community stored over the years in the Ben-Ezra synagogue, rediscovered in 1897) sheds light on the relations between Egypt and Eretz Israel. The Genizah documents include a guide to Jerusalem in Arabic, intended for the many Jewish pilgrims who came to the city.

In the late ninth century an important Karaite community was founded in Jerusalem, and another leading Karaite community came into existence in Cairo at the same time. In 1009 the Fatimid caliph al-Hakim ordered the destruction of all the Jewish and Christian houses of worship in his realm, including those in Jerusalem, but permitted their restoration eleven years later. A strong earthquake struck Jerusalem in 1033 and destroyed the city wall. Four decades later, in 1071 (or 1073), Jerusalem was conquered by the Seljuks (Sunni Muslims of Turkish descent), who ruled it until 1098, when the Fatimids retook the city and held it for a single year, until it fell to the Crusaders in 1099.

For a map of Jerusalem in this period see p. 210.

The Dome of the Rock ⟶

EARLY MUSLIM PERIOD

The Temple Mount

THE TEMPLE MOUNT'S sanctity stems from its selection as the site of Solomon's Temple. During the Second Temple period the entire precinct was fashioned as a huge plaza that rested on vaults and earth fill. On it stood the Temple, stoas, and other structures, all of which were destroyed during the Roman conquest in 70 CE. At that time the Mount acquired the general outline that it has retained to the present day. During the period of Byzantine-Christian rule, the Mount was left in ruins, as a symbol of the fulfillment of Jesus' vision and as testimony to the abasement of the Jewish people in contrast to the glory of Christianity. As time passed, Jewish law prohibited entry to the Temple Mount, due to its holiness. Nonetheless, the Mount never ceased to function as a spiritual focal point in the Jewish tradition, in which longings for the past were fused with yearnings for the future Redemption.

A tour of the modern-day plaza is mainly a visit to the huge mosque compound, with a shrine in its center – the Dome of the Rock (erroneously called the Mosque of Omar) – and dozens of Muslim religious structures, prayer installations, tombs of holy men, and mosques, the foremost of which is al-Aqsa mosque. The sanctity of the Temple Mount and Jerusalem in Islam draws upon their hallowed nature in Judaism and Christianity. In the early Muslim period, however, another dimension was added to this sacred status, when the Muslims began to identify the Temple Mount with the place from which Muhammad ascended to Heaven.

A new literary genre appeared in Islam: the *fada'il* (praise literature), consisting of paeans to a land or city, to a chapter of the Koran, or to certain commandments. A special "in praise of Jerusalem" literature already came into being in the early Muslim period, which contributed greatly to bolstering its image as a holy city. Nevertheless, it should be recalled that in Islam, Jerusalem ranks third in sanctity, after Mecca and Medina, and pilgrimage to Jerusalem is considered as an optional visit and not a religious obligation (*hajj*), as is the visit to Mecca.

The monumental construction on the Temple Mount of the Dome of the Rock and al-Aqsa mosque was conducted primarily in the time of the Umayyad caliphate, in the late seventh and early eighth centuries. These structures (especially the Dome of the Rock) are among the earliest and finest examples of Islamic architecture in the entire world. Muslim construction on the Temple Mount continued, on a smaller scale, in later periods. Especially noteworthy are the buildings from the Mamluk period and we will encounter some during this tour. A survey of these structures will complete Tour 14, which focuses on Mamluk Jerusalem. The Temple Mount precinct is currently under the supervision and administration of the Muslim *Waqf* (religious trust). This foundation fulfills religious, social, economic, cultural, and political functions in Muslim states and societies. The activity of the Waqf is supervised by the Supreme Muslim Council, which was established in 1921.

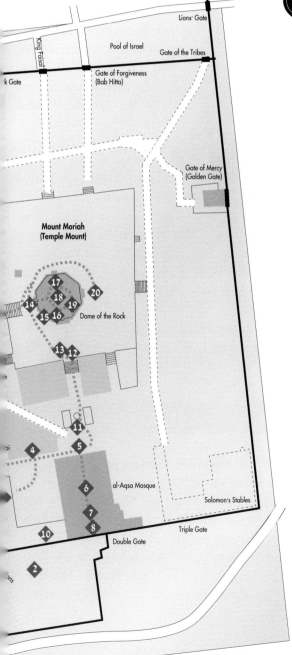

King Faisal

k Gate

Lions' Gate

Pool of Israel

Gate of the Tribes

Gate of Forgiveness
(Bab Hitta)

Gate of Mercy
(Golden Gate)

**Mount Moriah
(Temple Mount)**

17

18   19   20

14

15 16   Dome of the Rock

13 12

11

4   5

6   al-Aqsa Mosque

7

8

10   Triple Gate

Double Gate

Solomon's Stables

2

ns

0   100 m

↑
N

The route: the tour begins with a view of
the Southern and Western Wall
excavations close to the Dung Gate, and
continues onto the Temple Mount, where
it ends.

Duration of the tour: about two and a
half hours.

Public transportation: buses nos. 1 and 2
to the Western Wall; no. 38 (minibus) to
the Jewish Quarter – walk down from
there to the Dung Gate

By private car: the Jewish Quarter
parking lot, or the parking lot below
Dung Gate (outside the wall).

Visiting hours: Sun–Thu and Sat:
winter: 7:30 a.m.–10:30 a.m., 12:30 p.m.–
1:30 p.m.; summer: 8:30 a.m.–11:30 a.m.,
1:30 p.m.–3:00 p.m. On Fridays and
Muslim holidays the Temple Mount is
closed to visitors. Entry to the Mount is
free of charge, but there are entrance fees
for visits to al-Aqsa mosque, the Dome of
the Rock, and the Islamic Museum.

Notes: (1) weapons may not be brought
into the Temple Mount; (2) modest dress
is required; (3) those entering the
mosques are requested to leave their bags,
shoes and cameras at the entrance (there
are no cloakrooms).

A S WE STAND ON THE PATH connecting the Dung Gate with the entrance to the Western Wall plaza, we will look to the east, at the excavations at the foot of the Temple Mount.

The Umayyad caliphs who controlled the Muslim empire (660–750 CE) erected to the south and west of the restored Temple Mount plaza a series of opulent palaces, two whose ruins are visible from here ② ③. This was most probably the administrative compound, or Dar al-Imara (ruler's residence), which in Muslim cities was usually built alongside the mosque. The palaces share a common plan: at the center was located a paved courtyard with gardens, an irrigation system, and drainage channels. The courtyard was surrounded by porticoes, around which were series of rooms and halls, all forming a square plan. The rooms served as living quarters, bathing installations, and where various crafts were practiced. These palaces resemble those of the Umayyads in Syria and Eretz Israel

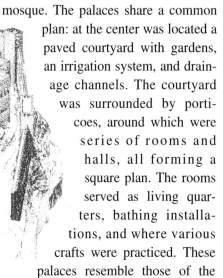

Proposed reconstruction of the Umayyad palaces

(for example, Hirbat al-Mafjar, Hisham's Palace near Jericho). Scholars are of the opinion that a small bridge connected the upper story of the ruler's palace with al-Aqsa mosque.

We will ascend to the Temple Mount through Maghribi Gate and, after purchasing tickets at the office ④, continue walking until we stand before the facade of the mosque.

W HAT IS THE SOURCE of the name **al-Aqsa**? An enigmatic verse in the Koran uses the following words to tell of a mysterious nocturnal journey by the

The Dome of the Rock is more magnificent than **al-Aqsa** mosque, but most scholars of Islam agree that the latter is of greater importance in the official Muslim religion, and is the key structure on the Temple Mount. Individuals come to pray at the Dome of the Rock, while public prayers are conducted in al-Aqsa mosque. In recent years women's prayers are conducted in the Dome of the Rock on Fridays.

prophet Muhammad: "Glory be to Him who carried His servant by night from the Holy Mosque [of Mecca] to the Further Mosque the precinct of which We have blessed" (Surah 17:1). The term "Further Mosque" (*al-masjid al-aqsa*) is unclear; later traditions identified it with the Temple Mount in Jerusalem, which is not mentioned in the Koran, and thus the mosque before us is known by that name.

Muslim tradition further relates that Muhammad made his nocturnal journey on a wondrous flying beast named "al-Burak," which is described as larger than a donkey but smaller than a mule; its body was like that of a horse, its horns were like the rays of the sun, its face like that of a beautiful woman, its nape was inlaid with diamonds, and its wings were those of a peacock. When Muhammad arrived at the Temple Mount, he ascended to Heaven, where he met Allah and illustrious personages from past generations.

The mosque was erected in the early eighth century by the Umayyad caliph al-Walid, above the system of vaults built by Herod when he extended the southern part of the Temple Mount. This made the mosque extremely vulnerable to earth-

Muhammad's nocturnal journey – Persian miniature, fourteenth century

quakes. These natural disasters that occurred in various periods (especially in the eighth and eleventh centuries) necessitated the continual rebuilding of wings of the structure that had been destroyed. The many renovations (which continue at present as well) have turned the mosque into a patchwork, and at times it is difficult to determine to which period each of its components belongs. Nothing remains of the original structure, whose shape is unknown, except for a small part of the southern wall. The facade of the mosque, built as a portico with seven arches leading to seven parallel halls inside the structure, was added by the Ayyubid ruler al-Mu'azzam Isa in 1217/8, as attested by an inscription above the central arch. The Ayyubids who wrested control of the city from the Crusaders were influenced by their architecture, and even incorporated in the facade Crusader decorative elements in secondary use.

The central arch is higher than the others, since it is located opposite the entrance to the nave of the mosque, which is wider and higher than the aisles. This arch is more highly embellished that the others, and is fashioned as a series of arches regressing inward, one of which features an engraved zigzag pattern that also appears in Crusader construction and Muslim construction from the Ayyubid period onward. Above the central arch is another element characteristic of Crusader architecture: small arches supported by colonnettes. Above the facade is a series of colonnettes resembling dentils, which are characteristic of Muslim construction and perhaps appear here as a simulation of the ornamentation in the facade of al-Azhar mosque that was built in Cairo in the tenth century.

We will remove our shoes and go inside to the nave . The nave and the three aisles on the east were renovated in 1938–42, and the ancient columns and capitals were replaced by marble columns brought from Italy, a gift from the Italian fascist leader Mussolini, "Il Duce." The blue wallpaper glued to the beams above the columns on both sides of the nave has replaced the original wooden carvings, which are presently on display in the Islamic Museum and the Rockefeller Museum.

The interior of the mosque is impressive in size and can accommodate up to 5,000 worshipers. In the past, however, it was twice as large, containing fifteen lengthwise halls (the nave and seven aisles on each side) built by the Abbasid caliphs when they reconstructed the Umayyad mosque following its destruction in an earthquake. The Abbasid structure collapsed in the earthquake of 1033, and when it was rebuilt by the Fatimid caliph al-Zahir two years later, it was reduced to its present shape.

Column capital from al-Aqsa

We will advance along the nave to the arch decorated with mosaics that separates it from the dome of the structure. The mosaics that had been installed by command of al-Zahir were covered by plaster, and were exposed once again only during the course of the renovations conducted in 1927. The dome of the mosque ❼, ornamented with mosaics featuring floral patterns, dates from the eleventh century. The stucco decorations in the upper part of the dome are from the Mamluk period. All of these ornamental features underwent renovations in later periods.

Facing us is the southern wall, the *qibla* ❽, with a *mihrab* – a niche showing the proper direction for prayer, toward Mecca, with decorations from the Ayyubid period in its center. Interestingly enough, for a period of about a year and a half, the Muslims initially prayed in the direction of Jerusalem, as Muhammad directed. When, however, Muhammad realized that the Jews refused to accept him as a prophet, he changed the direction of prayer toward Mecca, which was the holiest site of the Arab tribes in the Arabian Peninsula before the rise of Islam. To the east of the mihrab is the *minbar*, the pulpit upon which the preacher stands during prayers. This minbar replaces an earlier one that had been brought to Jerusalem by the Ayyubid Saladin after he had conquered the city from the Crusaders. That gem of Muslim art, made of ebony inlaid with ivory, without the use of nails, was consumed by flames in 1969 when a deranged Australian, who belonged to a Christian sect that sought to rebuild the Jewish Temple, set the mosque on fire. The remains of the minbar are on display in the Islamic Museum.

We shall now exit the mosque.

URING THE REIGN OF the Crusader king Baldwin II (1113–31), al-Aqsa mosque (which the Crusaders termed "Templum Solomonis" – Solomon's Temple) was given over to the knights of the Templar Order. The Templars renovated the structure and constructed additional buildings around it, some of which were subsequently destroyed. The Islamic Museum structure, along with that of the adjacent "Women's Mosque" 10, which is currently used as a Muslim theological center, also date to this period. Gigantic column capitals from the Fatimid period, which were removed from al-Aqsa mosque during the renovations conducted in 1938–42, lie near in the open space next to the entrance. The floral pattern on these capitals differs from that of the classical Corinthian capitals (see the illustrations for Tour 5).

Pottery and glass vessels, oil-lamps, censers, Muslim coins, and weapons (swords, daggers, and even rifles and pistols dating from the sixteenth century and later), are on display in the first hall. The lower level of the hall features an exhibition of copies of the **Koran**, with the largest, from the Mamluk period, in a display case in the center of the room.

The Mamluks developed the unique practice of writing **Korans** of exceptional size. They sought thereby to give expression to their religious piety, and possibly also to their worldview, which was founded on might and power. This vogue continued into the Ottoman period.

The second hall contains architectural and artistic elements removed from the Dome of the Rock and al-Aqsa mosque in the course of their various renovations. Above the entrance is a remnant of the metal grille that surrounded the Foundation Stone in the Crusader period, alongside which are the remains of the burnt Ayyubid minbar from al-Aqsa. On display along the southern wall are carved wooden beams from the early Muslim period that were removed from al-Aqsa mosque (another group of beams is exhibited in the Rockefeller Museum). The cannon standing at the end of the hall is the famous Ramadan cannon, which is fired every night during the month of Ramadan, close to Damascus Gate, to inform the faithful that the day's fast has ended. The Turkish cannon we see before us served faithfully until the end of World War II, when it was "retired" and replaced by a less ancient British cannon that dates only to 1918.

The Cup

Minbar al-Sayif

Upon leaving the museum, we turn to the north, toward the Dome of the Rock. On our way we pass by a goblet-shaped fountain ⑪ known as "al-Kas" (the Cup), which was built by the Mamluk emir Tankiz, the governor of Damascus in the fourteenth century. It is fashioned in the shape of his blazon, a goblet or cup. As in the past, the fountain is used for drinking and for purification before prayer. Purity is one of the central concepts in Islam. Before each prayer, a Muslim partially purifies himself by washing his face, his hands and arms up to the elbows, and his feet to the ankles. Before the Friday prayers a Muslim must engage in a full purification.

We will go up the stairs (an ascent of some four meters) to the *mastaba*, the raised platform on which the Dome of the Rock rests. The arches built at the top of the staircase ⑫ are called *mawazin* (scales). According to Muslim tradition, on the Day of Judgment scales will be suspended from the arches to weigh the souls of all people, in accordance with their good and evil deeds. To the west of the staircase is the Minbar al-Sayif (summer pulpit) ⑬, which was most probably built at the beginning of the Ayyubid period, making use of capitals and other Crusader elements. Another staircase was added, apparently in the Mamluk period. It seems that prayers for rain were offered at the summer pulpit: the congregation stood beside the minbar, and the preacher taught them the prayer, which they might have forgotten after several rainy years.

T HE DOME OF THE ROCK is popularly known as the "Mosque of Omar." How did the name of the caliph Omar ibn al-Khattab become attached to this structure?

The Arab force that accepted the surrender of Byzantine Jerusalem was led by one of Omar's officers, and not by Omar himself. Over the centuries, however, Muslim traditions came into existence which sought to embellish the story of the city's capture, and connected this event with Omar. According to one tra-dition, when Omar arrived at Jaffa Gate to accept the capitulation of the city from the Christian Patriarch Sophronius, he asked the churchman to lead him to the site of the Temple.

Dome of the Rock model

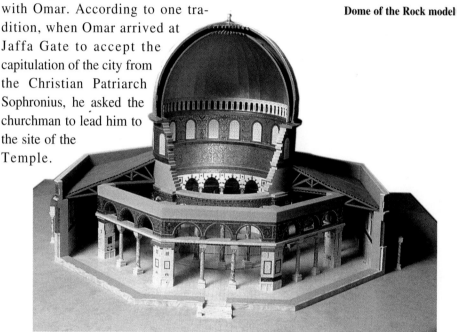

Sophronius tried to deceive Omar by taking him to various places, including the Church of the Holy Sepulcher and the Nea Church, but Omar was not fooled, and finally Sophronius was obliged to lead him to the Temple Mount. When Omar entered the precinct, he found it covered by piles of refuse. Using his cloak, he removed some of the refuse above the sacred rock, thus revealing it. This may be the source of the erroneous account that attributes the building of the Dome of the Rock to the caliph Omar.

Who then did build the Dome of the Rock (Qubbat al-Sakhra), and why? There appears to be a simple answer to the first question: the structure contains a large inscription bearing the name of the builder – the Abbasid caliph al-Ma'mun, who lived in the early ninth century. Surprisingly, though, the inscription gives 691 as the date of its construction, that is, about 120 years before al-Ma'mun's rise to power. A close examination of the inscription reveals that in al-Ma'mun's name the letters are closer together than in the other words, and appear on a darker background. We may conclude from this that al-Ma'mun deleted from the inscription the name of the original builder, and inserted his own name instead.

The real builder, whose name al-Ma'mun sought to efface, was the caliph Abd al-Malik, one of the Umayyads who ruled in Jerusalem before the Abbasid dynasty assumed power.

The second question is more difficult to answer. Some authorities maintain that the Dome of the Rock, the earliest monument in the Muslim world, was built as a counterweight to Mecca and Medina, which were ruled at the time by a dynasty that had rebelled against the Umayyads. According to another opinion, it was erected as a Muslim triumphal monument, which would offset the grand churches in Jerusalem, especially the Church of the Holy Sepulcher. A third view is that the structure (like the Great Mosque of Damascus) was erected to aggrandize Syria (including Eretz Israel), which had become the center of the Umayyad empire.

The eight sides of the original structure were paneled with marble. This type of ornamentation is also known from the late Byzantine period. Few of these panels have survived. Pay attention to the symmetrical geometric patterns formed by the veins in the marble. After being quarried, each block of marble was sawn widthwise into two "slices," and each "slice" was once again cut across its width, thereby producing four slabs, which were then placed together as a square to create a symmetrical pattern. The upper part of the octagon and the drum bearing the dome were decorated by Abd al-Malik with mosaics that did not withstand the ravages of time and were replaced, as from the sixteenth century, by a covering of colorful ceramic tiles. The current covering was applied in this century. The original gold-colored outer dome of the structure was replaced a number of times. In 1994 a new gold-plated exterior dome, weighing a total of 80 kilograms, was installed at a cost of $15,000,000. The plating is not more than .0023 mm thick, and the sheen of the gold was slightly muted during the plating so that the dome would not blind anyone gazing upon it. We will remove our shoes and enter the structure.

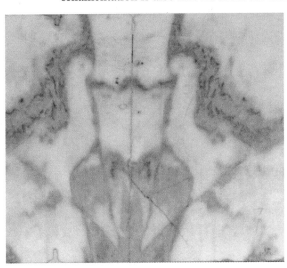

Marble decoration in the Dome of the Rock

Abd al-Malik invested in the construction of the Dome of the Rock a sum equivalent to the tax revenues from all Egypt for seven years. Nonetheless, he sought to reduce expenses by using **columns** taken from the ruins of earlier structures. Since the various columns were of different heights, the builders had to provide them with bases and marble additions above the capitals. The phenomenon of the secondary use of columns and capitals is known also from other sites in the Muslim world (such as the Great Mosque of Damascus), and expresses the triumph of Islam over the cultures that had erected the structures from which the architectural elements

We are standing in a peripheral corridor formed by the outer wall of the octagonal structure ⑮ and a series of pillars and **columns** ⑯ of octagonal plan, known as the intermediate octagon. A carved and painted marble band, dating from the Umayyad period, runs under the windows and on the interior of the outer wall. The columns of the intermediate octagon bear a beam made up of 24 parts, meant to stabilize the structure, and was decorated with gilded copper reliefs. In the center of each part of the beam is a floral decoration, with schematic geometric shapes at its edges. Most of the patterns are not repeated, a feature characteristic of Umayyad art. An inscription memorializing the construction project, in which the name of the caliph al-Ma'mun was inserted, is affixed on both sides of the upper portion of the intermediate octagon.

The inner side of the intermediate octagon is ornamented with realistic and imaginary floral patterns. The artists adapted the shape of the decorations to that of the surface on which they appear. Thus, for example, trees that extend upwards (some palm trees bearing fruit) appear on the narrow surfaces of the pillars, while chains of leaves and flowers are depicted on the parts of the arches facing the floor.

Beyond the intermediate octagon is another series of pillars and columns arranged in a circle ⟨17⟩ and bearing the drum that supports the structure's dome. Between and below the windows of the drum are mosaics, some with inlays resembling jewelry. The mosaics depict amphorae sprouting branches with a pair of wings above them. The amphorae, the jewelry decorations, and especially the triumphal wreaths are also known from Byzantine mosaic floors and served as symbols of royalty. The wings, on the other hand, appear as a symbol of the Persian Sassanid dynasty. The nascent Muslim art absorbed artistic elements from the cultures it defeated and incorporated them in a new, Islamic, style. According to one view, the use of these symbols of the conquered peoples expressed the victory of Islam over the Byzantines and the Sassanids.

The wooden dome above the drum is the inner dome of the structure, and is separated from the outer golden dome. The space between them provides an insulating layer that protects the ornamentations of the inner dome from meteorological changes. The dome, which was built in the eleventh century, was adorned three centuries later with stucco **Arabesques** painted in shades of red, black, and gold. The central part of the dome features red "loops," bearing patterns that widen downward. Two inscriptions incorporating decorations extend around the dome; one of them documents the work of the artists.

We will advance toward the center of the structure ⟨18⟩ to the ancient rock from which Muhammad ascended to Heaven. According to Jewish tradition, this is the Foundation Stone on which the world was founded, on which Abraham bound Isaac as a sacrifice, and is the site of the Holy of Holies (or the altar, in another version) in the First and Second Temples. The stone is surrounded by carved wooden latticework. The stone was not encompassed by a lattice in the Umayyad Dome of the Rock. However, following the Crusader conquest, when the structure was converted into the Templum Domini church, the need arose to protect the rock from souvenir hunters who chipped pieces from

In the Dome of the Rock we witness the first manifestation of the **Arabesque**. This is a style consisting of endlessly repeated abstract floral patterns. The Arabesque is characteristic of the later phases of Muslim art. The distinctive Arabesque abstract style is explained, inter alia, by the desire to avoid any naturalistic imitation of the Creation. Arabesques often include Arab script as an ornamental feature.

it. The rock was then covered with marble, an altar was placed on top of it, and a metal grille was erected around it. A place for the choir was constructed on the marble, and the walls were decorated with paintings depicting events in the history of the Temple. The Crusader grille was most likely removed upon the return of the Muslims to the city, who replaced the metal fixture with the current wooden one.

If you want to know the traditional location of the spot where Muhammad ascended to Heaven, look at the southwestern corner of the rock. Here stands a wooden cabinet containing a wooden chest in which two hairs from the prophet's beard are kept. According to Muslim tradition, the cabinet covers Muhammad's footprints in the rock.

We will end our visit by descending into the cave 19 concealed under the rock. A Muslim legend relates that when Muhammad ascended to Heaven the rock began to detach itself from the earth in order to accompany him, but the Archangel Gabriel prevented this, thus giving rise to the cave. The arch of the cave's entrance and the staircase were installed by the Crusaders, who identified this site as the place where the angel informed the priest Zacharias, the father of John the Baptist, that his wife Elisabeth was pregnant. The staircase is flanked by the

Sabil of Qayit Bey

David and Solomon prayer alcoves. Some visitors offer a personal prayer at these niches.

We will exit from the Dome of the Rock and pass to its eastern side, to an open structure covered by a dome  known as Qubbat al-Silsila (the Dome of the Chain). According to some authorities, this structure served as the model for the Dome of the Rock; however, it has ten sides, and its internal division differs from that of the Dome of the Rock. This structure apparently is a memorial erected in the late seventh century. A Muslim legend relates that the charmed "chain of judgment" hung here in ancient times. Litigants would approach and attempt to grasp it: a righteous and honest man would succeed, while it would evade the wicked.

The Sabil of Qayit Bey is located to the west of the platform on which the Dome of the Rock stands. This is a drinking fountain built in the fifteenth century by the Mamluk sultan Inal, but it was later renovated by Sultan Qayit Bey and thus bears his name. Its grille windows and dome decorated with reliefs, the incorporation of red stone in its construction, and the columns in the corners reflect the architecture of Mamluk Jerusalem in all its glory. South of the sabil is the Madrasa al-Ashrafiyya which was built as an institution for religious studies by Sultan Qayit Bey's predecessor. Qayit Bey ordered its destruction and rebuilt it in a quite opulent manner, beginning in 1480. This Mamluk madrasa is regarded as the third crowning jewel on the Temple Mount, together with the Dome of the Rock and al-Aqsa mosque.

From here we will continue southward, to the exit gate from the Mount. Here ends our tour, but those of us who wish to see Muslim art at its best are invited to visit the Rockefeller Museum, which is located close to the northeastern corner of the Old City, on Sultan Suleiman Street. On display there are eighth-century wooden beams from al-Aqsa mosque, as well as a breathtaking exhibition of decorations from the Umayyad Hirbat al-Mafjar (Hisham's Palace) near Jericho.

Madrasa al-Ashrafiyya

In 1099 the Christians reconquered Jerusalem after a siege of five weeks. These were Christians from Europe who had set out on a Crusade to the Holy Land in response to the call of Pope Urban II to free the holy places and the Eastern Christians from the infidels (the Muslims). The Crusader conquest was followed by the massacre of the city's Muslim and Jewish population, when some of the Jews were taken to Ashkelon to be sold as slaves. Godfrey of Bouillon, one of the leaders of the Crusade, was chosen to rule the Crusaders who had decided to remain in Eretz Israel, and was proclaimed "Advocate of the Holy Sepulcher." After more than a millennium, Jerusalem was once again a capital, this time of the Crusader kingdom.

The composition of the city's population completely changed. After the conquest and the slaughter of its inhabitants, many efforts were made to bring new settlers to the sparsely populated city. Thanks to various tax reductions or exemptions, and the later transfer of local Christians from Transjordan, the Christian population of Jerusalem increased. Jews were not permitted to dwell in the city, and the Jewish traveler Benjamin of Tudela wrote that only two Jews, who engaged in the dyeing of fabrics, were living in Jerusalem. The severance of Diaspora Jews from Eretz Israel, and especially their yearnings for Jerusalem, found expression in the compositions of Spanish-Jewish poets such as Rabbi Judah Halevi, who may even have come to Jerusalem. A legend relates that he met his death in the city when he was trampled by a mounted horseman.

The Muslim religious structures in the city were confiscated and converted into Christian institutions. The Church of the Holy Sepulcher became the focal point of the city, along with the Dome of the Rock, which now became a church. The orientation of the city's inhabitants was to the West, to their lands of origin. The area of the city in this period corresponded to that within the present-day walls, and a Crusader suburb sprang up on Mount Zion. The fortifications and streets from the late Muslim period retained their original functions. The systems of parallel streets and the markets established within the Cardo in the early Muslim period are still in use today. The various quarters of the city usually had a main thoroughfare, with most of the structures clustered around it. The quarters were generally named after the communities inhabiting them: the Syrians, the Armenians, and the various Christian military Orders (the Templars, the Hospitalers and the German Teutonic Knights). There was also the quarter of the Patriarch, whose residency was northwest of the Church of the Holy Sepulcher. The members of the various Orders were entrusted with guarding and assisting pilgrims and wayfarers. Our knowledge of this period is drawn from the testimonies of pilgrims (including Jews), contemporary maps, collections of documents from the churches and military Orders in the city, and the descriptions of historians from that time, such as William of Tyre. Various traditions regarding the life of Jesus sprang up in this period.

Crusader Jerusalem was a bustling city and its well-stocked markets provided for the needs of the inhabitants and pilgrims. Many religious structures of Romanesque or Gothic style were erected in the city. The Crusaders brought these styles with them from their lands of origin, but here they acquired a unique Eastern nuance.

In 1187 Saladin, the founder of the Ayyubid dynasty, besieged the city. Following negotiations, the Christians left Jerusalem, and it once again came under Muslim rule.

For a map of this period see p. 211.

For a map of this period see p. 211.

Arch in the Church of St. Mary of the Germans ⟶

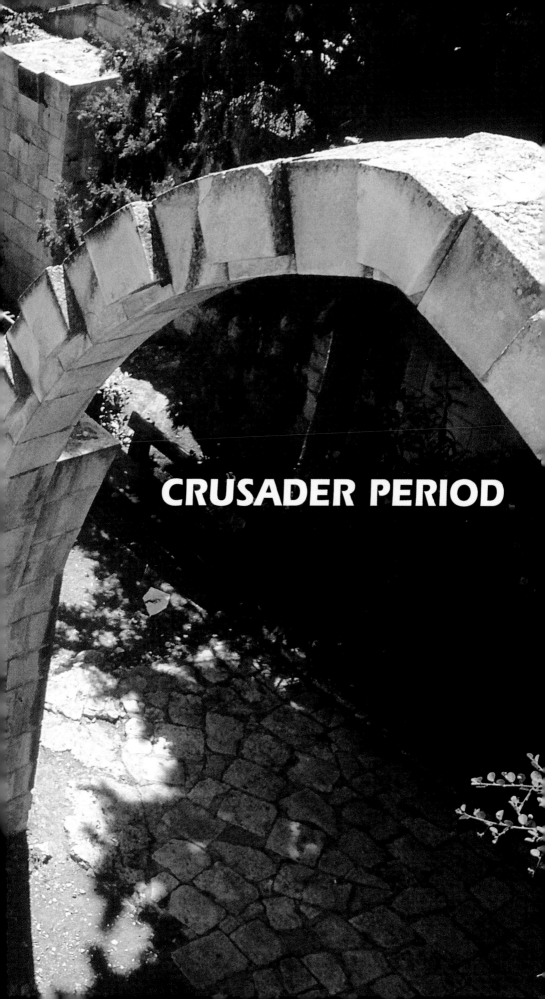

CRUSADER PERIOD

From Tancred's Tower to the Church of the Holy Sepulcher

THE RELIGIOUS FERVOR that gripped Christian Europe in the late eleventh century and provided the motivation for the Crusades exacted a bloody price from the Jewish communities in Europe. As the Crusaders headed for the Holy Land, they slaughtered thousands of Jews on their way. In a lament recited by some Jewish communities in the penitential prayers for the eve of Yom Kippur (Day of Atonement), Rabbi David bar Meshullam of Speyer describes the events of 1096:

O God, hold not your silence over my blood / ... infants and women together were sent to the pyre / ... the children writhe in agony, and struggle in their death throes, one atop the other ... / Tears from here and there spring and gush forth / And the slaughterers and the slaughtered moan, one over the other, the blood of the fathers and the sons touches and wells up / the blessing of the altar: "Hear, O Israel!" they cry out.

Three years later, when the Crusaders arrived in the Holy Land and conquered Jerusalem, they ruthlessly massacred the city's Jewish and Muslim inhabitants. On this tour we will trace the footsteps of the Crusaders, from one of the places where they assaulted the walls to the Church of the Holy Sepulcher – the focal point of their aspirations and the declared goal of their campaign.

After the establishment of Christian rule in the city, following more than 450 years of Muslim control of Jerusalem, and for the first time since the Second Temple period, the city became a capital once again, this time of the Crusader kingdom.

The Crusaders took vigorous steps to refurbish the city. A palace-fortress was erected as the residency of the Crusader kings, the city's fortifications were restored, streets were renovated, and the markets were roofed. Hostels and hospitals for pilgrims were built and structures were allocated for use by the various religious Orders.

What were the religious Orders in Jerusalem and where were they located? What architectural elements characterized Crusader construction? Where were the Crusader

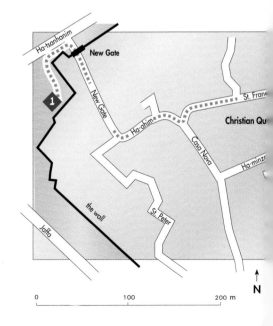

kings and heroes buried? How was the layout of the Church of the Holy Sepulcher changed? These questions will be the subject of this tour, during the course of which we will learn of ancient traditions, see exotic sites such as "the burial place of Adam," visit an enchanting Ethiopian "village" concealed by the domes of the Church of the Holy Sepulcher, and learn of the inflexible rules of the Status Quo that governs the life of the Christian communities in the holy places.

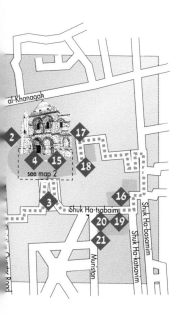

The route: the tour begins at Tancred's Tower, in the northwestern corner of the Old City wall, continues to the Church of the Holy Sepulcher, and ends at the Muristan in the Christian Quarter.
Duration of the tour: three to four hours.
Public transportation: buses nos. 6, 11, 18, 19, 20, 23, or any other line that reaches Safra Square (Jerusalem Municipality); from there one continues on foot to the corner of the Old City wall.
By private car: the Municipality parking lot or the David's Village parking lot.
Visiting hours: Church of the Holy Sepulcher: entire week: 4:30 a.m.–8:00 p.m. Closing time in the summer is 9:00 p.m.
Deir al-Sultan:
entire week: 4:30 a.m.–8:00 p.m.
Closing time in the summer is 9:00 p.m.
Church of the Redeemer: Tue–Sat: 9:00 a.m.–12:45 p.m., 2:00 p.m.–4:45 p.m. On Mondays the church is open only in the morning. Entrance fee for the bell tower.
Note: modest dress is required.

THE NORTHWEST CORNER of the city wall, which we are facing, was one of the points where the Crusaders concentrated their forces for the assault upon the city, in the first phases of the siege in the sweltering summer of 1099.

At the foot of the city wall we see the remains of a moat and above it are

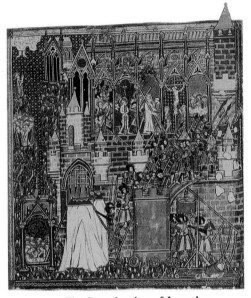

The Crusader siege of Jerusalem, medieval manuscript

particularly large stones that protrude from the wall. These are the remains of the base of a fortified tower, the continuation of which is situated in the basement of the Christian Écoles des Frères within the city walls. The large stones of the tower (which was built during or after the Crusader period) and its proximity to the Citadel (traditionally known as the Tower of David) led to its being called the Tower of Goliath by the Muslims. It is also known as Tancred's Tower, after the Norman Crusader commander from Sicily, who bivouacked here with his forces during the siege.

In the north the Crusader forces breached the walls near Damascus Gate. Using battering rams and siege towers several stories high, they rained arrows upon the defenders on the wall. A contemporary Crusader historian excitedly relates the events following the breaching of the wall:

It was impossible to look upon the vast numbers of slain without horror: everywhere lay fragments of human bodies, and the very ground was covered with the blood of the slain. It was not alone the spectacle of the headless bodies and mutilated limbs strewn in all directions that roused horror in all who looked upon them. Still more dreadful it was to gaze upon the victors themselves, dripping with blood from head to foot, an ominous sight which brought terror to all who met them (William of Tyre).

After the breakthrough, the Crusaders hastened to seize the Temple Mount (where they could quench their thirst from its cisterns, after weeks of a shortage of water). In the evening, after they had gained control

Mary's Arch

of the entire city, they made their way to the "Church of the Lord's Agony and Resurrection," that is, the Church of the Holy Sepulcher, to offer a prayer of thanksgiving.

We will head toward the New Gate (see Tour 16), enter the Old City, and continue to Christian Quarter Road. Here we will look on our left for a blocked gate ❷ topped by an arch (it may be difficult to spot the gate, which is usually partially covered by the embroidered dresses displayed for sale there). In the Crusader period the arch, known as Mary's Arch, and pulvinate decorations delineated an entrance leading to the rotunda of the Church of the Holy Sepulcher. The wall of the street in which we are standing is parallel to the western wall of the church. We will walk along the street and take the first turn to the left, continuing to the Church of the Holy Sepulcher.

CHURCH OF THE HOLY SEPULCHER   3

The Atrium

W E ARE STANDING at the entrance of the most important and sacred site in all Christendom. According to Christian tradition, the **Church of the Holy Sepulcher** is built over the site where Jesus was crucified, buried, and resurrected, thus proving his divinity. At the time, around 30 CE, this site was probably an abandoned quarry beyond the city walls, as Jewish (and Roman) burials were permitted only outside the city limits. Protestants do not accept this site as the location of the Crucifixion; from the end of the nineteenth century they identified the site of

◆ In some periods, Jews risked their lives when walking past the **Church of the Holy Sepulcher,** as is related by a Christian traveler from the sixteenth century: "One monk showed us... three dogs with the following special quality: when a Christian draws near to them, no harm will befall him, but if a Turk or Jew approaches them, his life is in danger, if no one comes to his aid. This was frequently proved by the exchange of garb" (Hans von Hirnheim, 1569).

Window in the facade of the Church of the Holy Sepulcher

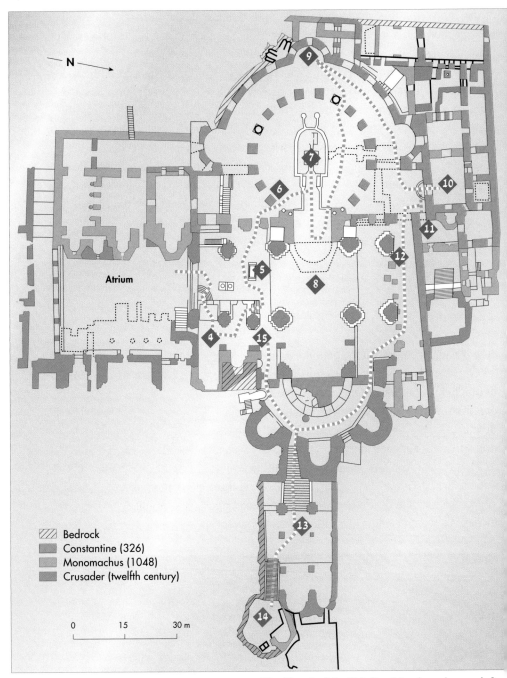

The Church of the Holy Sepulcher in various periods

Legend:
- ⬚ Bedrock
- ■ Constantine (326)
- ■ Monomachus (1048)
- ■ Crusader (twelfth century)

0   15   30 m

the Crucifxion as a hill north of Damascus Gate, which is known as the Garden Tomb. Nonetheless, on the basis of archaeological findings they acknowledge that the Garden Tomb is not from the Second Temple period (see Tour 21).

A pagan temple of Aphrodite was erected here in the reign of the Roman emperor Hadrian (117–38). Christian historians in later periods would claim that this was to prevent the early Christians, who were persecuted by the Romans, from visiting the site. A Christian tradition relates that in the time of the emperor Constantine the Great, who proclaimed Christianity to be the favored religion of the Roman Empire, his mother Helena came to Jerusalem, identified the location of Jesus' crucifixion and his tomb, found the remains of the Holy Cross, and then erected on the site the Anastasis (Resurrection) Church, which was inaugurated in 335. It was given the name "Church of the Holy Sepulcher" only in a later period.

The site was leveled, and a rotunda (also known as the Anastasis) was erected over the tomb. A basilica (a rectangular structure with rows of columns dividing it into a nave and flanking aisles), also called the Martyrium to commemorate Jesus' death as a martyr, was built to the east of the rotunda. The rotunda and the basilica were separated by an open garden surrounded by stone arches that was close to

Column capital in the facade of the Church of the Holy Sepulcher

the hill of the Crucifixion. The entrance to the entire precinct was in the east (in contrast with the present entrance) and faced the Cardo, the main thoroughfare of Jerusalem (see Tour 9). Over the course of time, the Byzantine church was destroyed and repaired a number of times. The Crusaders thoroughly renovated the structure in 1149 to mark the jubilee year of their conquest of the city. The plan of the Crusader church is fundamentally identical to that of the present-day church.

The Crusaders turned the basilica in the east into the monastery of the Augustinian Order, thereby reducing the length of the church. This also led to the roofing of the open garden, which became the Catholicon (the general prayer hall). In the entrance to the church, which was moved to the southern side in the eleventh century, the Crusaders built the two gates facing us. The gate on the right was later blocked when they were driven out of Jerusalem by the Muslims. To the left of the church facade the Crusaders added a bell tower whose upper part collapsed in the sixteenth century and has not been restored. Pay special attention to the arches above the entrance gates, which once again feature the pulvinate pattern that we saw in Mary's Arch.

Above the entrances are stone lintels that were once decorated with reliefs. The reliefs, which had become quite worn, were removed in 1930 and transferred to the Rockefeller Museum. The reliefs of the left lintel present various scenes from the life of Jesus, while those of the right lintel, which are of completely different style, depict intertwined floral ornamentations that incorporate nude human figures and imaginary animals.

In the upper story are two windows, whose shape is reminiscent of the entrances below. Note the ladder leaning against the right window: this is connected to the status quo in the church. As time passed, the various Christian communities acquired "possession" of parts of the church. The disputes between the communities regarding the boundaries of these possessions led to the formulation of agreements that established a permanent, binding state of affairs. To the present day, the church's activity is dictated by these status quo arrangements that leave nothing to chance: they determine the times of prayer for each community, the hours of the opening and closing of the church gates (by the Muslim Nusseibeh and Joudeh families who have held this honored office since the thirteenth century), the order of lighting the candlesticks and oil-lamps in the church, and even which floor tiles may be trodden on by the members of a specific community on their way from their place of prayer to the holy tomb. Every year before Easter, the heads of the different communities convene to discuss common problems pertaining to the church (repairs, cleaning, etc.), but there is so much mutual distrust that they generally cannot reach any decision. This is one of the reasons why the renovations in the church have been underway for such a long time, and why some parts of it look neglected. The last renovations were completed in 1997. Until 1831 the church gates would be opened only on special holidays, with the permission of the Muslim authorities; the rest of the year the gates were closed, and the Christian monks in the church were under "house arrest." Their food was brought up to them through the open window in the upper story, and the monks would use the ladder that we see in order to exit via the window. Since the ladder is specified in the status quo agreements, it may not be moved, even though it no longer serves any purpose.

We will cross the atrium surrounded by various religious structures belonging to the different Christian communities, and walk toward the gate of the church. In some of the columns to the left of the gate we can see a few nails embedded in the stone. In the past, it was the custom to hammer in iron nails that had been blessed, as a remedy for toothache, and the nails have remained there ever since. On the columns we discern reddish inscriptions from the fourteenth century, including the name "Dendulo." This person apparently was a member of the family of Doges of Venice, who, during a visit here, climbed a ladder in order to leave this "graffito." On the pavement to the right is a wood panel covering the tomb of Philip d'Aubigne, an English Crusader who was the tutor of King Henry III of England and a signatory to the **Magna Carta** in 1215. In his great humility, d'Aubigne, who died in 1236, requested to be buried here so that the pilgrims would tread on his grave.

We will enter the church and ascend the stairs to the right.

♦ The **Magna Carta** is the charter of rights
♦ granted to the barons in 1215 by the English
♦ king John Lackland, the brother of Richard
♦ Lion-Heart. This document, which limited the
♦ authority of the monarch, is considered to be
♦ the beginning of English constitutional law.

G OLGOTHA (or Calvary, from the Latin), which means "skull" in Aramaic, is, according to the New Testament, the site of the Crucifixion of Jesus (Matthew 27:33). Some claim that the name alludes to the shape of the hill of the Crucifixion, which bears some resemblance to a skull, while others link this name with the later tradition that the skull of Adam is buried here. Golgotha is divided between the Catholics (the southern part of the hill) and the Greek Orthodox (the northern part). The Catholic part is ornamented with modern dark mosaics that depict (from right to left) Station X of the Cross, where Jesus was stripped of his garments, and Station XI, where he was nailed to the cross. Visible in the ceiling is the sole remnant of an elliptic Crusader mosaic that presents Jesus as ruler of the world. In the sides of the altar opposite us, whose base is a bronze latticework, we see a heraldic shield with six balls. This was the ensign armorial of the Medici family from Florence, one of whose members donated the bronze latticework in 1588. Fashioned by Giovanni da Bologna, a Flemish sculptor resident in Italy, this is one of the most important artistic treasures in Israel.

To the left of the altar stands a statue of Mary mother of Jesus, adorned with a crown of sapphires and other gems. The crown has been stolen twice since 1967 and was replicated. The statue marks the spot where the suffering mother stood (Station XIII of the Cross) and beheld her crucified son. This event has been immortalized by many composers in works bearing the Latin name *Stabat Mater* (The Mother Stood).

We will advance to the left part of the hall, which is distinguished by a plethora of oil-lamps and paintings characteristic of the Eastern churches. The place where Jesus' cross stood is marked by a depression in the bedrock, visible here under a glass covering. This is Station XII on the **Via Dolorosa**. Pay special attention to the cleft in the rock that continues downward. The New Testament relates that when Jesus expired darkness reigned, the world trembled, and the curtain in the temple was miraculously rent (Luke 23:45). The twelfth-century Christian traveler Saewulf informs us: "The rock could no longer bear the death of its Creator without cleaving... and it is related that Adam [who was buried under the cross] arose from the dead because the blood of Jesus dripped on him."

In 1968 a sensational archaeological find at Givat Ha-mivtar in Jerusalem riveted the attention of laymen and scholars alike: the remains of the skeleton of a man from the Second Temple period who had been crucified were found in an ossuary. The nail by which he had been fixed to the cross was still present in his heel bone. This find is the only archaeological evidence of an act of crucifixion, which until this discovery had been known only from written sources and religious paintings. The bones of this

The **Via Dolorosa** is the route taken by Jesus on his way from the place where he was judged by the Roman procurator Pontius Pilate to the hill of Golgotha. The currently accepted route was already followed in the Middle Ages. It leads from the vicinity of the Lions' Gate to the Church of the Holy Sepulcher. Along the Via Dolorosa there are fourteen Stations of the Cross, which mark scenes of suffering during the successive stages of Jesus' journey to Golgotha. Some of these incidents are mentioned in the New Testament, while others appear in later traditions. The location of the Stations is indicated by signs placed along the Via Dolorosa.

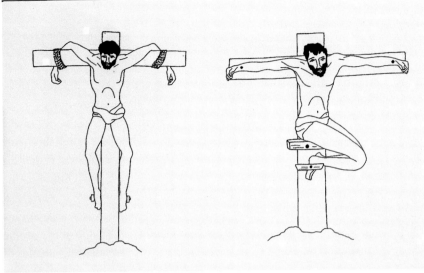

Proposed reconstructions of the Crucifixion

man (whose name, Johanan son of Hagakol, is engraved on the ossuary) were examined by anthropologists, who suggested two possible modes of crucifixion. Neither of these proposals corresponds to the manner in which the Crucifixion is traditionally depicted in paintings or sculpture.

We will descend from Golgotha and pass by the stone ◆5 on which Jesus' body was anointed with oil after he was taken down from the cross before being buried. According to some Christian traditions, this is Station XIII of the Cross, and not the place where Mary stood.

6   THE ROTUNDA

I N THE BYZANTINE PERIOD the rotunda which we have entered had a rounded dome, but this was replaced by the Crusaders with a dome in the shape of a truncated cone. This dome too was replaced in 1808 after a major fire had broken out in the church, and the new dome later underwent a number of renovations. The sepulcher of Jesus, which is situated in the center of the rotunda, is the fourteenth and final Station of the Cross. On both sides of the tomb ◆7, ornamented with an onion-shaped dome, we can discern elliptical holes in the walls. Through these holes the Holy Fire, which is miraculously ignited in the sepulcher on Easter, is passed forth to the masses of pilgrims tensely awaiting the performance of the miracle. The rock in which the tomb was hewn in the Second Temple period was later leveled when the area was prepared for the building of the church. Nothing remains of the rock-cut cave.

There are two chambers within the tomb: the first, the Chapel of the Angel, marks the place where an angel was revealed to the women who came to visit the grave three days after the burial of Jesus and found it empty, since Jesus had been resurrected (Luke 24:111). The inner chamber is the tomb itself. As we leave the tomb we see before us the Catholicon hall ◆8 which is held by the Greek Orthodox. Note especially the stone chalice on the floor of the hall. This is the

Tomb of Jesus

Omphalos marking the **center of the world** in Christian tradition

- Christianity assigned to the Church of the Holy Sepulcher certain Jewish traditions that were originally associated with the Temple Mount – namely that the **center of the world,** the burial site of Adam, the site of the binding for sacrifice of Isaac, and others. The transferral of these traditions from the Temple Mount to the Church of the Holy Sepulcher expresses the Christian view that regards this church as the new Temple.

(the Omphalos was recently shifted a few meters from where it had previously stood). We will walk around the rotunda and enter the small hall west of it  where the Syrian Christians conduct their prayers. A narrow entrance leads to a typical Second Temple period burial cave. In the beginning of the Christian era no importance was attributed to this cave, and the wall of the rotunda was built above it, which contributed to its preservation. Later Christian tradition has identified this spot as the tomb of Joseph of Arimathea, who donated a new tomb for the burial of Jesus (Mark 15:43). This tomb serves as proof that the site was used for burials in the Second Temple period.

We will return to the rotunda and enter the Catholic chapel ⑩ At its western end is a door behind which is Mary's Arch, that we saw on our way to the Church of the Holy Sepulcher. Upon leaving the chapel, we will ask permission to enter the room where the Catholics keep their vestments ⑪. Preserved in this room are the sword, cross, spurs, and a stone from the palace of Godfrey of Bouillon, the first Crusader king of Jerusalem.

Center of the world

We will now enter the ambulatory – the corridor encompassing the church. Here we see two colonnades supporting arches ⑫. The columns (some of them restored), bearing basket-like capitals, belong to the church found by the Crusaders found upon entering the city, and they bounded the open garden that had existed here. The row of columns bearing capitals with sculpted faunal depictions were added by the Crusaders when they closed off the garden and converted it into a chapel.

Continuing along the **ambulatory**, we descend the stairs to the Armenian Chapel of Helena ⑬ mother of the emperor Constantine (note the dozens of crosses carved alongside the stairs by pilgrims). On the floor of the chapel is a modern mosaic commemorating the massacre of the Armenians by the Turks

The term **ambulatory** is derived from the Latin verb *ambulo,* meaning "I walk." And indeed, we walk around the church in the ambulatory. The word ambulance is similarly derived.

during World War I. The mosaic depicts Armenian churches throughout the world surrounded by pairs of animals leaving Noah's Ark, that came to rest on Mount Ararat (identified as being in Armenia). Behind this chapel are the remains of an ancient quarry containing a small drawing of a ship with the Latin words: "*Domine ivimus* [Our Lord, we have come]," which were most likely inscribed by fourth-century pilgrims. Look up toward the dome of the chapel. We will later go up to the roof of the church and see the dome from the outside.

We will descend the stairs to the chapel dedicated to the discovery of the Cross ⑭. A Christian legend, several versions of which are known, relates that Helena, the mother of Constantine the Great, came to Jerusalem determined to find the location of the Cross. She assembled the Jews of the city and discovered that one of them, a person by the name of Judah, knew where Jesus had been

Crusader column capital in the ambulatory

Drawing of a ship discovered in the Church of the Holy Sepulcher

crucified but refused to reveal the site. Helena ordered that he be imprisoned, and threatened to starve him to death. A week later, the exhausted and frightened Judah agreed to lead Helena to the place of the Crucifixion. When she excavated the site, she found three crosses, because, as related in the New Testament, two thieves were crucified together with Jesus (Matthew 27:38).

In order to identify the **True Cross,** Helena ordered that the crosses be placed, one after the other, on the body of a young man who had just died. When the cross of Jesus was laid on the corpse, the young man came back to life. Judah, who was overcome by the manifest miracle, converted to Christianity and would later become the bishop of Jerusalem.

◆ Splinters from the **original**
◆ **Cross** are located in a large
◆ number of churches that
◆ are named after these
◆ remnants: Santa Cruz,
◆ Santa Croce, etc.

We will go back up to the ambulatory and enter beneath Golgotha, where we see the exposed bedrock.

THE CHAPEL OF ADAM 15

T HE CHAPEL, which is situated on the traditional **burial place of Adam**, exactly under the location of the Crucifixion, was much sought after as a burial site by the Catholic Crusader kings. The Greek Orthodox, however, who were hostile to the Catholics, destroyed these tombs at the first opportunity, during the course of the renovations carried out after the great fire in 1808. In 1867 Mark Twain visited the Church of the Holy Sepulcher. The famous author was very moved (in his own special way) by his encounter with the tomb of Adam, whom he thought was red-haired like himself:

◆ The **burial place of Adam** beneath the
◆ place of the Crucifixion is of
◆ theological significance in Christianity:
◆ Adam was born sinless, but he and
◆ his descendants have been tainted by
◆ the Original Sin of the eating of the
◆ fruit of the Tree of Knowledge. Jesus'
◆ death on the cross is perceived as
◆ atonement for the Original Sin,
◆ thereby creating the opportunity for
◆ salvation for all people.

There is no question that he is actually buried in the grave which is pointed out as his ... because it has never yet been proven that grave is not the grave in which he is buried. The tomb of Adam! How touching it was, here in a land of strangers, far away from home, and friends, and all who cared for me, thus to discover the grave of a blood relation.... I gave way to tumultuous emotion. I leaned upon a pillar and burst into tears. I deem it no shame to have wept over the grave of my poor dead relative. ... he did not live to see me ... And I alas, I did not live to see him. Weighed down by sorrow and disappointment, he died before I was born – six thousand brief summers before I was born (*The Innocents Abroad*, pp. 523-525).

We will exit the church and proceed via the southeastern doorway of the plaza to Shuk Ha-tsabaim Street, at the end of which is the Russian Alexander Nevsky Church 16. Visible in the basement of the church are remains of the columns of the Byzantine Cardo, one of the original entrances to the Byzantine Church of the Holy Sepulcher, and earlier remains of the Hadrianic temple of Aphrodite (see Tour 8). We will continue northward to Khan al-Zait Street, ascend the broad stairs to our left (parallel to the street), and walk along the winding alley to its end. Here we see a column attached to the wall denoting Station IX of the Cross, where Jesus fell for the third time on the way to Golgotha. To our right is the entrance of the Coptic church 🔟. We will ask permission to enter, and for a modest donation we will be able to carefully descend the rock-cut stairs that lead to a huge cistern hewn in the bedrock. This cistern apparently served as a reservoir for the temple of Aphrodite and the Byzantine Anastasis Church. After this, we will leave the church and pass through the entrance opposite us.

18   DEIR AL-SULTAN

WE ARE ON THE ROOF of the Chapel of Helena, that we visited earlier. The dome of the chapel is to our left. We will walk to the end of the courtyard and, after asking permission, go through the small opening on the left. We have entered a different world! Spread before us is a small African village of huts inhabited by Ethiopian monks. A single monk dwells in each meager hut. In the middle of the courtyard is a small garden – the "social center" – containing a large, ancient mulberry tree that was probably planted here in the early Ottoman period more than four hundred years ago. The Ethiopians, who formerly had "possession" of a small area of the Church of the Holy Sepulcher, were pushed out to the courtyard by the stronger communities, possibly as early as the sixteenth century. As we wander among the huts of the village, we will gain an idea of their ascetic humbleness and simplicity.

The Ethiopian precinct is called Deir al-Sultan (the Monastery of the Sultan),

Ethiopian holiday on the roof of the Chapel of Helena

after King Solomon, who is regarded by the Ethiopians as the founder of their royal dynasty (see Tour 19). In the Crusader period, this area contained the refectory and cloister of the monks of the **Augustinian Canonical Order**, and traces of the stone arches that stood here are still visible in the walls.

◆ The **Augustinian Canonical Order**
◆ was founded in the eleventh
◆ century, and its members
◆ undertook to live in accordance
◆ with regulations formulated in the
◆ spirit of the sermons of the Church
◆ Father St. Augustine.

At present, the roof of the Church of the Holy Sepulcher, like the Ethiopian chapels which we will shortly enter, is a bone of contention between the Ethiopian and Coptic communities, each claiming ownership of the site. In 1970 the matter was brought before an Israeli court, which ruled in favor of the Ethiopians. Following the signing of the peace treaty between Israel and Egypt, where most Copts live, the question of ownership was raised by the Egyptian government. The head of the Coptic church refuses to visit Israel until the property is returned to his community.

Painting in the Chapel of the Four Beasts

We will return to the courtyard surrounding the dome and walk to its southwestern corner. Here we pass through a low entrance that opens onto two Ethiopian chapels. The upper chapel is called the "Four Beasts" Chapel (Ezekiel 1:5), and the lower one, the "Angel Michael" Chapel. The style of both is characteristic of chapels of the Eastern, non-Catholic branch of Christianity. This is especially pronounced in the iconostasis, the reticulate wooden partition that separates the bema from the nave. There are some who claim that this partition is

Ethiopian monk in Deir al-Sultan

a vague allusion to the separation in the Temple between the Holy of Holies and the other parts. In the upper chapel, pay attention to the painting hanging on the wall, which depicts the visit of the Queen of Sheba to King Solomon. Some men in Solomon's entourage are portrayed as contemporary Hasidic Jews.

After leaving the chapel, we find ourselves once again at the entrance to the Church of the Holy Sepulcher. For a second time we exit through the southeastern entrance of the atrium, and walk along the street until we see to our right a blocked gate structure topped by an arch.

T HE PRESERVATION OF THE REMAINS of ancient buildings by incorporating them in new structures is not a modern invention. This method was already adopted a century ago in 1898 when the Germans built the massive Church of the Redeemer that stands before us. They incorporated in it the remains of the entrance gate of the St. Mary Latina church, which had been constructed by the Crusaders many centuries earlier. Look at the top of the arch and try to discern the details carved in it (although this is extremely difficult). The Crusader artist was commissioned to represent the months of the year, which he did by depicting the agricultural labors characteristic of them. Thus, for example, we see a reaper under the inscription "[Iu]nius" (that is, June), a person threshing grain in August, and someone harvesting grapes in September.

Ornamentation in the facade of the Church of St. Mary Latina

Symbol of the German Reich in the facade of the Church of St. Mary Latina

During the restoration and inauguration of the gate in 1898, the restorers engraved an eagle, the symbol of the German Reich, to the left of the arch, and added an armorial ensign on the right. These stones have undergone much weathering and the symbols now seem as if they were part of the original Crusader gate. This may serve as a warning for modern restoration architects to make a clear distinction between the restored structure and the adjoining modern additions, in order to prevent future confusion.

We will turn right, to the entrance of the Church of the Redeemer 20. Those of us who wish to may climb up to the top of the bell tower, for a view of the Old City. Evening concerts are held in the church (for details, see the bulletin board in the church).

Stone lion at the entrance to the Church of the Redeemer

We will continue south-ward along the street, and to our left we discover another doorway 21 decorated with a stone gable supported by two columns standing on a pair of lions, which apparently have survived from Crusader times. This is the entrance to the German Lutheran hostel, which contains the remains of a Crusader cloister incorporated in the late nineteenth-century German building.

The complex where we complete our tour is called Muristan (*bimaristan* is Persian for "hospital"). This was the residence of the Hospitaler knights, who had moved here from their previous abode on the Temple Mount. This Order, established during the First Crusade, is also called the **Order of St. John**, after John the Baptist. The church named after him, with its silver dome, stands here to the present day. These knights, entrusted with caring for the health of the Crusaders and the pilgrims, erected a hospital here.

Here our tour ends.

> ◆ The British branch of the **Order of St.**
> ◆ **John** founded the St. Johns'
> ◆ Ophthalmologic Hospital in Jerusalem in
> ◆ 1882, near the train station. Six years
> ◆ later the Order founded St. John's
> ◆ Ambulance service in Britain, which is
> ◆ still operative today.

From the Citadel to the Armenian Quarter

T HE IMPRESSIVE CHURCH of the Holy Sepulcher, which we visited in the preceding tour, was the building project that symbolized the essential sanctity of Jerusalem for the Christian Crusaders.

On this tour we will continue to encounter sacred sites that primarily commemorate famous events and figures in the annals of Christianity. We will also become acquainted with the German branch of the Order of Hospitalers, which built a hospital – where callous men served as nurses – in the city near the present-day Jewish Quarter. We will stroll through the centers of two of the non-Catholic Christian communities, the Monophysite Armenians and the Nestorian Syrians, which also were part of the city's diverse population.

While speaking of the city's inhabitants, we will attempt to learn something about their daily life: where, for example, did they purchase flour to bake their bread, or milk and eggs for breakfast? In addition to the city's permanent residents, many others also abided in the capital of the Crusader kingdom: visitors, merchants, and pilgrims. We will certainly want to know where the weary pilgrim could enjoy a cheap and satisfying lunch, and where was the best place to exchange the foreign coins he had brought with him for the local currency.

Nor will we ignore the Jewish aspect of life in the city. Although there was no Jewish community in Jerusalem during this period, except for a few individuals granted permission to dwell there at the pleasure of the Christian rulers', the Jewish traveler Benjamin of Tudela tells us of the wonderful tradition regarding the tombs of the Davidic line on Mount Zion, a tradition accepted to the present day.

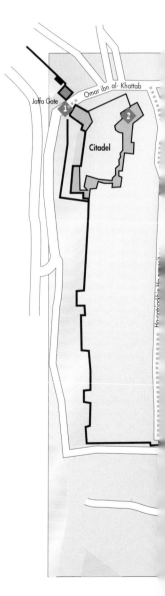

The route: the tour begins at Jaffa Gate, passes through the Jewish Quarter, continues to Mount Zion, and ends in the Armenian Quarter.

Duration of the tour: three to four hours.

Public transportation: buses nos. 3, 6,19, 20, 30, 38 to Jaffa Gate.

By private car: the parking lot in the Mamilla neighborhood (David's Village).

Visiting hours: Church of St. Mark: Mon–Sat: daytime hours. Prayers are conducted between 3:00 and 4:00 p.m. David's Tomb: Sun–Thur: 8:00 a.m.–6:00 p.m.; Friday: 8:00 a.m.–2:00 p.m.; Saturday: 8:00 a.m.–6:00 p.m. In the wintertime the site is closed one hour earlier.

Room of the Last Supper: all week: daytime hours.

Church of St. James: Mon–Sat: 3:00 p.m.–3:30 p.m. (during prayers)

Armenian Museum: Mon–Sat: 9:30 a.m.–5:00 p.m.

Note: modest dress is required.

David

Ha-shalshelet

St. Mark

Jewish Quarter

Misgav Ladach

Tiferet Israel

Jewish Quarter Road

Habad

Or Ha-hayyim

Ararat

Hayyei Olam

Beit El

Gilad

Mishmarot Ha-kehunah

Batei Mahase Square

Batei Mahase

Tiferet Yerushalayim Square

Ma-alot Ha-shalom

0   100   200 m

N

Jaffa Gate

JAFFA GATE, where we are standing, was built in the sixteenth century by the Ottoman sultan Suleiman the Magnificent. As early as the Crusader period, however, another gate, known as David's Gate, had stood here.

Most Crusader **maps** depict Jerusalem in the shape of a circle with its main streets intersecting to create the form of a cross. This model was probably influenced by the form of popular world maps in the Arab period that portray the world as an O-shaped body within which rivers form the letter T. Because of their form, such maps are known as "O-T maps" (also, these are the initials of the Latin *Orbis Terrarum* – circle of lands).

A visitor to Crusader Jerusalem could have been guided in his tours of the city by the descriptions of other travelers who had preceded him, but he would have been hard put to find a good city map. The contemporary **maps** depicting Jerusalem are generally unreliable, since their cartographers were influenced more by aesthetic and ideological considerations than the need to correspond to the reality. The most trustworthy map known to us from this period is the one kept in Cambrai, France, a reproduction of which appears on this page. Although this map, which was drawn in the twelfth century, depicts only the important buildings and main thoroughfares, it nevertheless provides us with a fairly good idea of the city's structure. And who knows – eight hundred years ago, a Crusader pilgrim may have stood where we are standing, with a copy of the map in his

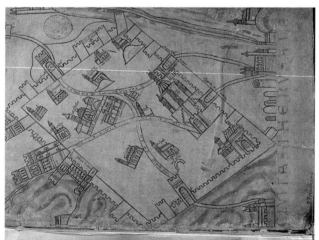

Cambrai map

hand, overcome by emotion at the thought of the adventure awaiting him in the holy city. Pay special attention to the tall gate tower in the upper portion of the map, with the inscription "Porta David," i.e., the David's Gate that was mentioned above. The artist even took pains to include the styled iron bolts that secured the gate.

We will proceed along the street to the stairs of the marketplace on David Street. The name of this street has not changed in the last eight hundred years, and in the Cambrai map it also appears as Via David (David Street). We will not enter the marketplace, but rather turn to the right, on a street that is not shown in the Cambrai map. To our right is the Citadel and David's Tower ❷ which is distinguished by its large stones (see Tour 30). David's Tower, whose base dates from the Herodian period, is also portrayed in the Cambrai map, with its name translated into Latin: Turris David. Its dimensions in the map undoubtedly reflect the impression made on the artist by the mighty tower. The Russian abbot Daniel, who visited Jerusalem seven years after the Crusader conquest, describes the strong impression left on him by a visit to the tower:

The tower that was also the residence of [King David] ... is built very high in an interesting manner of heavy stones.... It appears as if [made of] a single stone from its foundation up. It contains copious quantities of water, and has five gates of iron and two hundred steps leading to its top. It is virtually impregnable, and it is accounted the primary fortification of the city. It is heavily guarded, and it may be entered only under the closest supervision. By the grace of God, although I was not entitled to do so, I was permitted to enter this holy tower.

Note the moat protecting the Citadel wall, in which we see a glacis (sloping stone wall) resting on the lower part of the tower wall. The glacis was apparently built by the Crusaders to keep the enemy away from the wall and expose him to the arrows that rained down from above. What did the moat, glacis, wall, and tower protect? Perusal of the Cambrai map provides the answer: close to the tower we see a large structure called *curia regis*, which was probably the palace of the Crusader kings. The palace was located in the area of the present-day Citadel.

We will continue walking along the road, and turn left into St. James Street. The wall to our left ◆3 is the southern wall of the Crusader Church of St. Thomas. The church is in ruins, and we cannot enter it. From here we will advance and turn left along Ararat Street to Ha-ashurim Street.

ST. MARK'S MONASTERY 4

Ha-ashurim Street

WE HAVE ARRIVED at the center of one of the small communities in Jerusalem: the Syrian-Orthodox Christians. They are also known as Jacobites, after Jacob Baradai who was the leader of the community in Syria during one of its most trying times, after its repression in the sixth century by the Byzantine emperors. Incidentally, some people erroneously call this the "Assyrian" community. The Assyrians are another community, also called **the Nestorians,** who split off from mainstream Christianity in the fourth century. As a result of this error, the street on which the church is located is named "Ha-ashurim Street" – the Street of the Assyrians.

On entering the courtyard of the monastery compound, we may have the opportunity to see one of the priests wearing their distinctive headwear: a sort of black hood with twelve embroidered white crosses, corresponding to the number of Jesus' apostles. In the courtyard we can see cross vaults, attesting to the establishment of the compound in the Crusader period. These vaults continue into

◆ The **Nestorian** Christian communities follow the doctrine of Nestorius (fifth century), that the divine and human natures in the personality of Jesus are distinct, and therefore Mary was only the mother of the Messiah, but not of God. This interpretation was banned by the Church at the Council of Ephesus in 431.

Arch in St. Mark's Monastery

In the Church of St. Mark

Ornamentation in the Church of St. Mark

the church facing us, which we will now enter. According to a Syrian tradition, Jesus gathered his disciples here, and it was here that the Last Supper was held, following which Jesus was seized by the Roman soldiers and brought to trial. (This tradition is not accepted by the Roman Catholics, who believe the site of the Last Supper to be on Mount Zion, as we will learn in the continuation of the tour.) The Syrians believe that the apostle Mark (i.e. John), to whom Jesus entrusted his mother Mary before his death on the cross, dwelt in this house, and that Mary lived here after the Crucifixion.

It is believed that when Mary came to live here, she brought with her the font in which she had been baptized as an infant; this font is preserved in the monastery. A picture of Mary, which the Syrians claim was painted by Luke, one of the four authors of the Gospels, is displayed in the center of the southern wall of the church. Note especially the bases of the columns that are dated to the Byzantine period. On one of the columns we discern a sixth-century inscription written in the script of the religious works of the Syrian-Orthodox, who speak a dialect of Aramaic. The letters bear a slight resemblance to ancient Hebrew script. The Syrian community teaches its children about their ancient heritage and instructs them in Aramaic and their special script, so that they will not be forgotten.

The largest of the Syrian communities is in India, where they are called St. Thomas Christians. Other communities are found in Iraq, Syria, Jordan, Holland, Sweden, and New York. One of the bishops of the Jerusalem community purchased the first Dead Sea

Scrolls that were discovered in Qumran in 1947, and afterwards sold them to Professor E. L. Sukenik of the Hebrew University in Jerusalem. The small Jerusalem community, numbering only a few dozen souls, maintains not only the monastery in which we find ourselves, but also a small but important chapel in the Church of the Holy Sepulcher and a small chapel in Mary's Tomb in the Kidron Valley.

When the small group of Syrian churchmen go from their monastery to pray in the Church of the Holy Sepulcher, the **kavasses** preceding them beat loudly with their staffs, both to clear the way and to draw attention to the sacred procession. When the procession of the neighboring Armenians marches along the same route, they need not make so much noise, as their delegation is much larger.

We will leave the monastery, turn right to Habad Street, descend the stairs to the Cardo, and turn north on it to the roofed section with modern stores on the western side and a row of sealed vaults on the east.

Beginning in the Ottoman period, the **kavasses** (*qawass* in Arabic means bowman) accompanied the heads of the communities in the city wherever they went, and were entrusted with their security. They lead the processions in which the heads of the communities participate. In the past, two kavasses also accompanied the head of the Sephardi community in Jerusalem (the Rishon Le-Zion). The kavasses used to wear magnificent costumes, which looked like the dress uniforms of the Ottoman army. As time passed, they began to wear more simple garb, but the traditional hat and staff (and at times a sword) have been retained.

CRUSADER SHOPS AND MARKETS 5

THE CARDO (see Tour 9) had its beginnings in the Roman-Byzantine period, when it was the main thoroughfare of Jerusalem, and its central section was not covered. In the Crusader period sections of the early Cardo were roofed, the street was narrowed and shop structures were built in it, creating bazaars and marketplaces. The pointed arches of the shops around us attest to their construction in the Crusader period. During the archaeological excavations here, the western arches were cleared of their accumulated debris and refuse, and they once again became shops, as they had been eight centuries earlier. We will proceed northward along the Cardo, passing archaeological finds from the First and Second Temple and Byzantine periods (explanations are provided by the signs along the way), until we come to the David Street intersection 6. To our north we see three markets: Shuk Ha-katsavim (the Butchers' Market), Shuk Ha-basamim (the Spice-handler's Market), and Shuk Ha-tsorfim (the Gold and Silversmiths' Market), which occupy the same location as their counterparts in the Crusader period (and possibly even earlier).

Scene in an Old City market

The Spice-handlers' Market was the central market, and parallel to the Market of Bad Cookery. This name was given because of the unpleasant odors that emanated from the cheap restaurants that sold food to the pilgrims. An inhabitant of the city who wanted eggs for breakfast would turn west at the intersection onto David Street to the poultry market, which supplied dairy products, chickens, fish, and eggs. If he needed bread, he would have to walk to the end of the poultry market, head to the north of the Citadel where, close to the city wall, he would enter the grain market, with its adjoining small flour mill that served customers. There was also a special market in the city that sold only fish. Obviously, the markets were not intended only for the residents of the city but also for the many visitors, such as pilgrims or merchants from the wealthy cities of Italy. The stalls of the money changers were located alongside the market, to provide these merchants with local coinage. People from many nations lived in Crusader Jerusalem: Italians, Spaniards, Frenchmen, Germans, Englishmen, Syrians, Armenians, and even Hungarians. The city was bustling and crowded, and, it may be assumed, a bit too "fragrant" for modern sensibilities.

We will retrace our steps southward along the Cardo to its open section, go up to Jewish Quarter Road, cross the central square of the Jewish Quarter, and proceed to the end of Tiferet Israel Street, opposite the entrance to the ruins of the Church of St. Mary of the Germans.

7 CHURCH OF ST. MARY OF THE GERMANS

Misgav Ladach Street

THE HOSPITALER ORDER to which we were introduced in Tour 12 was led by the French, but some of its knights were German who began to seek independence for themselves in 1128. Their separate order was officially recognized by the Pope only in 1198, when Jerusalem was already under Muslim Ayyubid rule. Before this, in the twelfth century, when they were still in the city, the German Hospitalers established a center for themselves where they could speak their own language and follow their own customs. This center included a church, a medical center, and a hostel for the sick, the weary, and ordinary visitors.

The ruined hall that we entered from the street was the church of this compound. It has a basilican plan; note the two rows of columns that supported the ceiling and divided the hall lengthwise into a nave and two flanking aisles. The beautiful capitals, some of which are still affixed to the walls while others lie on the floor of the church, are called "elbow" capitals, since they jut out from the wall in the form of an elbow. The capitals are ornamented with a stylized leaf decoration, and they generally support a pointed arch. The

"Elbow" capital in the Church of St. Mary of the Germans

lodgings for pilgrims were located on the uppermost level, now occupied by a residential structure to the north of the church. To the south of the church was the two-story hospital. We will descend to it via the narrow staircase. You can picture to yourself the wooden divans covered by straw mattresses that must have been located here for the patients in the hospital, who were attended by male nurses.

Church of St. Mary of the Germans

Modern statue of a Hospitaler knight

After the Crusader period, the **hospital** became a place of both prayer and residence (*khankah*) for Muslim dervishes. As time passed, the structure fell into disuse, until it was mentioned once again in the survey

◆ The care of patients in medieval **hospitals** was usually limited to rest, heating
◆ (not always), and good food. The "diagnosis" of patients was made by the
◆ gatekeeper at the entrance, when, to be on the safe side, he would also
◆ hear the deathbed confession customarily recited by Christians. The halls
◆ and rooms contained beds, bedding, lamps, and at times a personal chest.
◆ Operations were generally not performed in the hospitals, but rather by
◆ private physicians for a fee.

conducted by the British in Jerusalem in 1867–69. Only a century later, after the Six-Day War, was the site excavated, cleared, and restored. We can rest for a while in the pleasant park at the bottom of the site.

We will retrace our steps and turn south on Jewish Quarter Road toward Zion Gate. At the turn in the road we will stop and look down at the remains of the reconstructed gate tower ◆8◆. A strange story is connected with this structure: as an inscription found here testifies, the tower, which defended the southern gate of the city, was built in 1212 by the Ayyubid al-Malik al-Mu'azzam, the nephew of Saladin who routed the Crusaders. It is known from the testimony of Arab historians (such as Ibn Wasil) that seven years after its construction, he ordered the destruction of the tower, along with all the city's fortifications. Ibn Wasil explains this surprising act by claiming that al-Mu'azzam, who greatly feared a renewed invasion by the Crusaders, preferred to demolish the city walls so as not to provide the Crusader forces with an easily defensible city.

On exiting from Zion Gate, we find ourselves on Mount Zion.

Remains of the Ayyubid Zion Gate

MOUNT ZION

I N THE BIBLE the name Zion is an appellation for the Temple Mount and Jerusalem, and only in the Middle Ages did it come to denote Mount Zion. Topographically, Mount Zion is part of the western hill of Jerusalem that was included in the city in the late First Temple and Second Temple periods, and was inhabited by the wealthy classes.

The mount is sanctified in both the Jewish and Muslim traditions as the burial place of King David, and in the Christian tradition as the site where the Last Supper was conducted, along with other events recorded in the New Testament. The Hagia Sion Church was built here in the Byzantine period. This church was destroyed by the Persians in 614 and later rebuilt by the Crusaders as the Church of St. Mary on Mount Zion, whose monastery included the Room of the Last Supper. The church was razed by al-Malik al-Mu'azzam as part of the "defensive measures" he took against the Crusader threat.

The renewal of Jewish settlement in Jerusalem after the Crusader period by Nahmanides (see Tour 15) most probably was centered on Mount Zion. Nahmanides founded a synagogue here, and the Jewish settlement extended from the Mount to the area of the present-day Jewish Quarter. Muslim hegemony of Mount Zion was established in the fifteenth and sixteenth centuries when the Franciscans were expelled from it. In the nineteenth and twentieth centuries, churches were built and Christian cemeteries established on the Mount

We will walk southward along the path. To our right is the massive stone structure of the Neo-Romanesque Dormition Abbey ⟨10⟩ The church memorializes the site where Mary mother of Jesus fell into eternal slumber (*dormire* in Latin means to sleep; the name is a combination of this root + Zion). Next to the cafeteria adjoining the church are a few remains of the Byzantine and Crusader churches that stood here. The current church structure, erected in 1910 by German Catholics, boasts a large and impressive modern mosaic depicting the Zodiac, symbols of Christian saints, and portrayals of prophets and saints.

To the left is an arch ornamented with a zigzag pattern. We will pass through it and ascend the stairs to the hall on the second floor. On the way we see a thick stone column standing close to one of the doorways. This column may possibly have belonged to the Byzantine Hagia Sion Church. We will now enter the Room of the Last Supper.

11 ROOM OF THE LAST SUPPER

O N THE LAST PASSOVER EVE of his life, Jesus arranged to celebrate the Seder night, in which the Paschal lamb is eaten. The New Testament relates:

Then came the day of the Unleavened Bread, on which the passover lamb had to be sacrificed. So Jesus sent Peter and John, saying, "Go and prepare the passover for

Room of the Last Supper

us, that we may eat it." They said to him, "Where will you have us prepare it?" He said to them, "Behold, when you have entered the city, a man carrying a jar of water will meet you; follow him into the house which he enters, and tell the householder, 'The Teacher says to you, Where is the guest room, where I am to eat the passover with my disciples?' And he will show you a large upper room furnished; there make ready." And they went, and found it as he had told them; and they prepared the passover (Luke 22:7-13).

Catholic tradition identifies that large upper room with the hall in which we are now standing. The New Testament further relates that in that upper room Jesus had his disciples drink the wine and eat the bread, which in Christianity came to symbolize the blood and flesh of Jesus, of which Christians partake during the Mass. The Latin name of the hall, Coenaculum, means "dining room."

Capital with sculpted pelicans

The structure itself is distinguished by fine cross vaults, possibly dating from after the Crusader period. It may have been built in the thirteenth century. Modern researchers have advanced the hypothesis that the structure is part of the church that stood here in the twelfth century. To the right of the entrance and painted on the wall is a heraldic shield containing the symbol of Regensburg in Germany.

As in David's Tomb, which we will shortly enter, here too we see a Muslim *mihrab* (prayer alcove) in the south wall facing Mecca, and the remains of a Muslim dome on the southwestern side of the hall.

Pay special attention to the capital of one of the columns of the Muslim dome. This is an early capital, possibly of Crusader origin, with an engraving of three **pelican chicks** pecking at their mother's heart. According to an ancient belief, the mother pelican sacrifices herself to feed her young, but later returns to life. This led to the pelican becoming a distinctive Christian symbol, exemplifying Jesus sacrificing himself for mankind and being resurrected after three days.

Leaving the Room of the Last Supper we return to the path, turning south on it to its end. We will pass through an arch decorated with a pulvinate pattern, and immediately turn left into the inner courtyard of David's Tomb.

◆ The idea of **pelican chicks** eating their
◆ mother's heart is already described in
◆ the pre-Christian bestiary literature. This
◆ story may have originated in the fact
◆ that the pelican chicks stick their heads
◆ into their mother's mouth to eat the
◆ masticated food stored in the pouch of
◆ her bill, which from a distance may give
◆ the impression that they are pecking
◆ away at the mother's internal organs.

HE INNER COURTYARD of the David's Tomb compound is encompassed by fourteenth-century vaults and was part of the cloister of the large Crusader monastery that existed until the sixteenth century, when the Franciscans were expelled from Mount Zion. From that time onward, the place served as a *khan*, or

Courtyard of David's Tomb

Interior of David's Tomb

roadside inn, for use by caravans that arrived at the city after the closing of the gates. We will enter the building, cross the synagogue, and enter the hall of David's Tomb. To be precise, the structure is the crypt below the Room of the Last Supper, and in its southern wall is a later Muslim prayer alcove facing Mecca. Beyond the wall, to the north, we see the large tombstone with its embroidered coverlet. Ashkenazi Torah scroll crowns from European Jewish communities that perished in the Holocaust stand on the coverlet, along with Sephardi Torah scrolls within wooden and metal cases. A rosette and leaves, remnants from the Crusader period, are engraved on the tombstone itself. Pay special attention to the finely drafted large stones of the northern wall and of the alcove built in it. Excavations conducted below the floor of the hall revealed remains of a mosaic reminiscent of the ones discovered in synagogues of the Byzantine period. There may have been a synagogue here, one of the seven mentioned in the writings of a French pilgrim known as the Bordeaux Pilgrim, who visited Mount Zion in 333. If so, the alcove may have housed its Torah Ark.

The earliest Jewish source mentioning the Tomb of David on Mount Zion is the Jewish traveler **Benjamin of Tudela** (1170), who tells of a miraculous event that befell two laborers engaged in construction work on Mount Zion, on the orders of the Patriarch of Jerusalem, fifteen years earlier:

Rabbi Benjamin ben Jonah, who came from the city of **Tudela** in Spain, spent the years 1165–73 on a lengthy journey. He left Spain and traveled through France, Italy, Greece, Turkey, Eretz Israel, Syria, Mesopotamia, the Persian Gulf, and Egypt. He recorded his experiences in a diary which is of great historical value. The reason for his setting forth on such a journey is not known. According to one opinion, he was a merchant; others, however, maintain that his goal of journeying to Eretz Israel coincided with his natural curiosity and wanderlust.

They were taking out the stones. They set up a stone, and they found there the mouth of a cave. One said to his fellow: "Let us go in and see if there is any money there."

They walked through the entrance of the cave until they came to a large palace built on marble columns covered with silver and gold. Before it was a gold table, scepter, and crown – this was the tomb of King David. To its left was the tomb of King Solomon as well, and all the kings of Judah are buried there. And in this place there are closed chests the contents of which are known to no man. The two men ran to enter the palace, but a tempestuous wind came from the mouth of the cave and smote them, and they fell to the ground as if dead, where they lay until the evening. And behold, a wind came and screamed in a loud voice, as if it were a human voice: "Arise, leave this place!" ... They went to the Patriarch ... and the Patriarch ordered that this place be sealed, and to hide it from humans to this day (A. Yaari, *Masa'ot Eretz Yisrael* [Eretz Israel Journeys], pp. 41-42).

Is it possible that David and the kings of his dynasty are buried on Mount Zion? The Bible attests that most of the kings of this dynasty were buried in the City of David (which is located south of the Temple Mount), and therefore their tombs cannot be located here. Nonetheless, modern research has raised the possibility that the last kings of the dynasty, whom we know were not interred in the City of David, were indeed laid to rest on Mount Zion. According to another opinion, it is not inconceivable that at least some of the monarchs buried in the City of David were later reburied on Mount Zion. This view is based on the extant tombstone of Uzziah king of Judah, which tells of the transfer of his bones from one place to another (see Tour 10).

Candle lighting in the courtyard of David's Tomb

We will return to the courtyard of the structure, turn right and then immediately left, and ascend the stairs to the roof of the building for a view of the entire Old City. Afterwards we will descend, leave the compound, walk back through Zion Gate and turn left along the road. To our left is the Old City wall, and to our right, the wall of the Armenian Quarter, which is the only quarter in the Old City enclosed by a wall. Further along to our right we see the entrance to the Armenian Museum 13, which documents (mainly with facsimiles and photographs) the treasures of the Armenian community. We will continue to the next gate on the right that leads into the Armenian Quarter and, if permitted by the monks, will enter the courtyard of St. James' Cathedral.

The Armenian Quarter

THE ARMENIANS are one of the oldest Christian communities, predating the emperor Constantine's recognition of Christianity in the early fourth century. One of the **Monophysite** communities, they come from Greater Armenia (bordering on Russia and Turkey) and Lesser Armenia (Cilicia, a small kingdom in what is now central Turkey). The Armenians were well represented in Jerusalem as early as the Byzantine period, as attested to by the beautiful Armenian mosaic floors and remains of monasteries from that period discovered in the city. Following the Muslim conquest, the notables of the Armenian community received a document guaranteeing the rights and security of the community. This document, which is preserved in the Armenians' archives, was signed by no less a dignitary than the caliph Omar.

The **Monophysite** Christians believe that Jesus had only a single, divine nature, while his human aspect was merely for appearance's sake. The sect's name is derived from its basic tenet: *monos* – one, *physis* – nature. The Monophysite view was banned by the Church at the Council of Chalcedon in 451.

The community experienced its greatest floruit in the Crusader period, thanks to its good connections with the Crusaders. The marriages of some Crusader kings to Armenian women and visits by Armenian princes to Jerusalem contributed to the firm establishment of the community and its ability to undertake its major building project: St. James' Cathedral, where we are standing. Armenian pilgrims and immigrants came to Jerusalem in all periods. This was the case after the Ottoman conquest in the sixteenth century, when Armenians were brought to the city on the initiative of the sultan Suleiman the Magnificent, and in the twentieth century, when many refugees, survivors of the Turkish massacre, arrived here. Families of Armenian ceramicists came to Jerusalem in the 1920s upon the initiative of Ronald Storrs, the governor of the city, in order to assist replating the Dome of the Rock with ceramic tiles.

In contrast to other Christian communities in Jerusalem, many of whose congregants are local Arabs, the Armenian community has preserved its national "purity" – one cannot be affiliated with the Armenian Church without belonging to the Armenian people and accepting its culture. The church named after St. James commemorates two Christian saints by this name who died for their faith. One was the brother of Jesus of Nazareth and the first bishop of Jerusalem, and the other was the apostle James the Greater (the brother of the apostle John) who fell victim to Herod Antipas' sword (Acts 12:2). James the Greater's head was severed and buried here, while his body was interred where he frequently preached, in Spain. The tomb containing the remains of James' body became an important pilgrimage site in medieval Europe, and the Spanish city of Santiago (= St. James) de Compostela was built around it. The differences between the two saints were blurred and they merged in various traditions.

Before entering the church, take note of the engraved stone tablets bearing Armenian inscriptions. The tablets incorporated in the facade of the church were donated by visiting pilgrims. To our right we see wooden boards and iron sheets held by chains. These devices, known as *nakos* or *simandron*, replaced the church bells during the period when the Ottoman authorities forbade the ringing of the bells. These would be struck with special staves in order to summon the public to prayers.

Ceremony in the Cathedral of St. James

We will pass through the entrance whose pointed arch shape – like the pointed head-wear of the Armenian clergy – is meant to remind us of the shape of Mount Ararat. The church still retains its basilican plan from Crusader times and is roofed by a large central dome. Pay special attention to the columns: some bear capitals with engravings of fauna, a feature characteristic of Crusader capitals.

Opposite us in the eastern wall, above the altar, is a seventeenth-century throne dedicated to James the brother of Jesus, and alongside it is a simpler throne on which the Armenian Patriarch sits during services. The Patriarch may sit on the major throne only once a year, for the ceremony dedicated to the latter. We will pass through the entrance in the southern wall leading to the chapel dedicated to the city of Echmiadzin, where Jesus was revealed to Gregory, patron saint of the Armenians who influenced them to accept the Christian faith. In the Crusader period the entrance through which we passed had been the original entrance to the church, and in its inner part we can discern the familiar Crusader pulvinate ornamentation. Only in the seventeenth century was the original entrance closed, when it became a chapel. The fine bluish ceramic tiles decorating the chapel were brought here from Kutahya, Turkey, in the eighteenth century by the Patriarch Gregory, known as "the Chainbearer." During his time, the Armenian community found itself in financial straits because of heavy debts and the burden of taxes. The Patriarch decided to take an exceptional step to arouse public opinion in Armenia and obtain contributions to save the Jerusalem community: he hung a heavy iron chain around his neck and walked through Armenia in this fashion for four years. This unconventional "show" proved to be very successful as many hearts and purses were opened to the energetic Patriarch. The sum that was collected sufficed not only to cover the community's financial obligations, but also made possible the restoration of Armenian religious buildings in Jerusalem and the encompassing of the entire Armenian Quarter with a wall. These donations also served for the purchase of 8,000 ceramic tiles, which were also used in the ornamentation of the Echmiadzin Chapel.

We will leave the chapel and go to the exit from the church. On the way, take a look at the doorways in the northern wall. One of them, with wooden doors finely crafted with mother of pearl and tortoise-shell ornamentations, leads to the St. James Chapel where, according to tradition, the saint's head is buried. This chapel is the most sacred place in the church.

We will exit to the street and turn right to Jaffa Gate, where the tour ends.

The rule of the Ayyubid Muslims in Egypt came to an end in 1250, when they were replaced as the ruling dynasty by the Mamluks, the commanders of the Ayyubid army. In 1260 the Mamluks conquered Palestine, and during the course of the ensuing three decades they drove the last of the Crusaders from the country, particularly from the coastal plain.

The Arabic word mamluk means "slave," and the Mamluks, who were of Central Asian origin, were sold in their youth by slave traders to the Ayyubid Muslim rulers of Egypt to serve in their army. Along with their rigorous military training, they were also instructed in the fundamentals of Islam, to which they converted. As time passed, the status of the Mamluks would radically change, and they became the ruling nobility in Egypt, Syria, and Eretz Israel. In this period, all of Eretz Israel suffered from neglect, and large parts of it, especially the coastal cities, were left in ruins so that they would be indefensible if the Crusaders were to invade the coasts and gain control of these cities.

The ruined walls of Jerusalem were similarly not rebuilt, most probably for this same reason. The city was distant from the major roads and had a relatively inferior status. Its religious standing, however, was enhanced in this period, and the Temple Mount and its surroundings experienced a surge of construction, with the establishment of schools for religious studies. These and other charitable and religious institutions were filled with scholars of Islam and Muslim mystics. Hostels were erected in the city, as well as grand tombs, all constructed in the unique and rich Mamluk style. We learn of the character of the city in this period mainly from the descriptions provided by the Jerusalem historian, the qadi (judge) Mujir al-Din. The years of Mamluk rule were characterized by peace and tranquility. The city was not encompassed by walls, and through its streets passed many Muslim pilgrims from all parts of the Arab world, for whom religious colleges, hostels, and places for seclusion and prayer were built.

After some ninety years of Christian rule, in which Jews were forbidden to live in the city, the Mamluks permitted them to settle in Jerusalem. It seems that they took up residence in the vicinity of Mount Zion. A small Christian community also lived in Jerusalem at this time, partly around the Church of the Holy Sepulcher and partly in the Mount Zion area. An important source regarding the renewal of the Jewish community in the city is a letter sent by Nahmanides to his son in 1267, in which he describes the sorry state of Eretz Israel and its Jewish inhabitants. This was after the Mongol invasion of Eretz Israel in 1260, which left ruin and destruction in its wake, before being eventually repelled by the Mamluks. Many Jews came to the city, including Eshtori ha-Parhi, whose writings and descriptions of the country constitute an important source for our understanding and knowledge of the period. Even though Jews were permitted to settle in the city once again, the Mamluks exhibited a rigid attitude toward minorities, and enacted special legislation against them, such as the obligation to dress in distinctive garb.

For a map of Jerusalem in this period see p. 212.

MAMLUK PERIOD

Mamluk Buildings

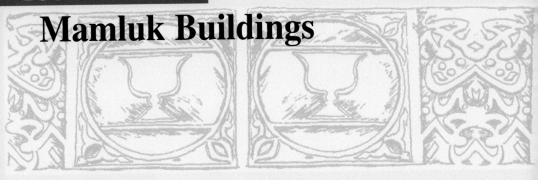

JERUSALEM IN THE MAMLUK PERIOD was a partially walled city on the periphery of the empire. Despite the secondary rank that the city held, entire streets, religious buildings, and bathhouses were built in it, reflecting the investment of large sums of money and much decorative skill.

What explanation can be given for the massive construction in the city at that time? This phenomenon undoubtedly had its roots in the Muslim conception of Jerusalem as the third most holy city, after Mecca and Medina. This building activity, however, was also motivated by other factors, that we will learn about during the tour. The major construction effort was concentrated on the Temple Mount (see Tour 11), in the adjoining areas to the west and north, and in extensive parts of the area now known as the Muslim Quarter, which was built and fashioned in its present layout in the Ayyubid and Mamluk periods.

A series of extensive vaults was built over the low area to the west of the Western Wall, on which streets leading to the Temple Mount were laid, flanked by dwellings, mosques, and *madrasa*s (religious colleges). This raised the ground level outside the Temple Mount to that of its plaza.

On this tour we will visit a Mamluk khan, glimpse the madrasas of the period, learn of the Mamluks' methods for evading the strict inheritance laws and become acquainted with the later history of some of these structures.

Some Mamluk buildings are currently being used for various purposes such as dwellings or store-rooms, while others are in a state of neglect.

We will walk down from Jaffa Gate to the beginning of Ha-shalshelet (The Chain) Street, which is the continuation of David Street.

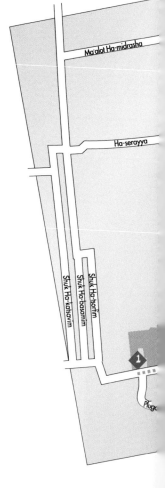

The route: the tour begins at Khan al-Sultan on Ha-shalshelet Street, and continues along this street. From there we go down to al-Wad and Sha'ar Ha-barzel Streets, and end the tour on Ma'alot Ha-midrasha Street.

Duration of the tour: about two hours.

Public transportation: buses nos. 3, 6, 19, 20, 30 to Jaffa Gate; no. 38 (minibus) to the gates of the Citadel. Enter the Old City, go down David Street, and continue on Ha-shalshelet Street to Khan al-Sultan.

By private car: The Mamilla neighborhood (David's Village) parking lot.

Note: modest dress is required.

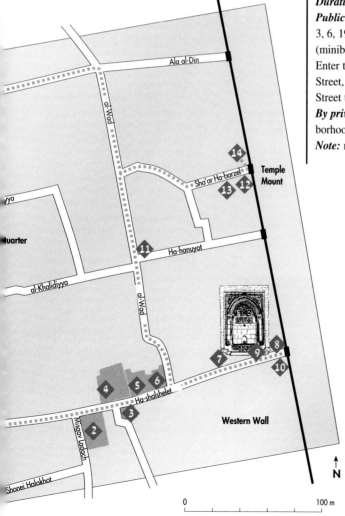

Ala al-Din

al-Wad

14

Sha'ar Ha-barzel

Temple Mount

13 12

'ya

Quarter

11 Ha-hanuyot

al-Khalidiyya

al-Wad

7 9 8

10

4 5 6

Ha-shalshelet

3

Misgav Ladach

2

Western Wall

Shonei Halakhot

0   100 m

N

Ha-shalshelet Street

ROM HA-SHALSHELET STREET we enter the long passageway leading through the ancient *khan* or inn (hotel), for merchants and wayfarers who came to the city. The royal khan was built in 1386/7 by order of the Mamluk sultan Barquq, the first Mamluk sultan of Circassian origin. Barquq sought to improve the city's condition, expressed in the civil building projects he undertook for the public welfare. Thus, for example, he built the Sultan's Pool and repaired the aqueduct bringing water from the Arrub spring to the city (see Tour 7).

The establishment of the khan at this location, very close to the market center of Jerusalem, undoubtedly contributed to the commercial life of the city. The Jerusalem judge **Mujir-al-Din**, who lived in the city in the late fifteenth century, relates that the khan was a great commercial success, and its annual revenues from providing lodging and services for the merchants, in the amount of four hundred *dinars*, were used for the maintenance of al-Aqsa mosque.

The covered passageway formerly contained a dedicatory inscription des-

David Street. Painting by Gustav Bauernfeind (nineteenth century)

- In 1495–96 the Jerusalem judge **Mujir-al-Din** wrote a detailed history of Jerusalem and Hebron, in which he described dozens of sites, streets, and markets in the city as well as the structures on the Temple Mount. This work is exceptional, because writers in the Mamluk period did not give detailed documentation to Eretz Israel and its cities, relating to them rather as part of Syria. In the period of Jordanian rule, a tombstone was erected for this historian at the foot of the Mount of Olives, next to the Church of Mary's Tomb.

cribing the construction of the khan by Barquq. In the upper stories flanking the

passageway we see porches with decorated bases, above which are the entrances to small rooms that were used as lodgings or shops. At the end of the passageway, on the left, is a narrow staircase leading to the porches. We can go up the stairs and gain an impression of the humbleness of the rooms, whose only source of light and air is the square opening

Khan al-Sultan

above the doors. Some claim that the passageway was already built in the Crusader period and was later incorporated in the khan of Barquq. We exit from the passageway to the khan's large courtyard, that is surrounded by rooms on two stories. It seems that the rooms on the first floor served as storerooms and stalls for animals, while the merchants themselves used the rooms on the second floor during their stay in the city.

In the northern wall of the courtyard, between the two arches, is an Arabic inscription from 1736, the year in which the khan apparently underwent renovations. Turn around to the exit. On the way out, note the large wooden beam at the top of the gate, with sockets for the pivots of the missing door. The protrusion of the gate's arch protected the pivots, only allowing the door to open inward. If the gates of the khan had to be closed quickly because of some external threat, this could be done from inside, with no need for anyone to go outside and expose himself to danger.

We will return to Ha-shalshelet Street and walk down it until we pass the corner of Misgav Ladach Street.

MADRASA AL-TASHTAMURIYYA 2

Ha-shalshelet Street, corner of Misgav Ladach Street

B EFORE US is a *madrasa* that was built in 1382/3 by the emir Tashtamur. He served the Mamluk sultans so successfully in the second half of the fourteenth century that Sultan Barquq married his daughter. As often happened, however, Tashtamur later fell into disfavor with his masters and for some

unknown reason was arrested and sent to prison in Alexandria. When he was released, his position improved considerably and he was sent to live as a deposed emir (*batal* in Arabic) in Damietta, Egypt. He was later appointed governor of Safed for a certain period. In 1382, when he was 48 years old, the emir grew weary of the perversity of imperial politics whose honey and gall he had tasted. He resigned from his duties, and asked to reside in Jerusalem, with no official position. Tashtamur lived in the city for about two years, until his death at the age of 50; he was buried in a room of the building that he had constructed, which also contains a *mihrab* (an alcove showing the direction for prayer). Tashtamur's son is also interred here. This is a good opportunity to learn one of the reasons for the many Mamluk building projects in Jerusalem, despite the city's inferior political status.

Entrance to Madrasa al-Tashtamuriyya

According to Mamluk law, a son could not inherit his father's property, and it was feared that after the latter's death his possessions would be confiscated by the authorities. The Mamluks therefore sought means to overcome this problem. One way was construction in Jerusalem. A Mamluk father would erect some building in the city and dedicate it as a *waqf* (religious trust), since the authorities would usually refrain from confiscating waqf structures. The father would then appoint his son as custodian or financial director of the waqf, thus ensuring the son's economic future. In the process, Jerusalem benefited from many construction projects.

The structure before us contains a number of architectural elements characteristic of many Mamluk buildings. Stone "benches" flank the entrance. On the lintel appears a geometric pattern (guilloche), carved in the stone, and in its upper part is a sort of concave semi-dome, and drop-like *mukarnas* ornamentations.

The term *waqf* has two meanings: stoppage/cessation, and also trust. The reference is to the "stoppage" of the financial transfer of a certain property, and its dedication for a declared purpose, usually charity. A waqf can be either a family or a public trust. The administration of the Jerusalem Waqf is currently responsible for waqf properties intended for public purposes, such as mosques, holy sites, schools, orphanages, etc. One of its major sources of income is the entrance fee to the mosques.

The entrance area is fringed by a cornice, as are the pair of windows to its west and next to it are other characteristic decorative elements: iron bars arranged in a grid pattern with spheres at the connections, and the dedicatory inscription dating the construction of the madrasa, around which is a gray and white guilloche.

The tombstones of Tashtamur and his son are located behind the windows (the tomb structure is called *turba* in Arabic), and behind it is a typical madrasa, built as four *iwans* (halls) arranged in a cruciform pattern around a central room or unroofed courtyard.

Characteristic Mamluk latticework

3 BARKA KHAN

Ha-shalshelet Street, corner of Ha-kotel Street

THE PRESENT NAME of the building where we are standing is al-Khalidiyya, which reveals its connection to the famous al-Khalidi family that has lived in Jerusalem for many generations. The building's association with the al-Khalidi family, however, is fairly recent, dating only from the late nineteenth century, when it became their library. When the structure was built in the thirteenth century it was called Barka Khan, since it contains the tombstones (as you can

Inscription in the facade of Barka Khan

see if you look through the window bars) of a man named Barka Khan and his two sons. Who was Barka Khan? In the 1240s the Egyptian ruler al-Malik al-Saliah Ayyub recruited regiments of Hwarizmians (a people originating from the south of the present-day Commonwealth of Independent States). These Hwarizmians put an end to Crusader rule in Jerusalem in 1244, and the Ayyubids regained control of the city. The Mamluk sultan Baybars would later marry the daughter of a Hwarizmian commander, and their son, who is buried here, was Barka Khan. The tomb before us may have been built by his mother. The upper inscription above the central window, the last line of which is in Persian, expresses the prayer of the builders of the tomb in poetic and stirring language:

In the name of Allah the merciful and compassionate... Oh God, grant us that which was promised by your servants and do not relent upon us on the day of resurrection for you do not renounce your promise... This is the tomb of the servant needful of God's mercy and forgiveness Barka Khan, may God illumine his resting place. He died on Friday, the first day of Muharram in the **year** 644 [=18 May 1246]... May Allah forgive him and his parents... pure did they emerge from the chaos and have become impure. Serene did we come into [the world] and anxious have become fearful. We were created out of the black soil, fire and water, and afterwards we returned to the soil.

◆ The Muslim **year** is a lunar year of approximately 354 days, in contrast to the solar year which consists of approximately 365 days. The Muslim year count begins from 622 CE, the year of Muhammed's *hejirah* (migration) from Mecca to Medina. Thus, for example, 1999 is parallel to 1419/20 in the Muslim calendar.

The structure, which was built in 1246, was renovated in the Mamluk period at the end of the fourteenth century. Incorporated in its facade is a guilloche pattern above the window. In a technique known in Arabic as *ablak*, which also is very characteristic of Mamluk buildings, the masons used stones of different colors.

Above the entrance in the western part of the facade we can see an arch in typical Romanesque style and below it an arch with a zigzag pattern. These two elements already appear in Crusader and Ayyubid construction, and an example of this combination is visible in the facade of al-Aqsa mosque. The structure was recently cleaned and restored by the Muslim Waqf.

We will enter Ha-kotel Street, which adjoins Barka Khan, and turn to face Ha-shalshelet Street. From here we can

Romanesque arch in facade of Barka Khan

see the domes of another structure ◆4 facing Barka Khan and known as al-Kilaniyya. Visible in the central dome are round apertures that provide the interior with light and air. This building, which was erected in 1352, houses the tomb of (take a deep breath) Hajj Jamal al-Din Bahlawan, son of the Emir Shams al-Din Tubad Shah, son of Shams al-Din Muhammad al-Kilani al-Lahiji. Adjoining this structure on the east is another building known as al-Tazziyya.

Ornamented door in al-Kilaniyya

AL-TAZZIYYA

Ha-shalshelet Street

AL-TAZZIYYA IS EASILY identified by the barred window and above it a guilloche pattern, a building inscription, and medallions featuring a cup in relief, the symbol of the emir Taz who is buried here. Taz, like the emir Tashtamur whom we have already encountered, was a high-ranking official in the Mamluk empire (the governor of Aleppo in Syria), who fell out of favor with the sultan. He was arrested and later sent into exile as a batal in Jerusalem. In 1361 he built the madrasa and tomb before us. The dismissal of officers who

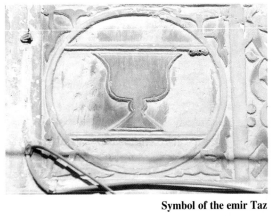

Symbol of the emir Taz

had acted improperly and their banishment to an obscure city or outpost on the periphery of the empire was a common practice of the Mamluk authorities. Due to its inferior political status, Jerusalem was a convenient place of exile. Feelings of guilt and remorse (either real or feigned) in these exiles motivated some of them to atone for their misdeeds and to contribute to Islam, which had redeemed them in their youth from the lands of the infidels, by building madrasas and other religious structures in Jerusalem.

We will continue to walk down Ha-shalshelet Street to the corner of

Ha-madregot Street. To our left we see an Arabic inscription, only the left part of which has survived.

Corner of Ha-madregot Street

A CITY THAT WAS OF MARGINAL importance to the Mamluks usually benefited from its distance from the ups-and-downs of government and other dangers that threatened the proud and rich centers of the empire. This tranquility, however, was sometimes accompanied by neglect on the part of the central government, which had neither the time nor the desire to attend to the basic needs of such remote cities. It was quite understandable, therefore, that when in 1480 the inhabitants of Jerusalem saw some six hundred workers hewing out of the hillside the course for an aqueduct that would lead water to the thirsting city, they were certain that they were dreaming. So relates Felix Fabri, a Dominican monk who visited Eretz Israel at the time:

The work of Hezekiah did not resemble that of the Sultan [Qayit Bey], who not only dug in the bedrock... but also split mountains over great distances, in order to bring water to there ... The Saracens [Muslims], the Jews, and the Christians, all wonder what the Sultan had in mind to do for Jerusalem, that he should spend so much money and do so much in order to supply it with water. The Saracens think that he intends to transfer the seat of government from Babylon in Egypt [i.e., from Cairo] to Jerusalem (M. Ish-Shalom, *Christian Travellers to the Holy Land*, pp. 253-254).

Indeed, the one responsible for this great undertaking was none other than the Mamluk sultan Qayit Bey, one of the few sultans who visited the city. The fruits of this visit were the construction (actually, the renewal and restoration) of the aqueduct, and the building of the Qayit Bey fountain and the Madrasa al-Ashrafiyya on the Temple Mount (see Tour 11).

The last part of the aqueduct extended along Ha-shalshelet Street, bringing water to the Temple Mount. The partially destroyed inscription next to which we are standing was affixed here to commemorate the royal waterworks.

We will continue walking to the end of Ha-shalshelet Street, passing on the way another tomb ❼, that of the dowager (*khatun* in Turkish) Turkan, who was buried here in 1352/3. Note the

Facade of Turkan Khatun

Fountain near the Gate of the Chain

beautiful geometric engravings in the stone of the tomb's facade.

At the end of the street we come to the Gate of the Chain 8 that leads to the Temple Mount. The double gatehouse that was built in the Crusader period and was then known as the Beautiful Gate was later renovated in the Ayyubid period, at which time fragments of the Crusader sculpture were incorporated in the bases of the gate's domes. The excavations of the facade of the gate revealed a magnificent staircase 9 dated to the Roman period and next to it is a *sabil* (drinking fountain) that was built (according to the inscription it bears) in the reign of Suleiman the Magnificent (1537). Pay special attention to the trough in the lower part of the sabil. This is most likely a sarcophagus from the Roman period that was included in the Ottoman fountain. The rosette ornamentations and the zigzag arch above the inscription also may have been taken from earlier structures by the Ottomans and incorporated in the sabil.

We will now look at the impressive structure located to the right of the Gate of the Chain. We can use our "expertise" to identify the Mamluk building elements that indicate the period in which it was erected: the ablak, the drops, the conch, the stone guilloches, and the stone "benches" flanking the entrance. This is the al-Tankiziyya building.

10   MAHKAMA AL-TANKIZIYYA

At the end of Ha-shalshelet Street

THE EMIR TANKIZ, who erected the madrasa facing us in 1328/9, served for many decades as the governor of Damascus on behalf of the Mamluk Sultan al-Mansur Muhammad ibn Qala'un, and we know of many building projects undertaken in Eretz Israel at his initiative. He established the khan in Jaljulia (north of Rosh Ha-ayin), the Nabi Yamin khan near Kfar Saba, a hospital in Safed, whose location cannot be determined, and other structures in Gaza, Hebron, and Nablus. In Jerusalem, Tankiz built the "Cup" on the Temple Mount (see Tour 11), the minaret of the mosque near the Gate of the Chain, and other projects. The Arab geographer al-Umari (died 1349) praised Tankiz and noted: "He restored Jerusalem to the status of a city, instead of its former condition as a neglected and forgotten place."

Contemporary documents describe this structure as a college for the teaching

later building addition

shell-like ornamentation

tear drops engraved in stone

black and white stone guilloches

decorative inscription

stone "bench"

Al-Tankiziyya

of Islamic traditions or as a *khankah*, a hostel for **Sufis** and **dervishes**, rather than as a madrasa. In this period, however, the distinctions between these terms are somewhat blurred. The madrasa was named al-Tankiziyya after Tankiz, whose heraldic shield we see in the facade: a goblet within a round medallion. The meaning of this symbol is unclear, and apparently the goblet bears no connection to Tankiz's position. It is noteworthy that the structure is built over early large vaults adjoining the Western Wall, as is the eastern part of Ha-shalshelet

◆ The **Sufis** are the adherents of Muslim mysticism. The first Sufis
◆ wore a simple wool garment (*suf* in Arabic), which is the source of
◆ the movement's name. They engage extensively in fasting, prayer,
◆ and immersion, in order to draw as close to God as possible.
◆ From the twelfth century, Sufi orders were established and given
◆ the name **dervishes**, which means "poor," "mendicant" in Persian.

Ceiling decorations in the facade of al-Tankiziyya

Street. Anyone visiting the Western Wall tunnel (see Tour 4) passes under these vaults on his way to the tunnel.

Several Mamluk sultans stayed in this building while visiting Jerusalem. In the Ottoman period the building assumed a new function: it became a courthouse in which trials were conducted and judges resided. For this reason it is called the *Makhkama* (courthouse).

Since 1968 the building has been used as a base of the Border Police, and it may be entered only with special permission. We will have to make do with a description of the atmosphere that pervaded the building in the late nineteenth century, which appears in the memoirs of Gad Frumkin, who would later become a Supreme Court justice during the British Mandate:

The courtyard of the Makhkama is a vaulted courtyard which has, opposite its entrance, windows that face the Western Wall. Through the iron lattices of these windows one can calmly gaze from above at the Wall.... There were two large rooms in this courtyard. On the right, the chamber of the *qadi*, that is, the religious judge, and opposite it is the chamber of the *bash-katib*, the chief scribe, and with him two or three secretaries.... At times I had to accompany one of the female members of the family who had some litigation concerning a claim for alimony, which in those days was subject to the jurisdiction of the Muslim religious court. It was then inconceivable that a woman would go out by herself, but even a young boy would suffice as her escort. The courtyard was always filled with litigants and the curious, including "professional" witnesses who were wont to offer their services to a person in his time of distress and testify on his behalf, as would be required, if one of the parties would be willing to pay the witness his fee... (*The Way of a Judge in Jerusalem*, p. 36).

Around the central courtyard are four halls arranged in a cruciform pattern, similar to the plan of Madrasa al-Tashtamuriyya. This plan was typical mainly of large madrasas in Muslim cities of the late Middle Ages.

Before leaving the courtyard of the Makhkama we should recall that there are other impressive Mamluk buildings on the Temple Mount, which are mentioned in Tour 11. Visitors are not permitted to enter the Temple Mount through the Gate of the Chain, and those wishing to enter the precinct must proceed to the Maghribi Gate to the south of the Western Wall plaza. We, at any rate, will continue on the route that passes to the west of the Mount, and we will therefore retrace our steps along Ha-shalshelet Street. We will go down the stepped alley to al-Wad Street, and continue along this street until the right turn to the covered Cotton Merchants' Market **11**, at the end of which is another Mamluk gateway to the Temple Mount. This street of shops was built by Tankiz in 1336/7 and its wares included cotton imported from the coastal plain. A distinctive feature of this street are the two Mamluk bathhouses. One, Hammam al-Ayn (the Spring Bathhouse) was operative until the 1980s, and the other, Hammam al-Shifa (the Healing Bathhouse), is still in use. Both may have been built on the sites of ancient bathhouses, possibly dating from the Roman period. A Muslim legend tells of a Muslim pilgrim who came to Mecca, and when he bent down to the waters of the sacred Zamzam spring, the copper cup in his hand slipped out of his grasp into the spring and was lost. Later in his journey, when he reached Jerusalem, he went to bathe in Hammam al-Shifa. Suddenly, the copper cup was miraculously revealed to him, on the floor of the bathhouse.

We will continue along al-Wad Street and turn right onto Sha'ar Ha-barzel Street, also built in the Mamluk period. We can walk along this street to the gate that leads to the Temple Mount. Among the various buildings here we will mention two: Madrasa al-Arghuniyya, on the southern side of the iron gate  which was built on the initiative of Arghun al-Kamil in the fourteenth century. Arghun was the governor of Aleppo in Syria and

Symbol of Arghun al-Kamil

was arrested and imprisoned in Alexandria by order of the Mamluk ruler. He was sent to Jerusalem as a batal, where he died a few months after the construction of the madrasa had begun. Above the entrance we see the heraldic symbol of Arghun. In the 1930s Muhammad Ali Jinnah, leader of the Muslim League in India, and Musa Kazim al-Husseini, President of the Muslim Supreme Council, were buried here. In April 1948 Abd al-Qader al-Husseini, leader of the Arab irregular forces who was killed in the battle for the Kastel outpost during the War of Independence (see Tour 37), was buried here. The building currently serves only as a residence.

To the right of Madrasa al-Arghuniyya we see the facade of Madrasa al-Muzhiriyya , which was built in the late fifteenth century by Abu Bakr ibn Muzhir, who was commander of the army and also employed in the "letter writing" office in Cairo. In the facade of the madrasa, mainly above the pair of barred windows, we see teardrop decorations and colorful guilloches. This particular combination of colors in the structure is quite rare in Jerusalem Mamluk construction. A few years ago, the Muslim Waqf invested much effort renovating the madrasa and finding stones to match the colors of the original masonry, but the facade was once again destroyed by vandals.

Facade of Madrasa al-Muzhiriyya

To the north of the iron gate we see a small entrance leading to a courtyard. To the east of the courtyard is a massive wall, which is a section of the upper course of the Western Wall that remained exposed despite the dense Mamluk construction close to the Temple Mount. Its two lowest courses may be from the

Ummayad period, and the upper courses apparently were added in the time of the Mamluks. This small section of the wall, which is about 175 m north of the Western Wall plaza, is known as "The Small Wall." No special importance was attributed to this wall in former generations, but in recent decades the Jews of Jerusalem have been accustomed to pray and light candles here.

We will return to al-Wad Street and walk to the north, turn left onto Ma'alot Ha-midrasha Street and stop by a large structure with three entrances, the easternmost of which is blocked at the bottom.

The Small Wall

15 TUNSHUQ'S PALACE

Ma'alot Ha-midrasha

THE IMAGE OF TUNSHUQ, the woman who built the magnificent building next to which we have stopped, is a mysterious figure. We know that she was the Turkish concubine, and possibly the wife, of a wealthy man named Muzafar al-Din, who, some say, was a local Mamluk ruler. Mujir al-Din relates that Tunshuq, who arrived in Jerusalem in 1391/2 and died in 1398, supported the followers of the Qalandriyya Order, whose *zawiyya* was located in the center of the Mamila cemetery. The palace before us was also called Muzafariyya (after her husband), and was dedicated by Tunshuq to this order. She spared no effort to adorn the building in accordance with the finest Mamluk architectural tradition: construction with stones of reddish hues, guilloches, *mukrans*, engravings of birds and flowers above the gates, and selected verses from the Koran. The structure would eventually be incorporated in the large complex erected to the south of it by Hatski Sultana, wife of the Ottoman sultan Suleiman the Magnificent, who built the city's walls. This fact gave the building its second name: Hatski Sultana. In the 1870s the building became a *saraya* (palace, government office building) of the Ottoman government, serving as the residency of the Pasha, a courthouse and the offices of the police commander. We will not enter the building with its many halls that presently functions as a Muslim orphanage, with a workshop for the production of rattan furniture. We will rather call upon the amusing

> *Zawiyya* (angle, corner, small mosque) is the name given to a structure in which Sufis conducted their ceremonies. In the Middle Ages there were several zawiyyas in Jerusalem, on the fringes of the Temple Mount and in the Muslim Quarter, around courtyards. Each such courtyard would serve as a gathering point for Muslims from different countries (a zawiyya of Indians, of Afghans, etc.) or for the members of a certain Sufi order.

recollections of Justice Gad Frumkin, as he tells of what went on in the saraya in late Ottoman period:

The grandeur of "royalty" infused this group of buildings... The long passageway... was divided into two parts: one was a clean and spacious courtyard... as soon as you entered it, you encountered two rooms, to the right and to the left, whose entrances were covered by screens of heavy cottonwool blankets in the winter and the summer, so that the cold and noise would not enter them. These were the offices of the district police commander to the right, and the commander of the gendarmerie to the left. Nearby, on the sides of the courtyard, stood guards... who would frequently lean their rifles against the wall, while they themselves would socialize with the other policemen... just to engage in worthless conversation. When they sensed some movement from behind the screen, they would immediately hasten to their posts, seize their weapons, and present arms with a great deal of noise and cries of "*Salaam dur!*" when the commander of the police or the gendarmerie commander would pass through the courtyard in response to an urgent summons from the Pasha. A similar salutation awaited the commanders on their return from the Pasha to their offices. And if there was a new commander, he would frequently cross the courtyard for his pleasure, to enjoy the "military honor" that they afforded him.... (*The Way of a Judge in Jerusalem*, p. 36).

Opposite the palace we see the tomb that Tunshuq erected for herself 16. This structure bears a dome and a railing with stylized dentils which repeat themselves in a fixed geometric pattern. This ends our tour.

Mamluk cavalryman

Historical Maps

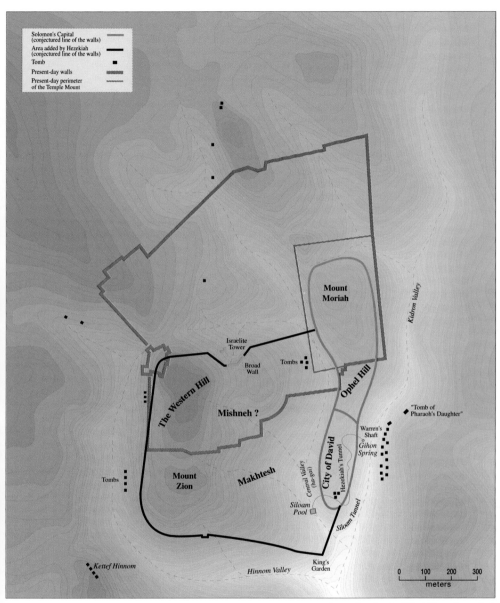

Legend:
- Solomon's Capital (conjectured line of the walls)
- Area added by Hezekiah (conjectured line of the walls)
- Tomb
- Present-day walls
- Present-day perimeter of the Temple Mount

Mount Moriah

Kidron Valley

Israelite Tower

Broad Wall

Tombs

The Western Hill

Ophel Hill

"Tomb of Pharaoh's Daughter"

Mishneh ?

Warren's Shaft

Gihon Spring

City of David

Hezekiah's Tunnel

Central Valley (ha-gai)

Tombs

Mount Zion

Makhtesh

Siloam Pool

Siloam Tunnel

Kettef Hinnom

Hinnom Valley

King's Garden

0   100   200   300
meters

Jerusalem in the First Temple period

207

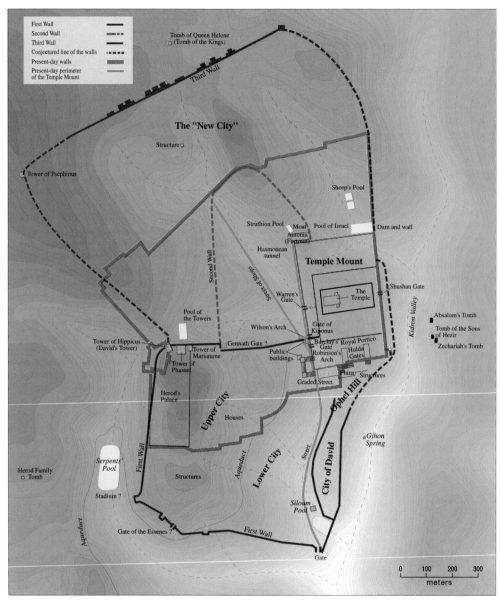

Jerusalem in the Second Temple period

First Wall
Second Wall
Third Wall
Conjectured line of the walls
Present-day walls
Present-day perimeter
of the Temple Mount

Tomb of Queen Helene
(Tomb of the Kings)

Third Wall

The "New City"

Structure

Tower of Psephinus

Sheep's Pool

Struthion Pool   Moat   Pool of Israel   Dam and wall
Antonia
(Fortress)

Hasmonean
tunnel

Temple Mount

Shushan Gate

Warren's
Gate

The
Temple

Absalom's Tomb

Tomb of the Sons
of Hezir

Zechariah's Tomb

Pool of
the Towers

Wilson's Arch   Gate of
Kiponus

Tower of Hippicus
(David's Tower)

Tower of
Mariamme

Gennath Gate ?

Barclay's Royal Portico
Gate
Robinson's Hulda
Arch   Gates

Public
buildings

Tower of
Phasael

Plaza Structures

Graded Street

Herod's
Palace

Upper City

Houses

Ophel Hill

Gihon
Spring

First Wall

Serpents'
Pool

Aqueduct

Lower City

Street

City of David

Herod Family
Tomb

Stadium ?

Structures

Siloam
Pool

Aqueduct

Gate of the Essenes ?

First Wall

Gate

Kidron Valley

Street of Shops

Second Wall

0   100   200   300
meters

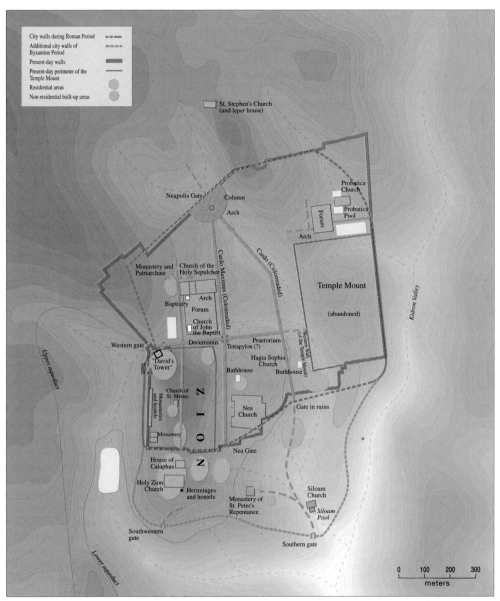

St. Stephen's Church
(and leper house)

Probatica
Church

Neapolis Gate

Column

Arch

Forum

Probatica
Pool

Arch

Monastery and
Patriarchate

Church of the
Holy Sepulcher

Temple Mount

(abandoned)

Baptistry

Arch

Forum

Church
of John
the Baptist

Western gate

Decumanus

Praetorium

Tetrapylon (?)

Hagia Sophia
Church

"David's
Tower"

Bathhouse

Bathhouse

Church of
St. Menas

Monasteries
and hostels

Nea
Church

Gate in ruins

Monastery

Nea Gate

House of
Caiaphas

Holy Zion
Church

Hermitages
and hostels

Monastery of
St. Peter's
Repentance

Siloam
Church

Siloam
Pool

Southwestern
gate

Southern gate

Cardo Maximus (Colonnaded)

Cardo (Colonnaded)

Western Wall
(of the Temple Mount)

Kidron Valley

Upper aqueduct

Lower aqueduct

Z I O N

0   100   200   300
meters

Jerusalem in the Roman-Byzantine period

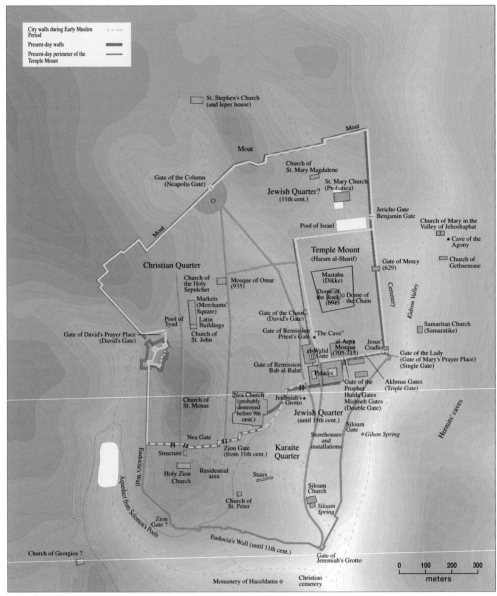

St. Stephen's Church (and leper house)

Moat

Moat

Moat

Church of St. Mary Magdalene

Gate of the Column (Neapolis Gate)

St. Mary Church (Probatica)

Jewish Quarter? (11th cent.)

Jericho Gate
Benjamin Gate

Church of Mary in the Valley of Jehoshaphat

Pool of Israel

● Cave of the Agony

Temple Mount
(Haram al-Sharif)

Gate of Mercy (629)

Church of Gethsemane

Christian Quarter

Church of the Holy Sepulcher

Mosque of Omar (935)

Mastaba (Dikke)

Dome of the Rock (691)

Dome of the Chain

Cemetery

Kidron Valley

Markets (Merchants' Square)

Latin Buildings

Gate of the Chain (David's Gate)

Samaritan Church (Samaritike)

Pool of Tyad

Church of St. John

Gate of Remission Priest's Gate

"The Cave"

al-Aqsa Mosque (705-715)

Jesus' Cradle

Gate of the Lady (Gate of Mary's Prayer Place) (Single Gate)

Gate of David's Prayer Place (David's Gate)

al-Walid Gate

Gate of Remission Bab al-Balat

Palaces

Gate of the Prophet

Akhmas Gates (Triple Gate)

Church of St. Menas

Nea Church (probably destroyed before 9th cent.)

Jeremiah's Grotto

Hulda Gates
Mishneh Gates (Double Gate)

Hermits' caves

Jewish Quarter (until 11th cent.)

Siloam Gate

Nea Gate

Zion Gate (from 11th cent.)

Karaite Quarter

Storehouses and installations

Siloam Gate

Gihon Spring

Eudocia's Wall

Structure

Holy Zion Church

Residential area

Stairs

Siloam Church

Aqueduct from Solomon's Pools

Zion Gate ?

Church of St. Peter

Siloam Spring

Eudocia's Wall (until 11th cent.)

Church of Georgios ?

Gate of Jeremiah's Grotto

0   100   200   300

meters

Monastery of Haceldama ◇

Christian cemetery

Jerusalem in the Early Muslim period

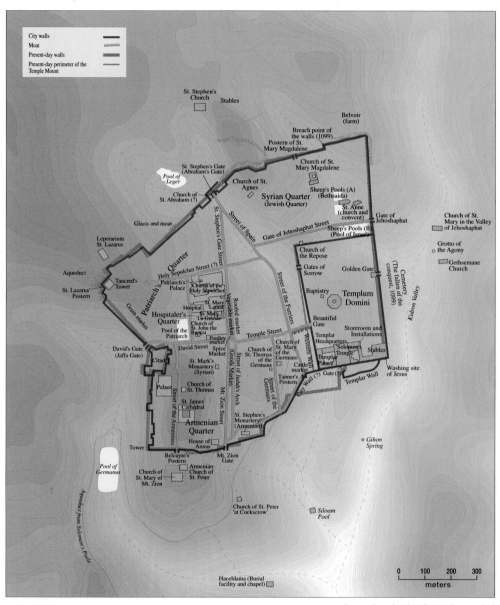

Jerusalem in the Crusader period

City walls
Moat
Present-day walls
Present-day perimeter of the Temple Mount

St. Stephen's Church
Stables
Belvoir (farm)
Breach point of the walls (1099)
Postern of St. Mary Magdalene
Church of St. Mary Magdalene
St. Stephen's Gate (Abraham's Gate)
Church of St. Agnes
Pool of Leger
Sheep's Pools (A) (Bethsaida)
Church of St. Abraham (?)
Syrian Quarter (Jewish Quarter)
St. Anne (church and convent)
Gate of Jehoshaphat
Church of St. Mary in the Valley of Jehoshaphat
Glacis and moat
St. Stephen's Gate Street
Street of Spain
Gate of Jehoshaphat Street
Sheep's Pools (B) (Pool of Israel)
Grotto of the Agony
Leperarium St. Lazarus
Church of the Repose
Gethsemane Church
Aqueduct
Quarter
Holy Sepulcher Street (?)
Gates of Sorrow
Golden Gate
Tancred's Tower
Patriarch's Palace
Church of the Holy Sepulcher
Street of the Furriers
Baptistry
Templum Domini
St. Lazarus' Postern
Patriarch's Quarter
Hospital
St. Mary Latina
St. Mary 'la Grande
Grain market
Hospitaler's Quarter
Church of St. John the Baptist
Vegetable market
Rooted market
Beautiful Gate
Storeroom and Installations
Cemetery (The fallen of the conquest, 1099)
Kidron Valley
Pool of the Patriarch
Poultry market
Temple Street
Templar Headquarters
'Solomon's Temple'
Stables
David's Gate (Jaffa Gate)
David Street
Spice Market
Greek Market
Street of Judah's Arch
Church of St. Thomas of the Germans
Church of St. Mary of the Germans
Templar Palace
Washing site of Jesus
Citadel
St. Mark's Monastery (Syrian)
Cattle market
Templar Wall
Palace
Street of the Armenians
Mt. Zion Street
Tanner's Postern
City Wall (?)
Gate (?)
Church of St. Thomas
Street of the Germans
Western Wall
St. James' Cathedral
St. Stephen's Monastery (Armenian)
Armenian Quarter
Gihon Spring
House of Annas
Tower
Belcayre's Postern
Mt. Zion Gate
Pool of Germanus
Armenian Church of St. Peter
Church of St. Mary of Mt. Zion
Church of St. Peter 'at Cockscrow'
Siloam Pool
Aqueduct from Solomon's Pools
Haceldama (Burial facility and chapel)

0   100   200   300
meters

Jerusalem in the Crusader period

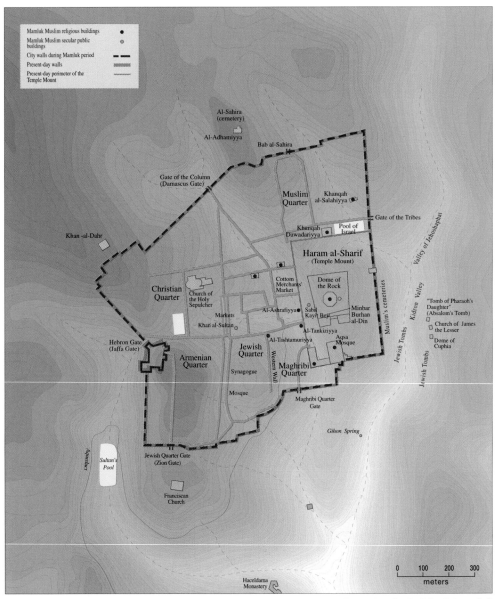

Jerusalem in the Mamluk period

Mamluk Muslim religious buildings •
Mamluk Muslim secular public buildings ⊙
City walls during Mamluk period
Present-day walls
Present-day perimeter of the Temple Mount

Al-Sahira (cemetery)
Al-Adhamiyya
Bab al-Sahira
Gate of the Column (Damascus Gate)
Muslim Quarter
Khanqah al-Salahiyya
Khan -al-Dahr
Khanqah Dawadariyya
Pool of Israel
Gate of the Tribes
Haram al-Sharif (Temple Mount)
Cottom Merchants' Market
Dome of the Rock
Christian Quarter
Church of the Holy Sepulcher
Al-Ashrafiyya
Sabil Kayit Bey
Minbar Burhan al-Din
Markets
Al-Tankiziyya
Khan al-Sultan
Al-Tashtamuriyya
Aqsa Mosque
Hebron Gate (Jaffa Gate)
Jewish Quarter
Armenian Quarter
Synagogue
Western Wall
Maghribi Quarter
Mosque
Maghribi Quarter Gate
Gihon Spring
Sultan's Pool
Jewish Quarter Gate (Zion Gate)
Franciscan Church
Haceldama Monastery
Valley of Jehoshaphat
Kidron Valley
Muslim's cemeteries
Jewish Tombs
Jewish Tombs
"Tomb of Pharaoh's Daughter" (Absalom's Tomb)
Church of James the Lesser
Dome of Cuphia
Aqueduct

0 100 200 300
meters

Index to Volume One